Tim Harford writes 'The Undercover Economist' column for the *Financial Times*, and his 'Dear Economist' column is published in *Men's Health*. His writing has also appeared in *Esquire*, *Forbes*, *New York Magazine*, *Wired*, the *Washington Post* and the *New York Times*. His other books include *The Logic of Life* and *Adapt*. Harford is a visiting fellow at Nuffield College, Oxford, and Cass Business School, London. He was the winner of the 2006 Bastiat Prize for economic journalism. Harford presents the popular BBC Radio 4 show *More or Less*, which won the 2010 Royal Statistical Society award for excellence in journalism. He lives in London with his wife and two daughters.

'What made for dull school textbooks comes alive in his capable hands ... This book will come as a welcome wake-up call. If nothing else, it should make you a much more savvy shopper ... Any student at GCSE level being taught by a bored economics teacher who should be teaching media studies should definitely make a bee-line for it, as indeed should people who know a lot about economics; if only to learn how to write in the hope of making the "dismal science" less so' *Express*

'*The Undercover Economist* is an excellent Undercover Introduction to Economics. If you think that sounds boring, you probably ought to read it' *Financial Times*

'Economists do indeed think differently from the rest of us. This book gives an excellent introduction as to quite why they do' *Telegraph*

'As lively and witty an introduction to the supposedly "dismal science" as you are likely to read' *The Times*

'If you want a quick overview, you can't do better than *The Undercover Economist*' *Wall Street Journal*

'A playful guide to the economics of everyday life ... *The Undercover Economist* succeeds in taking the chalk dust out of the subject' *The Economist*

The Undercover Economist

The Undercover Economist

TIM HARFORD

ABACUS

ABACUS

First published in Great Britain in 2006 by Little, Brown
This paperback edition published in 2007 by Abacus

39 40 38

Copyright © Tim Harford 2006

The moral right of the author has been asserted.

A CIP catalogue record for this book
is available from the British Library.

ISBN 978-0-349-11985-4

Typeset in Janson by M Rules
Printed and bound in Great Britain by
Clays Ltd, Elcograf S.p.A.

Papers used by Abacus are from well-managed forests
and other responsible sources.

MIX
Paper from
responsible sources
FSC® C104740

Abacus
An imprint of
Little, Brown Book Group
Carmelite House
50 Victoria Embankment
London EC4Y 0DZ

An Hachette UK Company
www.hachette.co.uk

www.littlebrown.co.uk

First edition:
To Deborah Harford, Fran Monks and Stella Harford –
family ... past, present and future.

Second edition:
To my family

Contents

Acknowledgements

Peter Sinclair got me into economics; Tony Courakis, Simon Cowan, Stan Fischer, Bob Garhart, Paul Klemperer, Brendan McElroy, Hyun Shin, Bill Sjostrom and many others helped me along the way. I am grateful to them all.

At Shell, Ged Davis let me work part-time while I produced the first draft of the book. I was flattered by his reluctance and grateful for his support. Other colleagues at Shell were inspirational, especially Betty-Sue Flowers, Anupam Khanna, Cho Khong, Michael Klein, Doug McKay and John Robinson.

At the *Financial Times*, Pilita Clark, Andy Davis, Chris Giles, Andrew Gowers, John Kay, John Willman and Martin Wolf gave me opportunities and then made sure I didn't waste them.

David Bodanis, Felicity Bryan, Penny Dablin, Moore Flannery, Juri Gabriel, Mark Henstridge, Diana Jackson, Oliver Johnson, John Kay, Cho Khong, Paul Klemperer, Stephen McGroarty, Doug McKay, Fran Monks, Dave Morris, Rafael Ramirez, Jillian Reilly, John Robinson, Tim Savin, Martin Wolf and Andrew Wright improved the book with their comments.

Sally Holloway, my agent, has been superb. I have been very lucky to work with my editors Tim Whiting and Iain Hunt, along with Tim Bartlett and Kate Hamill on the North American edition – all four have been excellent.

Most importantly, emotional support came from Paul Domjan,

Diana Jackson, my wife Fran Monks, 'Uncle' Dave Morris and Jillian Reilly. Above all I have to thank Andrew Wright, a genius, without whom the book could never have been finished, and David Bodanis, an inspiration, without whom it would never have been started.

Acknowledgements for the second edition

Cosmina Dorobanţu and Kelly Chen provided excellent research assistance for the second edition; Cosmina not only updated a huge number of out-of-date statistics but she also discovered and fixed several embarrassing statistical errors in the first edition – the only person to spot them. As always, Andrew Wright's perceptive editing was invaluable. Above all I am hugely grateful to my readers for their enthusiasm, questions and comments.

Preface to the second edition

When I was first writing *The Undercover Economist* – mostly in 2002, although the first edition emerged in the US in 2005 – I would never have dreamed that eight years later, I would be writing a preface to a new edition. I have a great deal of good luck and about a million readers to thank for that, and I am counting my blessings.

Since I wrote the book, the world has changed and so have I. I have tried to preserve as much as possible of the original book rather than surrendering to hindsight bias, but I have tried to update as many of the statistics and examples as possible as seamlessly as I can. (Occasionally I have used footnotes to highlight changes between the first edition and this one – especially if the changes have either proved me right or made me look silly.)

A more substantial change has been to replace Chapter 6 – which was originally about the dot-com bubble – with a new chapter about the banking crisis that began in 2007. The dot-com bubble, alas, now seems fairly benign in comparison with the banking crisis, and it felt impossible to publish a second edition without trying to make sense of it all.

If you enjoy this book, you may also enjoy my weekly column for the *Financial Times*, also named 'The Undercover Economist' and inspired by the book. The column, my other articles, and other resources for econophiles, are available at my website: timharford.com. I'm also on Twitter: @TimHarford.

Introduction

I would like to thank you for buying this book, but if you're anything like me you haven't bought it at all. Instead, you've carried it into the bookshop café and even now are sipping a cappuccino in comfort while you decide whether it's worth your money.

This is a book about how economists view the world. In fact, there might be an economist sitting near you right now. You might not spot her – a normal person looking at an economist wouldn't notice anything remarkable. But normal people look remarkable in the eyes of economists. What is the economist seeing? What could she tell you, if you cared to ask? And why *should* you care?

You may think you're enjoying a frothy cappuccino, but the economist sees you – and the cappuccino – as players in an intricate game of signals and negotiations, contests of strength and battles of wits. The game is for high stakes: some of the people who worked to get that coffee in front of you made a lot of money, some of them made very little and some of them are after the money in your pocket right now. The economist can tell you who will get what, how and why. My hope is that by the time you finish this book, you'll be able to see the same things. But please buy it first, before the shop's manager throws you out.

Your coffee is intriguing to the economist for another reason:

she doesn't know how to make a cappuccino, and she knows that nobody else does either. Who, after all, could boast of being able to grow, pick, roast and blend coffee, raise and milk cows, roll steel and mould plastics and assemble them into an espresso machine and, finally, shape ceramics into a cute mug? Your cappuccino reflects the outcome of a system of staggering complexity. There isn't a single person in the world who could produce what it takes to make a cappuccino.

The economist knows that the cappuccino is the product of an incredible team effort. Not only that, there is nobody in charge of the team. Economist Paul Seabright reminds us of the pleas of the Soviet official trying to comprehend the Western system: 'Tell me ... who is in charge of the supply of bread to the population of London?' The question is comical, but the answer – nobody – is dizzying.

When the economist drags her attention away from your coffee and looks around the bookshop, the organisational challenges are even greater. The complexity of the system that made the shop possible defies easy description: think of the accumulated centuries of design and development, from the paper upon which the books are printed to the spotlights that illuminate the shelves to the software that keeps track of the stock, not to mention the everyday miracles of organisation through which the books are printed, bound, stored, delivered, stacked and sold.

The system works remarkably well. When you bought this book – you have bought this book by now, haven't you? – you probably did so without having to give instructions to the bookshop to order it for you. Perhaps you did not even know when you left your home this morning that you were going to buy it. Yet by some magic, dozens of people took the actions necessary to fulfil your unpredictable desires: me, my editors, marketers, proofreaders, printers, paper manufacturers, ink suppliers and many others. The economist can explain how such a system works, how companies will try to exploit it and what you as a customer can do to fight back.

Now the Undercover Economist is gazing out of the window at the traffic jam outside. To some people, the jam is merely an irritating fact of life. To the economist, there is a story to tell about the contrast between the chaos of the traffic and the smooth running of the bookshop. We can learn something from the bookshop that will help us avoid traffic jams.

While economists are constantly thinking about the things going on around them, they are not limited to discussing local matters. If you cared to engage one in conversation you might talk about the difference between bookshops in the developed world and libraries in Cameroon, which have eager readers but no books. You might point out that the gap between the world's rich countries and the world's poor countries is huge and appalling. The economist would share your sense of injustice – but she could also tell you why rich countries are rich and poor countries are poor, and what might be done about it.

Perhaps the Undercover Economist seems like a know-it-all, but she reflects the broad ambition of economics to understand people: as individuals, as partners, as competitors and as members of the vast social organisations we call 'economies'.

This breadth of interest is reflected in the eclectic tastes of the Nobel Prize committee. Since 1990, the Nobel Prize in Economics has only occasionally been awarded for advances in the obviously 'economic' things, such as the theory of exchange rates or business cycles. More often, it has been awarded for insights less obviously connected with what you might have thought was economics: human development, psychology, history, voting, law and even esoteric discoveries such as why you can't buy a decent second-hand car.

My aim in this book is to help you see the world like an economist. I will tell you nothing about exchange rates or business cycles, but I will unlock the mystery of second-hand cars. We'll look at the big issues, such as how China is lifting a million people a month out of poverty, and the little ones, such as how to avoid paying too much money in the supermarket. It's detective work all the way, but I'll teach you how to use the investigative tools of the economist. I hope that by the end of the book, you'll be a more savvy consumer – and a more savvy voter too, able to see the truth behind the stories that politicians try to sell you. Everyday life is full of puzzles that many people do not even realise are puzzles, so above all, I hope that you will be able to see the fun behind these everyday secrets. So let's start on familiar territory by asking, who pays for your coffee?

1

Who Pays for Your Coffee?

The long commute on public transport is a commonplace experience of life in major cities around the world, whether you live in New York, Tokyo, Antwerp or Prague. Commuting dispiritingly combines the universal and the particular. The particular, because each commuter is a rat in his own unique maze: timing the run from the shower to the station turnstiles; learning the timetables and the correct end of the platform to speed up the transfer between different trains; trading off the disadvantages of standing room only on the first train home against a seat on the last one. Yet commutes also produce common patterns – bottlenecks and rush hours – that are exploited by entrepreneurs the world over.

Like all London stations at rush hour, Waterloo is packed full of sleep-deprived, tetchy travellers. There are seventy-four million of them a year, half of them with their heads in the air trying to find a departure board, the other thirty-seven million staring fixedly straight ahead as they push their way out.

This second group – which includes me – is made up of people who are not easily turned aside from their paths. They want to get out of the noise and bustle, around the gormless, shuffling tourists, and to their desks just slightly before their bosses. They do not welcome detours. But there is a place of peace and bounty which can tempt them to tarry for a couple of minutes. In this oasis, rare delights are served with smiles by attractive and exotic men and women – today, a charming barista whose name badge reads 'Jacinta'. I am thinking, of course, of the AMT coffee kiosk.

Even if you've never heard of AMT coffee, you'll know exactly what I am talking about. You find the same kind of thing all over the planet – and catering to the same desperate commuters. The coffee shop within ten yards of the exit from Washington's Dupont Circle metro station is called Cosi. New York's Penn Station boasts Seattle Coffee Roasters just by the exit on to Eighth Avenue. Commuters through Shinjuku Station, Tokyo, can enjoy a Starbucks without leaving the station concourse.

An AMT double-shot cappuccino is cheaper than a coffee from some of these bigger names on the market, yet it's hardly cheap. But of course, I can afford it. Like many of the people stopping at that coffee shack, I earn the price of that coffee every few minutes. None of us care to waste our time trying to save a few pennies by searching out a cheaper coffee at 8.30 in the morning. We want coffee, we want it now – and there are seventy-four million of us. This is why the location of the coffee bar is important.

The position of the AMT coffee bar in Waterloo Station is advantageous, not just because it's located on the most efficient route from the platforms to the main station exit, but because there are no other coffee bars on that route. It's hardly a surprise that they do a roaring trade.

If you buy as much coffee as I do you may have come to the conclusion that somebody is getting filthy rich out of all this. If the occasional gripes in the newspapers are correct, the coffee in that cappuccino costs pennies. Of course, the newspapers don't tell us the whole story: there's milk, electricity, cost of the paper cups – and the cost of paying Jacinta to smile at grouchy customers all day long. But after you add all that up you still get something a lot less than the price of a cup of coffee. According to economics professor Brian McManus, mark-ups on coffee are around 150 per cent – it costs forty cents to make a one dollar cup of drip coffee and costs less than a dollar for a small latte, which sells for $2.55. So somebody is making a lot of money. Who?

You might think that the obvious candidates are Alistair, Allan and Angus McCallum-Toppin, the founders of AMT. But the answer can't be as simple as that. The main reason that AMT can charge £1.55 for a cappuccino is that nobody else has a kiosk next door charging £1.45. So why is nobody next door undercutting the AMT kiosk? Without wishing to dismiss the achievements of the entrepreneurial McCallum-Toppins, cappuccinos are not in fact complicated products. There is no shortage of drinkable cappuccinos (sadly, there is no shortage of undrinkable cappuccinos either). It wouldn't take much to buy some coffee machines and a counter, build up a brand with a spot of advertising and some free samples, and hire decent staff. Even Jacinta is replaceable.

The truth is that the AMT bar's most significant advantage is its location on the desire line of seventy-four million commuters. It is in the very best spot that a coffee bar could possibly be located. And it is safe to assume that AMT has an agreement with its landlord that direct competitors will not be allowed right next door. To set up a rival coffee bar you will either have to go somewhere else, or wait until the current contract has expired. The nice margin that AMT makes on its cappuccinos is mostly due neither to the quality of the coffee nor to the staff: it's location, location, location.

But who controls the location? Look ahead to the negotiations for the new rental agreement. The landlord is the owner of Waterloo Station concourse, Network Rail. Network Rail is talking to the AMT brothers but also to the representatives of Costa Coffee, Ritazza, Aroma, Pret a Manger, Café Nero, Starbucks and half a dozen other wannabe 'coffeepreneurs'. The Network Rail manager can sign an agreement with each one of them, or can sign an exclusive agreement with only one. She'll quickly find that nobody is very keen to pay much for a space next to twelve other coffee bars, and so she will get the most advantage out of the exclusive agreement.

In trying to work out who is going to make all the money, simply remember that there are thirteen coffee bar entrepreneurs on one side of the negotiating table and on the other side is a manager who owns a single, perfect coffee-bar site. Thirteen against one is likely to be bad odds for the thirteen. By playing them off against each other, the Network Rail manager should be able to dictate the terms, and force one of them to pay pretty much all their expected profits. Everything they would otherwise have expected to earn should go on the rent bill.*

There's a pattern here. The power of scarcity has come up twice in two pages. First, AMT has the power to charge high prices

---

*To my sorrow, AMT no longer has the concession to sell coffee in Waterloo station. But I am pleased to note that my theory about the negotiation between coffee bars and Network Rail appears to have something in it. AMT has been replaced by Café Nero. Lots of new concessions have opened up over the years – you can now buy cornish pasties, baguettes, sushi, donuts and boiled sweets within a few yards of the Café Nero kiosk. However, the nearest specialist coffee bar, a Costa Coffee, is some way off, next to a different exit. Another Café Nero stakes out the station's east exit. On the level below, Starbucks has the London Underground exit covered. There are forty-five food and drink outlets in the station, but the coffee bars could not be further apart.

because of the scarce location of the coffee kiosk. Second, Network Rail has the power to charge high rents because there is only one location and lots of companies are eager to use it to sell coffee.

This is pure armchair reasoning. It's reasonable to ask if it's actually true. After I once explained all of the principles involved to a long-suffering friend (over coffee), she asked me whether I could prove it. I admitted that it was just a theory. A couple of weeks later she sent me an article from the *Financial Times* which relied on industry experts who had access to the accounts of coffee companies. The article began, 'Few companies are making any money in the UK coffee bar market' and concluded that one of the main problems was 'the high costs of running retail outlets in prime locations with significant passing trade'. It seems that armchair reasoning is the easy way to get to the same conclusion.

The economists' way of thinking about the world isn't guaranteed to produce the right answer. But it gives insights about the world which apply far more generally than any industry analyst's accounting: if there's a profitable deal to be done between somebody who has something unique and someone who has something which can be replaced, then the profits will go to the owner of the unique resource.

Strength from scarcity

Browsing through the old economics books on the shelf at home, I dug out the first analysis of twenty-first-century coffee bars. Published in 1817, it explains not just the modern coffee bar but much of the modern world itself. Its author, David Ricardo, had already made himself a multimillionaire (in today's money) as a stockbroker, and was later to become an MP. But Ricardo was also an enthusiastic economist, who longed to understand what had happened to Britain's economy during the recent Napoleonic wars: the price of wheat had rocketed, and so had rents on agricultural land. Ricardo wanted to know why.

The easiest way to understand Ricardo's analysis is to use one of his own examples. Imagine a wild terrain with few settlers but plenty of fertile meadow available for growing crops. One day an aspiring young farmer, Axel, walks into town and offers to pay rent for the right to grow crops on an acre of good meadow. Everyone agrees how much grain an acre of meadow will produce, but they cannot decide how much rent Axel should pay. Because there is no shortage of land lying fallow, competing landlords will not be able to charge a high rent ... or any significant rent at all. Each landlord would rather collect a small rent than no rent at all, and so each will undercut his rivals until Axel is able to start farming for very little rent – just enough to compensate for the landlord's trouble.

The first lesson here is that the person in possession of the desired resource – the landlord in this case – does not always have as much power as one would assume. And the story doesn't specify whether Axel is very poor or has a roll of cash in the false heel of his boot, because it doesn't make any difference to the rent. Bargaining strength comes through scarcity: settlers are scarce and meadows are not, so landlords have no bargaining power.

That means that if relative scarcity shifts from one person to another, bargaining shifts as well. If over the years many immigrants follow in Axel's footsteps, the amount of spare meadowland will shrink until there is none left. As long as there is any, competition between landlords who have not attracted any tenants will keep rents very low. One day, however, an aspiring farmer will walk into town – let's call him Bob – and will find that there is no spare fertile land. The alternative, farming on inferior but abundant scrubland, is not attractive. So Bob will offer to pay good money to any landlord who will evict Axel, or any of the other farmers currently farming virtually rent-free, and let him farm there instead. But just as Bob is willing to pay to rent meadowland rather than scrubland, all of the meadow farmers will also be willing to pay not to move. Everything has changed, and quickly: suddenly the landlords have acquired real bargaining power, because suddenly farmers are relatively common and meadows are relatively scarce.

That means the landowners will be able to raise their rents. By how much? It will have to be enough that farmers earn the same farming on meadows and paying rent, or farming on inferior scrubland rent-free. If the difference in productiveness of the two types of land is five bushels of grain a year, then the rent will also be five bushels a year. If a landlord tries to charge more, his tenant will leave to farm scrubland. If the rent is any less, the scrub farmer would be willing to offer more.

It may seem odd that the rents changed so rapidly simply because one more man arrived to farm the area. This story doesn't seem to explain how the world really works. But there is more truth to it than you might think, even if it is oversimplified. Of course, in the real world, there are other elements to consider: laws about evicting people, long-term contracts and even cultural norms, such as the fact that kicking one person out and installing a new tenant the next day is just 'not done'. In the real world there are more than two types of farmland, and Bob may have different options to being a farmer – he may be able to get a job as an accountant or driving a cab. All these facts complicate what happens in reality; they slow down the shift in bargaining power, alter the absolute numbers involved and put a brake on sudden movements in rents.

Yet the complications of everyday life often hide the larger trends behind the scenes, as scarcity power shifts from one group to another. The economist's job is to shine a spotlight on the underlying process. We should not be surprised if, suddenly, the land market shifts against farmers; or if house prices go up or down dramatically; or if the world is covered by coffee bars over a period of just a few months. The simplicity of the story emphasises one part of the underlying reality – but the emphasis is helpful in revealing something important. Sometimes relative scarcity and bargaining strength really do change quickly, and with profound effects on people's lives. We often complain about symptoms – the high cost of buying a cup of coffee, or even a house. The symptoms cannot be treated successfully without understanding the patterns of scarcity which underlie them.

'Marginal' land is of central importance

The shifts in bargaining power don't have to stop there. While the farming story can be elaborated indefinitely, the basic principles remain the same. For example, if new farmers keep arriving, they will eventually cultivate not only the meadowland but also all of the scrubland. When a new settler, Cornelius, walks into town, the only land available will be the grassland, which is even less productive than scrubland. We can expect the same dance of negotiations: Cornelius will offer money to landlords to try to get onto scrubland, rents will quickly rise on scrubland, and the differential between scrubland and meadow will have to stay the same (or farmers would want to move), so the rent will rise on meadow too.

The rent on meadowland, therefore, will always be equal to the difference in grain yield between meadowland and whatever land is available rent-free to new farmers. Economists call this other land 'marginal' land because it is at the margin between being cultivated and not being cultivated. (You will soon see that economists think about decisions at the margin quite a lot.) In the beginning, when meadowland was more plentiful than settlers, it was not only the best land, it was also the 'marginal' land because new farmers could use it. Because the best land was the same as the marginal land, there was no rent, beyond the trivial sum needed to compensate the landlord for his trouble. Later, when there were so many farmers that there was no longer enough prime land to go around, scrubland became the marginal land, and rents on meadows rose to five bushels a year – the difference in productivity between the meadowland and the marginal land (in this case, the scrubland). When Cornelius arrived, the grassland became the marginal land, meadows became yet more attractive relative to the marginal land, and so the landlords were able to raise the rent on meadows again. It's important to note here that there is no absolute value: everything is relative to that marginal land.

Back to coffee bars

A nice story, but those of us who like Westerns may prefer the gritty cinematography of *Unforgiven* or the psychological isolation of *High Noon*. So, David Ricardo and I get no prizes for our screenwriting, but we might be excused, as long as our little fable actually tells us something useful about the modern world.

We can start with coffee bars. Why is coffee expensive in London, New York, Washington or Tokyo? The common-sense view is that coffee is expensive because the coffee bars have to pay high rent. David Ricardo's model can show us that this is the wrong way to think about the issue, because 'high rent' is not an arbitrary fact of life. It has a cause.

Ricardo's story illustrates that two things determine the rent on prime locations like meadowland: the difference in agricultural productivity between meadows and marginal land, and the importance of agricultural productivity itself. At £1 a bushel, five bushels of grain is a £5 rent. At £200,000 a bushel, five bushels of grain is a £1-million rent. Meadows command high rents only if the grain they help produce is also valuable.

Now apply Ricardo's theory to coffee bars. Just as meadowland will command high rents if the grain it produces is valuable, prime coffee-bar locations will command high rents only if customers will pay high prices for coffee. Rush-hour customers are so desperate for caffeine and in such a hurry that they are practically price-blind. The willingness to pay top whack for convenient coffee sets the high rent, and not the other way around.

Spaces suitable for coffee kiosks are like meadows – they are the best-quality property for the purpose, and they fill up quickly. The ground-floor corner units of Manhattan's Midtown are the preserve of Starbucks, Cosi and their competitors. Near Washington DC's Dupont Circle, Cosi has the prime spot at the southern exit, and Starbucks has the northern one, not to mention staking out territory opposite the adjacent stations up and down the Metro line. In London every station hosts one of the big-name coffee chains. These spots could be used to sell second-hand cars or Chinese food, but they never are. This isn't because a train station is a bad place to sell a Chinese meal or a second-hand car, but because there is no shortage of other places with lower rents from which noodles or cars can be sold – customers are in less of a hurry, more willing to walk or order a delivery. For coffee bars and similar establishments selling snacks or newspapers, cheaper rent is no compensation for the loss of a flood of price-blind customers.

Portable models

David Ricardo managed to write an analysis of cappuccino bars in train stations before either cappuccino bars or train stations existed. This is the kind of trick that makes people either hate or love economics. Those who hate it argue that if we want to understand how the modern coffee business works, we should not be reading an analysis of farming published in 1817.

But many of us love the fact that Ricardo was able, nearly two hundred years ago, to produce insights that illuminate our understanding today. It's easy to see the difference between nineteenth-century farming and twenty-first-century frothing, but not so easy to see the similarity before it is pointed out to us. Economics is partly about modelling, about articulating basic principles and patterns that operate behind seemingly complex subjects like the rent on farms or coffee bars.

There are other models of the coffee business, useful for different things. A model of the design and architecture of coffee bars could be useful as a case study for interior designers. A physics model could outline the salient features of the machine that generates the ten atmospheres of pressure required to brew espresso; the same model might be useful for talking about suction pumps or the internal combustion engine. Today we have models of the ecological impacts of different disposal methods for coffee grounds. Each model is useful for different things, but a 'model' that tried to describe the design, the engineering, the ecology and the economics would be no simpler than reality itself and so would add nothing to our understanding.

Ricardo's model is useful for discussing the relationship between scarcity and bargaining strength, which goes far beyond coffee or farming and ultimately explains much of the world around us. When economists see the world, they see hidden social patterns, patterns that become evident only when one focuses on the essential underlying processes. This focus leads critics to say that economics doesn't consider the whole story, the whole 'system'. How else, though, could a nineteenth-century analysis of farming proclaim the truth about twenty-first-century coffee bars, except through grossly failing to notice all kinds of important differences? The truth is that it's simply not possible to understand anything complicated without focusing on certain elements to reduce that complexity. Economists have certain things they like to focus on, and scarcity is one of them. This focus means that we do not notice the mechanics of the espresso machine, nor the colour schemes of the coffee bars, nor other interesting, important facts. But we gain from that focus, too, and one of the things we gain is an understanding of the 'system' – the economic system, which is far more all-encompassing than many people realise.

A word of caution is appropriate, though. The simplifications of economic models have been known to lead economists astray. Ricardo himself was an early casualty. He tried to extend his brilliantly successful model of individual farmers and landlords to explain the division of income in the whole economy: how much went to workers, how much to landlords and how much to capitalists. It didn't quite work, because Ricardo treated the whole agricultural sector as if it were one vast farm with a single landlord. A unified agricultural sector had nothing to gain from improving the land's productivity with roads or irrigation, because those improvements would also reduce the scarcity of good land. But an individual landlord in competition with the others would have plenty of incentive to make improvements. Tied up in the technical details, Ricardo failed to realise that thousands of landlords competing with each other would make different decisions than a single one.

Ricardo, of course, is not the only one to have let economic models beguile him. Quantitative analysts at the cutting edge of finance leaned too heavily on rigorous-seeming models of risk in 2006 and 2007, only to find out later they had destroyed the banks for which they worked – and a good chunk of the world economy. We'll find out more in Chapter 6 about why this happened. It's perhaps worth pointing out that economic models are not the only ones to have this flaw. For instance, engineers and architects use models of the laws of physics to help them build bold new structures. These models are not always successful: the award-winning Kemper Arena collapsed, with no loss of life, just twenty-four hours after hosting the American Institute of Architects Convention. The laws of physics are not to blame – merely the fact that sometimes what the models leave out is more important than what they include.

So no model can explain everything. But we are about to discover that Ricardo's model goes further than Ricardo himself could ever have imagined. It doesn't just explain the principles behind coffee bars and farming. If applied correctly, it shows that environmental legislation can dramatically affect income distribution. It explains why some industries naturally have high profits, while in other industries high profits are a sure sign of collusion. It even manages to explain why educated people object to immigration by other educated people, while the less skilled complain about immigration by other unskilled workers.

Different reasons for high rent

Do you care if you get ripped off?

I do. A lot of things in this life are expensive. Of course, sometimes that expense is a natural outcome of the power of scarcity.

For instance, there are not many apartments overlooking Central Park in New York or Hyde Park in London. Because so many people want them, those apartments are expensive, and a lot of people end up being disappointed. There is nothing sinister about that. But it's not nearly so obvious why popcorn is so expensive at the cinema – there was no popcorn shortage last time I checked. So the first thing we might want to do is to distinguish between different reasons for things being expensive.

In Ricardo's terms, we would like to know the different causes of high rents. Knowing this about meadows is only mildly interesting (unless you are a farmer) but takes on a sudden significance when applied to the question of why your flat's rent seems so extortionate, or whether banks are ripping us off. But we can start with meadows and apply what we learn more widely.

We know that rents on the best land are determined by the difference in fertility between the best land and the marginal land. So the obvious reason that rents might be high is that the best land produces very valuable crops relative to the marginal land. As mentioned a couple of pages ago, five bushels of grain is a £5 rent at £1 a bushel, but at £200,000 a bushel, five bushels of grain is a £1-million rent. If grain is expensive, it's only natural that the scarce meadows that produce it will also be expensive.

But there's another way to drive rent on meadows up, and it is not nearly so natural. Let's say landlords get together and manage to persuade the local sheriff that there should be what in the UK is called a 'green belt', a broad area of land around the city on which property development is very strongly discouraged by tough planning regulations. The landlords claim that it would be a shame to cover beautiful wild land with farms, and so farming on the land should be made illegal.

The landlords stand to benefit hugely from such a ban, because it would drive up the rents on all legal land. Remember that rents on meadowland are set by the difference between the productivity of such land and the productivity of the marginal land. Ban farming on that marginal land, and the rent on meadows will jump; where once the alternative to paying rent and farming on meadows was to farm on grassland rent-free, now there is no alternative. Farmers are much more eager to farm on meadows now that farming on the grassland is illegal, and the rent they're willing to pay is much higher too.

So we've found two reasons why rents might be high. The first is that it's worth paying a lot for good land, because the grain that good land produces is so valuable. The second is that it's worth paying a lot for good land because the alternatives that should be available are not.

Those readers currently renting property in London may have furrowed brows at this point. London is surrounded by the original Green Belt, created in the 1930s. Is that why property in London is so expensive to rent or buy – not because it's so much better than the alternative, but because the alternative has been made illegal?

It is a combination of both: it is certainly true that London is unique, and a better place to put plush flats or office buildings than Siberia, Kansas City or even Paris. Rents are high, in part, for that reason. But another reason why property in London is expensive is because of the Green Belt. One effect is to keep London from sprawling out across the surrounding region – which many people think is a good idea. The other effect is to transfer a massive amount of money from London tenants to London landlords: the Green Belt keeps rents and house prices in London much higher than they would be, in exactly the same way as a ban on grassland farming keeps rents on meadow and scrub much higher than they would otherwise be.

This is not an argument against the Green Belt. There are lots of benefits in having London's population capped at fewer than nine million people, instead of nineteen million or twenty-nine million. But it is important that when we are weighing the pros and cons of legislation like the Green Belt, we understand that its effects are more than simply to preserve the environment. Office rents in London's West End are higher than in Manhattan or central Tokyo – in fact, the West End is the most expensive place in the world to rent an office. The Green Belt has made property in London scarce relative to the people who want to use it, and of course, strength comes from scarcity.

Now it's time for your first economics test. Why would improvements in the quality and price of the commuter train services that bring people into London's mainline stations, such as Waterloo, from the surrounding suburbs please anyone who rents a property in central London? And why might the city's landlords be less enthusiastic about such improvements?

The answer is that improved public transport increases the alternatives to renting a place in the city. When a two-hour commute becomes a one-hour commute, and people are able to get a seat on the train instead of standing, some decide they'd rather save money and move out of central London. Vacant apartments then appear on the market. Scarcity lessens, and rents fall. Improving commuter services wouldn't just affect commuters; it would affect everyone involved in London's property market.

Are we being ripped off?

One of the problems with being an undercover economist is that you start to see 'green belts' of one kind or another all over the place. How can we tell the difference between things that are expensive because they are naturally scarce, and things that are expensive because of artificial means – legislation, regulation or foul play?

Ricardo's model can help here, too. We need to appreciate a hidden parallel between natural resources, like fields or busy locations, and companies. Fields are ways of turning stuff into different stuff: manure and seed into grain. Companies are the same. A car manufacturer turns steel, electricity and other ingredients into cars. A petrol station turns pumps, big tanks of fuel and land into petrol in your tank. A bank turns computers, advanced accounting systems and cash into banking services. Without perpetrating too much intellectual violence, we can replace 'rent' with 'profit' throughout Ricardo's model. Rent is the return landlords receive from their property; profit is the return company owners earn from *their* property.

Let's use banking as an example. Imagine that one bank is very good at producing banking services – it has a fantastic corporate culture, a strong brand and has developed the best specialised banking software. Good people work there and other good people join just to learn from them. All this adds up to what economist John Kay (who explicitly invokes Ricardo's model) calls a 'sustainable competitive advantage', meaning the sort of edge over the competition that will produce profits year in and year out.

Let's call this überbank Axel Banking Corporation.* A second bank, Bob's Credit and Debt, is not quite so competent: the brand is less trusted, the corporate culture is so-so. It's not bad, but it's not great either. A third bank, Cornelius's Deposit Enterprises, is extremely inefficient: it has a terrible reputation, the tellers are rude to the customers and control of expenses is non-existent.

---

*As I work on the second edition in late 2010, it strikes me that choosing banks for this example – rather than, say, brewers or carpet weavers – was not one of my better decisions. Oh well. The analysis still stands, even if half the banks don't.

Cornelius's bank is less efficient than Bob's outfit and grossly incompetent compared with Axel's Banking Corporation. All this should remind us of the three types of land: meadowland, which is very efficient at producing grain; scrub, which is less efficient; and grassland, which is even less efficient.

Axel's bank, Bob's bank and Cornelius's bank compete to sell banking services by persuading people to open accounts or take out loans. But Axel's bank is so effective that it can either produce banking services more cheaply or produce better-quality services for the same cost. At the end of each year, Axel's bank will earn large profits, and Bob's bank, which serves its customers with less ease, will make something rather more modest, and Cornelius's bank will just break even. If the banking market was tougher, Cornelius's bank would go out of business. If the banking market started to get more attractive, Cornelius's bank would start to make a profit, and a new bank, even less efficient than Cornelius's, would enter the business. The new bank would be the marginal bank, just breaking even.

Without repeating every step of the analysis, we can remind ourselves that the rent on meadowland was set by comparison with the productivity of meadows to that of the marginal grassland. In the same way, Axel's profits are set in comparison with Cornelius's bank, the marginal bank, which we know should expect to make little or no profits: company profits, like rents, are determined by the alternatives. A company with stiff competition will be less profitable than a company with incompetent rivals.

You are probably thinking of a flaw in the analogy: the acreage of meadows is fixed, but companies can grow. But that's only partly true; companies cannot grow overnight without diluting their reputation and the other capabilities that made them successful. On the other hand, while acreage cannot change, the distinctions between different types of land will shift over time as irrigation, pest control and fertiliser technology develops. Ricardo's model, which ignores these changes over time, will explain trends in agricultural prices over decades but not over centuries, while it will explain corporate profitability over years, but not decades. As with many economic models, the analysis will work well for a certain time scale – in this case, the short and medium term. For other time scales, different models are needed.

This is all very well ... but what does it have to do with corporate profiteering?

The newspapers often point to high corporate profits as a sign that the consumer is being screwed. Are they right? Only sometimes. Ricardo's analysis suggests that there are two reasons why average profits of an industry like banking might be high. If customers really value great service and reputation, both Axel and Bob will make a lot of money (Cornelius's bank is the marginal bank and can expect very little). Newspaper hacks will be able to complain about excessive profits. If customers place only a small value on great service, Axel and Bob will be only moderately more profitable than Cornelius (still the marginal bank, still making very little), and average profits should be low. The commentators will be silent. But the motives and strategies used by the industry haven't changed – the only thing that changed was that customers put a premium on great service. Nobody is ripping anybody off; instead, Axel and Bob are being rewarded because they are offering something both scarce and highly valued.

But high profits are not always earned so fairly; sometimes the newspaper outrage is justified. There's a second explanation for high corporate profits. What if a kind of banking 'green belt' completely excluded Cornelius's bank from the market? In the real world there are lots of reasons why potential new companies cannot enter a market and compete. At times the consumers have only themselves to blame: new firms struggle to enter the market because customers will deal only with established companies. John Kay shows that certain 'embarrassing' products, including condoms and tampons, are highly profitable because new entrants find it hard to create a buzz about their products. More frequently, the firms themselves lobby their governments asking to be protected from competition, and many governments around the world grant monopoly licences, or are highly restrictive of entry into 'sensitive' industries like banking, farming or telecommunications. Whatever the reason, the effect is the same: established companies, free of competition, enjoy high profits. In fact, because of the similarity between the rents that can be charged on land with few substitutes and the profits enjoyed by a firm with few competitors, economists often call those profits 'monopoly rents'. It may be a confusing term, but you can blame David Ricardo's model and the lack of imagination shown by economists ever since.

If I want to know whether I am being ripped off by supermarkets, banks or drug companies, I can find out how profitable those industries are. If they are making high profits, then initially I am suspicious. But if it seems that it is fairly easy to set up a new company and compete, I become less suspicious. It means that the high profits are caused by a natural scarcity: there are not many really good banking organisations in the world, and good banking organisations are much more efficient than bad ones.

Resource 'rents'

Landlords and executives are not the only people who like to avoid competition and who like to enjoy monopoly rents. Trade unions, lobby groups, people studying for a professional qualification and even national governments like them too. Every day people all around us are trying to avoid competition or reap the rewards of others who have succeeded in doing so. Economists call this type of behaviour 'creating rents' and 'rent-seeking'.

It's not easy to do this. It turns out that the world is a naturally competitive place, and it is no simple matter to steer clear of competition. This is fortunate, because although competition is uncomfortable if you are on the wrong end of it, it is pleasant to be on the right end, as the customer. We all benefit when we are interacting with people who are competing to offer us jobs, newspapers or vacations in the sun, just as our mythical landlords benefited from competition between Bob and Axel.

One way of preventing competition is by controlling a natural resource such as farmland. There is only so much good farmland in the world, and only revolutions in agricultural techniques can change that. But farmland is not the only finite natural resource in the world. Another example is oil. Some parts of the world can produce oil cheaply, most notably Saudi Arabia, Kuwait, Iraq and other Gulf states. Other parts of the world can produce oil more expensively – Alaska, Nigeria, Siberia and Alberta. And there are many parts of the world that have oil that is so expensive to extract that nobody is even thinking of doing so. At the moment, places like Alberta produce the marginal oil.

The history of the oil industry is a case study in Ricardo's theory of rents. Until 1973, the world's oil supply was produced by 'oil meadows', largely in the Middle East. Despite the incredible value of oil to the industrialised economies, the price of oil was very low – less than $10 a barrel in today's money, because there was plenty of it available at very low costs. The Organisation of Petroleum Exporting Countries, OPEC, which was sitting on most of the oil meadows, decided in 1973 to take some of its own meadows out of commission, by ordering each member country to restrict oil production. Oil prices leapt to $40 a barrel, and then to $80, in today's money. They stayed high for years, because in the short run there were few alternative sources of oil. (The equivalent in Ricardo's world would have been to abruptly halt the cultivation of meadowland, leaving a delay before grassland could be cleared and ploughed, thereby causing a temporary grain shortage, raising rents.)

At $80 a barrel, plenty of alternatives looked cheap and were adopted over the years: producing electricity using coal instead of oil; building cars that gave better mileage; and exploring for oil in places like Alberta and Alaska. More and more 'energy scrubland' and 'energy grassland' was being cultivated. To keep prices high, OPEC was forced to accept a smaller and smaller share of the world oil market. Eventually Saudi Arabia broke ranks in 1985 and expanded production. Prices collapsed in 1986, and until just a couple of years ago the price of oil has roughly tracked the cost of production from marginal fields in places like Alberta – around $15–20 a barrel. In the last couple of years we have been tripped up by a combination of unexpectedly high demand in China with disruptions in Saudi Arabia, Iraq, Nigeria and Venezuela, all of which have caused oil prices to rise to more than $50 a barrel and beyond. Yet even at the much lower prices prevailing in the 1990s, the oil produced from the cheapest fields in Saudi Arabia and Kuwait, at a cost of a couple of dollars a barrel, was almost pure profit.*

*The oil price spike in the late 2000s – with an all-time high of $147 per barrel in 2008 – has revealed that in the medium term, oil fields are not the only source of scarcity. Oil companies found that the price of vital equipment – such as floating drilling rigs – rose sharply as everyone tried to respond to the high oil prices at once. The cost of producing oil in marginal places, which many people had assumed was constant, also rose. In Ricardo's world, the shortage might have been of ploughs and fertiliser. Scarcity can pop up in unexpected places.

When does crime pay?

A lot of the world's economy isn't closely linked to limited natural resources. That means that people have to find other ways to prevent competition.

One popular method is through violence, which is particularly popular in the drug trade and other organised crime. Drug dealers prefer not to have competitors driving down the price of drugs. Conceivably, by shooting or beating up enough people, a criminal gang could discourage rival gangs from entering the market and thus enjoy large profits. This is illegal, of course, but so is dealing in drugs; if you're risking prison anyway, there is little point in using half measures. If drug dealers want to enjoy strength from scarcity, they have to go to some lengths to make the competition scarce. Meanwhile, their customers are hardly likely to complain to the police about being ripped off.

Unfortunately for your average drug gang, even violence may not be enough to earn profits. The difficulty is that guns and aggressive young men are both in plentiful supply. Any gang making good money is tempting other gangs to muscle in on its territory – and there will be plenty of contenders. Economist Steven Levitt and sociologist Sudhir Venkatesh managed to get hold of the accounts of one American street gang. It turns out that the 'foot-soldiers' sometimes take home as little as $1.70 an hour. Promotion prospects are good, considering the rapid turnover of gang membership (people leave, or get killed, quite often); but even considering these prospects, the average wage is less than $10 an hour. This is not much given that over a four-year period, the typical gang member can expect to be shot twice, arrested six times and has a one-in-four chance of being killed.

Some criminal enterprises are more successful. Mafia groups

often get involved in legitimate businesses, such as wholesale laundry, which can make big profits only if entry is deterred. One way to deter entry is to threaten rivals. This is fairly easy, since laundry trucks and laundries themselves are much easier to find and damage than a bag of cocaine. It's even easier to threaten customers. Fans of *The Sopranos* know that the Mafia provides overpriced laundry services to restaurants as a way of extorting money. The reasons are clear enough: restaurants are particularly vulnerable to extortion because it doesn't take much disruption to put off customers, while collecting the extorted cash by providing an expensive service makes the protection money tax deductible. Profitable businesses usually attract competition, but in this case the competition reckon that there must be a safer way to make a living.

This suggests that it isn't violence as such that creates barriers to entry and sustainable profits – it's the effectiveness of an organisation. Axel's bank had it and Cornelius's didn't; the typical street gang lacks it, the Mafia seems to have it in spades.

'Conspiracies against the laity'

Luckily, in genteel corners of the developed world we are usually sheltered from people who use violence to keep out competition. But it does not mean that people have not worked out other ways to keep competitors at bay.

Trade unions are an obvious example. The purpose of a union is to prevent workers from competing with each other for jobs, driving down wages and conditions. If there is a lot of demand for electricians and few people who can do the job, then the electricians have strength from scarcity and should have excellent pay and conditions, with or without a union. If more and more electricians set up shop, this strength is sapped. The new electricians play the role of Bob the farmer. The trade union is designed partly to bargain collectively, but partly to block too much entry into the profession.

As mass-mechanisation spread in the nineteenth century, the incentive to unionise was considerable. Workers were a plentiful commodity: all gathered together in urban concentrations, easily substitutable for each other. Without unionisation, wages could be kept very low. With it, competition could be excluded and wages would rise – for the lucky ones inside the union. In the United States, trade unions were kept at bay by the law: anti-trust laws designed to prevent collusion between large companies were also directed against unions. But as the political climate changed, these laws were ruled inapplicable and trade unions grew in strength.

If trade unions were especially successful, then we might expect unionised industries to enjoy enormous salaries, and there have been times and places – such as the American car industry in the 1960s and 1970s – when this has been true. But trade unions face several obstacles to this kind of success. When unions are perceived as making unreasonable demands, causing prices to rise to a level that's deemed unacceptable by a large portion of the public, the public in turn puts pressure on politicians to regulate the unions. Sometimes the unions have their scarcity challenged by international competition, as in the case of American car workers, who enjoyed excellent wages and job security until the Japanese car industry used more efficient methods and started putting American manufacturers under pressure.

In the case of shrinking industries like the British shipbuilders or the car industry in the United States, available jobs are disappearing at such a rate that trade unions have great trouble maintaining their scarcity value; the union can never threaten to cut off the supply of workers fast enough to keep pace with a vanishing demand.

In other industries it is not shrinking demand but powerful employers that curtail the power of the unions. In the United States, Wal-Mart has tremendous bargaining power: there were only two unionised Wal-Marts in North America in the spring of 2004, when Wal-Mart announced that one of them, a branch in Quebec, would be closed because the union was damaging its business model. Another Canadian branch of Wal-Mart, in Weyburn, Saskatchewan, acquired a union late in 2008 – but only after four years of legal challenges from Wal-Mart. In the United Kingdom, teachers' wages were kept low for years – and declining relative to average earnings – in spite of the fact that there was a shortage of qualified teachers. This is because the government, the single employer, has massive bargaining power. Ordinarily, when there is a shortage of workers, competition between employers would bid up wages. Only a monopoly employer could possibly maintain a situation where there is a serious shortfall of teachers but salaries do not rise to respond. The teachers have some strength from scarcity, but in this case the government has more.

Other professionals, like doctors, actuaries, accountants and lawyers manage to maintain high wages through other means than unionisation, erecting virtual 'green belts' to make it hard for potential competitors to set up shop. Typical virtual green belts will include very long qualification periods and professional bodies that give their approval only to a certain number of candidates per year. Many of the organisations that are put forth to protect us from 'unqualified' professionals in fact serve to maintain the high rates of the 'qualified' to whom we are directed. In fact, many of us, informally, are happy to seek legal advice from experienced professionals who lack the formal qualification – even medical advice from medical students, foreign doctors or alternative therapists. But the legal and medical professions do their best to limit the supply of fully qualified professionals and outlaw any low-cost substitutes: if you can't afford the rent on meadow, the scrub and the grassland are forbidden. Small wonder that George Bernard Shaw said that the professions were 'all conspiracies against the laity'.

And now for something controversial

Immigration has always been an emotive issue and although national security has recently become a concern, the debate continues to revolve around an old question: do immigrants steal our jobs? They may steal your job, but they certainly haven't stolen mine.

Well-educated workers with jobs requiring skill and training, along with businesses in need of cheap labour, tend to welcome immigration as part of an enriching process which adds to each nation's economic and cultural life, while poorly educated workers tend to reject any further immigration by unskilled immigrants on the grounds that 'they steal our jobs'. Perhaps that's too much of a caricature, but it makes sense from a self-interested viewpoint.

As one of those skilled workers I dislike resistance to immigrants and would like to see more immigration. But then, I would, wouldn't I? If you need skilled and unskilled labour together to get useful work done, then it is in my direct interests to see more unskilled workers come to the country, and directly against the interests of the unskilled workers who are already here.

Imagine me and my fellow well-educated citizens as landowners, but instead of 'meadow' read 'degree'. My skills and qualifications are a resource, just as a meadow is a resource. But are my skills a *scarce* resource? Imagine that I go to work for Tesco's management team. When my skills (let's not be too specific about what they are supposed to be) are combined with the hard work of store assistants and shelf-stackers, we're a productive team. Who gets to enjoy the proceeds depends on whose abilities are scarce. If the country is short of unskilled shelf-stackers, their wages will have to rise to attract people into the job. But if the country is short of skilled managers and full of unskilled shelf-stackers, I'll be paid well for my scarcity value, just as landlords were paid well for scarce land once enough farmers showed up.

Some blame resistance to immigration on the racism of the uneducated. An alternative, and more convincing, theory suggests that everybody is acting in his own self interest. New workers are good for people who have assets that become relatively scarcer, whether those assets are meadows or degrees; but it is understandable if new workers are loathed by established ones. In fact, the people who are most harmed by new immigration are the previous group of immigrants, who find their wages nailed to the floor.

The facts support the application of Ricardo's theory to immigration. Skilled immigrants lower the wages of skilled natives, and unskilled immigrants lower the wages of unskilled natives. In the UK, the salaries of nurses in the National Health Service have been kept low by the influx of thirty thousand foreign nurses; immigrants in the UK are nearly 50 per cent more likely than natives to have a university degree. In contrast, in the United States, which takes in a far higher percentage of low-skilled immigrants than the UK does, it is unskilled wages that have stayed low: the income of unskilled workers has barely kept pace with inflation for the last forty years.

What should economists do?

We've been thinking like economists throughout this chapter. But what does that mean? We've used one major economic model to deepen our understanding of a variety of situations. The chapter has moved from some objective-sounding analysis of who makes money from the cappuccino business to the dangerous political territory of planning restrictions and immigration.

Some economists would claim that there is no difference between their analysis of coffee rents and their analysis of immigration. In an important sense, that's true. Economics is in many ways just like engineering; it will tell you how things work and what is likely to happen if you change them. The economist can show that allowing lots of skilled immigrants will help control the gap between skilled and unskilled wages, while allowing unskilled immigrants will do the reverse. What societies and their leaders do with the information is another matter.

Yet the fact that economics itself is a tool for objective analysis doesn't mean that economists are always objective. Economists study power, poverty, growth and development. It is hard to wield the models that underlie such subjects and remain unmoved by the real world behind them.

So economists often step beyond their role as engineers of economic policy and become advocates. David Ricardo, for example, was an early campaigner for free trade. He was encouraged by his friend, James Mill, to run for parliament; he won a seat in 1819 when he campaigned for repeal of the Corn Laws, which severely restricted the import of grain. Ricardo's theories had demonstrated clearly that the Corn Laws were shovelling money into the pockets of landlords at the expense of everyone else in the country. Ricardo was not content simply to observe the effects of the Corn Laws, he wanted to abolish them.

Economists come to similar conclusions today about protectionist laws, which, as we will see in Chapter 9, protect privileged pressure groups at the expense of the rest of us in the developed world and the developing world alike. Billions of people could benefit from better economic policies. Millions are dying because of bad ones. Sometimes the logic of economics is so compelling that it's impossible for economists not to take a stand.

2

What Supermarkets Don't Want You to Know

On a sunny day in London you can purchase a cappuccino and sip away as the capsules on the Eye, the capital's landmark Ferris wheel, rotate high above you, occasionally passing between you and the sun ... one of life's simple pleasures.

Everywhere you look around the Eye you can see vendors with scarce resources, trying to exploit that scarcity. There is only one coffee bar in the immediate area, for instance. There is also a lone souvenir shop doing brisk business. But the most obvious example is the London Eye itself. It towers over most of London's most famous buildings and is the world's largest observation wheel. The scarcity power is clearly considerable, but it is not unlimited: the London Eye may be unique, but it is also optional. People can always choose not to go. Further along the river, the Millennium Dome was similarly unique, 'the largest fabric structure in the world', boasted the local authority. Yet the Dome proved a commercial disaster because uniqueness alone wasn't enough to persuade people to pay enough to cover the vast costs of its construction. (Eventually it was converted into a music and sports arena. It really helps to have a sensible business plan.) Businesses with scarcity power cannot force us to pay unlimited prices for their products, but they can choose from a variety of strategies to make us pay more. It's time for the Undercover Economist to get to work and find out more.

The only coffee provider beside the London Eye wields plenty of scarcity power over the customer. It's not innate, but is reflected glory from the amazing setting. As we know, because customers will pay high prices for coffee in attractive locations, the coffee bar's rent will be high. Their landlords have rented out some of this scarcity value to a coffee bar, just like the owners of Manhattan's skyscrapers, or train stations from Waterloo to Shinjuku. Scarcity is for rent – at the right price.

But how should the bar's managers exploit the scarcity they are renting from the London Eye? They could simply double the price of a cappuccino. Some people would pay the new price, but many would not. Alternatively, they could cut prices and sell much more coffee. They could cover wages and ingredients by charging as little as 60p a cup. But unless they were able to increase their sales dozens of times over, they'd not make enough to cover their rent. That's the dilemma: higher margins per cup, but fewer cups; or lower margins on more cups.

It would be nice to sidestep that dilemma, by charging 60p to people who are not willing to pay more and £5 to people who are willing to pay a lot to enjoy the coffee and the view. That way they would have the high margins whenever they could get them and still sell coffee at a small profit to the skinflints. How to do it, though? Have a price list saying, 'Cappuccino, £5, unless you're only willing to pay 60p'?

Cappuccino for the lavish   £5.00
Cappuccino for the thrifty   60p

It does have a certain something, but I doubt it would catch on with the coffee-buying public of London's South Bank. So coffee bars have to be more subtle.

For years the incumbent coffee bar was Costa Coffee, who in the early 2000s used to have an elegant strategy: Costa offered 'Fair Trade' coffee to anyone willing to pay an extra 10p. Fair trade coffee comes with a promise to offer good prices to coffee farmers in poor countries. But there is no guarantee that any particular price premium paid by a consumer is the same as the price premium received by the coffee producer. At the time the fair trade premium received by farmers was between 40p and 55p per pound of coffee. That relatively small premium was enough nearly to double the income of a farmer in Guatemala, where the average income was less than $2000 a year. But since the typical cappuccino is made with just a quarter-ounce of coffee beans, the premium paid to the farmer should have translated into a cost increase for Costa of less than a penny a cup.

Of the extra money that Costa charged, more than 90 per cent did not reach the farmer. Their suppliers, Cafédirect, told me that they did not get a cut, so the money went to Costa's bottom line – unless using the fair trade coffee somehow increased their costs hugely. The truth is that fair trade coffee wholesalers could pay two, three or sometimes four times the market price for coffee in the developing world without adding anything noticeable to the production cost of a cappuccino, because coffee beans make up such a small proportion of that cost. Charging an extra 10p gave the impression that that was the cost of the fair trade coffee, but a customer who reached that conclusion would have been wrong. A certain Undercover

Economist made some inquiries. Costa eventually worked out that the whole business gave the wrong impression, and at the end of 2004 began to offer fair trade coffee on request, *without* a price premium. Costa abandoned the premium of fair trade coffee because it was bad public relations, not because it was unprofitable.

But *why* was it profitable to charge a higher mark-up on the cost of production on fair trade coffee than on normal coffee? Certainly not because Costa objected to the whole idea of fair trade and tried to discourage such idealistic behaviour with their pricing. The reason has nothing to do with fair trade at all: it's because fair trade coffee allowed Costa to find customers who are willing to pay a bit more if given a reason to do so. By ordering a fair trade cappuccino, you sent two messages to Costa. One message may or may not have interested them:

'I think that fair trade coffee is a product that should be supported.'

The second message is the one that they were straining to hear: 'I don't really mind paying a bit extra.'

This immediately gave Costa the information they were looking for. They know that socially concerned citizens tend to be less careful with their cash in coffee bars, while unconcerned citizens tend to keep their eyes on the price.

Cappuccino for the concerned   £1.85
Cappuccino for the unconcerned   £1.75

Costa's strategy was designed to get maximum value out of the scarcity power they rented from the London Eye. They were torn between raising prices and losing customers, or lowering prices and losing margins. If they had to charge the same price to every customer, they would simply have had to guess the best trade-off between the two options. But if they could charge a high price to the lavish (or concerned) and a low price to the thrifty (or unconcerned), then they could enjoy the best of both worlds. And there is no need to worry on Costa's behalf that this strategy has now been denied to them. Several years on, Costa still has plenty of alternative ways to identify customers for a price increase. Nor is there anything unusually Machiavellian about Costa Coffee. Any well-run business would seek to charge each customer the maximum price he'd be willing to pay – and they do.

Take a Starbucks, any Starbucks. For the sake of argument, take the Starbucks in St Pancras Station in London. As of late 2010, the price list looks like this:

Cappuccino	£2.10
Hot Chocolate	£2.25
Caffé Mocha	£2.40
White Chocolate Mocha	£2.80
Venti White Chocolate Mocha	£3.40

Or, to translate:

Cappuccino – no frills	£2.10
Hot Chocolate – no frills	£2.25
Mix them together – I feel special	£2.40
Use different powder – I feel very special	£2.80
Make it huge – I feel greedy	£3.40

Starbucks isn't merely seeking to offer a variety of alternatives to customers. It's also trying to give the customer every opportunity to signal that they've not been looking at the price. It doesn't cost much more to make a larger cup, to use a flavoured syrup or to add chocolate powder or a squirt of whipped cream. Every single product on the menu above costs Starbucks almost the same to produce, down to the odd few pence or so.

Does this mean that Starbucks is overcharging all of its customers? No. If so, a regular cappuccino or hot chocolate would cost £3.30, and you could have all the frills you wanted for 10p. Perhaps Starbucks would like to do that, but they can't force price-sensitive customers to pay those prices. By charging wildly different prices for products that have largely the same cost, Starbucks is able to smoke out customers who are less sensitive about the price. Starbucks doesn't have a way to identify lavish customers perfectly, so it invites them to hang themselves with a choice of luxurious ropes.

There is also, incidentally, one more drink on offer at Starbucks that you won't see on the menu, which is cheaper than the traditional offerings:

The Invisible Cappuccino   £1.90

We'll find out more about why the Invisible Cappuccino exists, and how to order one, later in the chapter.

There's one born every minute: two ways to find him

There are three common strategies for finding customers who are cavalier about price. Let's cover two for now, and leave the best for last.

The first is what economists call 'first degree price discrimination', but we could call it the 'unique target' strategy: to evaluate each customer as an individual and charge according to how much he or she is willing to pay. This is the strategy of the used-car salesman or the estate agent. It usually takes skill and a lot of effort; hardly surprising, then, that it is most often seen for items that have a high value relative to the retailer's time – cars and houses, of course, but also souvenirs in African street stalls, where the impoverished merchant will find it worth bargaining for some time to gain an extra pound.

Now, however, companies are trying to automate the process of evaluating individual customers to reduce the time it takes. For instance, supermarkets accumulate evidence of what you're willing to pay by giving you 'discount cards', which are needed to take advantage of sale prices. In return for getting a lower price on certain items, you allow the stores to keep records of what you buy and then in turn offer you coupons for discounts on products. It doesn't work perfectly, because supermarkets can only send 'money off' vouchers, not 'money on' vouchers. 'Money on' vouchers have never been a success.

When technology allows, firms with scarcity power may use highly sophisticated methods to target customers. It's no secret any more that internet retailers such as Amazon can identify each customer by putting a tracing device called a 'cookie' on her computer. Amazon used to tailor their prices based on their records of individual customers. The company really was able to offer 'money on' vouchers: two customers buying exactly the same product would be offered different prices based on what, if anything, they had previously bought. Even though it would be more difficult than for online sales, supermarkets could, with the right technology, do the same thing – each customer could have an identity tag, and price labels would change according to who was looking at them.

Of course, the 'unique target' approach is unpopular. In Amazon's case, customers started to realise that if they deleted the cookies on their computers, they were offered different, often lower prices. And when they found out what the company was doing, there was an outcry. Like Costa, Amazon has promised not to do it any more.

Interestingly, people tend not to object nearly so much to the second approach, the 'group target' strategy, which is to offer different prices to members of distinct groups. Who could complain about reduced bus fares for children and the elderly? Surely it must be reasonable for coffee shops to offer a discount to people who work nearby, and for tourist attractions to let locals in for a lower rate? It often *seems* reasonable because people in groups who pay more are usually people who can afford more, and that's because people who can afford more are usually people who care less about price. But we shouldn't forget that this is a convenient coincidence. Companies trying to increase their profits and get the maximum value out of their scarcity are interested in who is *willing* to pay more, rather than who can *afford* to pay more.

For instance, when Disney World in Florida offers admission discounts of over 50 per cent to locals, they're not making a statement about the grinding poverty of the Sunshine State. They simply know that for a reduced price, locals are more likely to come regularly. But tourists will probably come once, and once only, whether it is cheap or expensive.

This example gets to the heart of things and tells us what we really mean by 'price sensitivity' or 'being lavish' or 'being cavalier about prices'. The important concept is this: when I raise the price, how much do my sales fall? And when I cut the price, how much do my sales rise? Economists tend to call this 'own-price elasticity'. Personally I think 'price sensitivity' is a bit more descriptive.

Tourists visiting Florida are less price-sensitive than locals, which means that if Disney World raises its prices, locals are more likely to skip a day at the park. By the same token, if the admission price falls, locals may make repeat visits in a way that tourists probably won't. Being rich is sometimes connected with being insensitive to prices, but not always. Business-class air travel is expensive, because companies are willing to pay, and airlines have the scarcity power to take advantage of that fact. Business telephone calls are inexpensive, because although companies would be willing to pay, there is too much competition around for any phone company to force them to.

The same is true of discounts at coffee bars for local workers. The AMT coffee bar in Waterloo station in London used to knock 10 per cent off the cost of your coffee if – as I did at the time – you worked locally. This wasn't because the local workers were poor; they included top government officials and the extravagantly remunerated employees of the gigantic oil company Shell. The discount reflected the fact that local workers are price-sensitive despite being rich. Commuters who pass through Waterloo in a hurry see only one or two coffee bars and are willing to pay high prices for convenience. Local workers pop out of the office at 11 a.m. for coffee and could walk in any direction. They can buy from several cafés, all equally convenient, all of which they will have had a chance to sample. They are bound to be more price-sensitive, even if they are rich.

The 'individual target' strategy is difficult, partly because it requires a lot of information and partly because it tends to be very unpopular. Despite the difficulties, however, it's so profitable that companies always explore new ways to do it. The 'group target' strategy of discounts for students or locals is less effective but easier to put into action, and it's usually socially acceptable, even welcomed. Either will deliver more profits than simply treating all customers as a homogenous mass.

The third way: turkeys voting for Christmas

The cleverest and most common way to persuade turkeys to vote for Christmas is the 'self-incrimination' strategy – the one Costa Coffee and Starbucks both use when they persuade some of their customers into confessing that they are not sensitive to price. To get customers to give themselves away, the company has to sell products that are at least slightly different from each other. So they offer products in different quantities (a large cappuccino instead of a small one, or an offer of three for the price of two), or with different features (with whipped cream or white chocolate or fair trade ingredients), or even in different locations, because a sandwich in a station kiosk is not the same product as a physically identical sandwich in an out-of-town superstore.

It's reasonable to ask how common this tactic really is. Because the products are different, you never quite know whether the firm is using a price-targeting trick or merely passing on added costs. It could be that it really does cost 10p more to put fair trade coffee in a cappuccino; maybe cans of whipped cream are expensive to refrigerate and troublesome to clean and the staff hate using them; perhaps large cups of coffee take longer to drink, and so the charge is for table space not coffee – in which case, charging a higher price is not a strategy to get me to incriminate myself but simply the coffee bar passing its costs through to me. But I think it's safe to say that companies are always alert for ways to squeeze the maximum advantage out of whatever scarcity power they have, and price-targeting is the most common way to do that. If it looks like price-targeting, it probably is.

Although use of this strategy is hard to prove, there's plenty of circumstantial evidence around if you know where to look. For instance, the premium you pay for a large cappuccino instead of a small one is the same whether you drink it in the café or take it away. (Except for my favourite coffee shop, the Monmouth in Covent Garden. They are short of space, and will charge a mark-up for a large cappuccino if you drink it in the shop. However, they charge less for take-out coffee, and it comes in only one size. I have decided they are far too nice to try to make profits.) That doesn't make sense if it's a charge for taking up space. So we have good reason to believe that coffee bars try for a 'self targeting' strategy, charging high prices to customers who demonstrate a willingness to pay them.

Coffee bars are not alone

Supermarkets have turned price-targeting into an art, developing a vast array of strategies to that end. Above the main concourse

How far would you walk to save 30p?

About 500m is all that separates two Marks & Spencer stores with somewhat different pricing policies. But for most city dwellers it's just not worth the walk.

of Liverpool Street station, there's a Marks & Spencer 'Simply Food' store, catering for busy commuters on the way in and out of London. We know all about the scarcity value of train stations by now, so perhaps it shouldn't surprise us to find that this shop isn't cheap, even compared with another branch of Marks & Spencer merely 500 metres or so away, at Moorgate.

I picked up five products at random in the Liverpool Street store and managed to locate four of them in the Moorgate store. Every single one was about 15 per cent cheaper there. Big salads were down from £3.50 to £3.00, sandwiches from £2.20 to £1.90. But even when such discrepancies come to light, few City workers would be willing to stray that distance to save 30p. A bold and effective piece of price-targeting.

Other supermarkets are more circumspect about their pricing policy. Going undercover once again, I made a comparison between the smallish Sainsbury's supermarket in Tottenham Court Road in the heart of London's West End, and the large store in Dalston, one of East London's less prosperous neighbourhoods. It was harder to find examples of identical products selling for different prices, although by no means impossible. Does this mean that Sainsbury's doesn't price-target as much as M&S? Not at all. They simply go about the whole process with more finesse.

When researching Sainsbury's, my approach was the same as with M&S: walk into the shop and see what caught my eye. As you probably know, what catches our eyes as we walk into the supermarket is no coincidence; it's the result of careful planning designed to throw attractive but profitable products in the path of customers. What constitutes an attractive product depends on who those customers are. In Tottenham Court Road the obvious goods were all quite expensive: Tropicana orange juice at £1.95 a litre, Tropicana 'Smoothies' at £1.99 for 100ml, 750ml of Vittel mineral water at 80p, and so on. It wasn't that these products were more expensive in Tottenham Court Road than in Dalston (only the Vittel was), it was just that in Dalston cheaper substitutes sprang into view far more readily.

For instance, I couldn't find inexpensive orange juice in the Tottenham Court Road store, but in Dalston, Sainsbury's own brand of fresh chilled juice was sitting next to the Tropicana at about half the price, and the concentrated juice was almost six times cheaper than the Tropicana. Brand-name pasta was the same price in both shops, but only in Dalston was it sitting next to Sainsbury's pasta, which again was almost six times cheaper. The effect was to target the whole Tottenham Court Road store at shoppers who are indifferent to prices, but to aim the Dalston stores at shoppers with a sharper eye for a bargain – while of course giving any price-blind Dalston shoppers plenty of opportunity to show their true colours.

Price-gouging the natural way

The best price-targeters pair their efforts to improve profits with apparently virtuous behaviour. We've seen how Costa Coffee trumpeted its commitment to fair trade while using it to identify customers with money to burn. It's also good business to offer discounts to the elderly and to students (translation: charge higher prices to people likely to have jobs). Who but a cynic – or an economist – could object to such commendable behaviour?

The favoured game at the moment has to be price-gouging the natural way, riding the bandwagon of organic food. Despite a lull in sales during the recent recession, organic food has been catching on for a variety of reasons, including the fact that in the wake of repeated food health scares, many people think organic food is better for them, or at least won't kill them. The supermarkets have come to the rescue with a plentiful supply of organic products that happen to be marked up far above their additional costs to the supermarket. In British supermarkets, these are often stacked together, apparently for the convenience of the organic shopper but also to the advantage of the supermarkets, who thereby reduce the risk that organic shoppers will notice the price of the typical alternative. In Washington DC's Wholefoods store, just across the street from Starbucks, the vast and luxurious fruit and vegetable section contains both organic and conventionally grown produce side by side ... but always side by side with a completely different product. The organic bananas are next to the 'conventional' (that is, non-organic) apples; the organic garlic is next to the conventional onions. You will never find the organic bananas next to the conventional bananas, or the organic garlic next to the conventional garlic. The price-comparison would be too sobering.

But is expensive organic food really part of a price-targeting tactic? Organic food should be more expensive: it costs more to produce and, with a shorter shelf life, it is also more expensive to distribute than the standard product. But as with your cappuccino, raw ingredients are only a small part of the price of most food on the supermarket shelves. For example, in the UK, organic milk commanded a premium at the farm gate of just three pence a litre in 2008; as a shopper, you'll pay around fifteen pence a litre extra. We should not be surprised that supermarkets are taking the opportunity afforded by the organic food movement to zap customers with well-aimed price increases. My recommendation, if you are convinced of the merits of organic food, is not to let food retailers exploit your enthusiasm: vote with your wallet by supporting any retailer – or direct supplier – who brings the price of organic and non-organic food closer together.

Bargain shopping and bargain stores

When I lived in Washington DC, I was across the street from the Wholefoods supermarket. On hearing this, people would comment on how wonderful the store is: Wholefoods prides itself on being 'The World's Leading Natural and Organic Food Supermarket', touts its community involvement and offers a jungle of fresh fruit and vegetables alongside hormone-free steaks, European cheeses and beers and luxury chocolates. It's a fun place to shop and offers great food. But my acquaintances also complain about how expensive Wholefoods is. But ... is it really expensive?

That depends on what you mean by expensive. Presumably people have some price comparison in mind. A fair one would be to compare prices in Wholefoods with prices in Safeway just five blocks away, a store known to the locals as 'Soviet Safeway' because of the small range of products and the harsh decor. Compare the price of the typical Wholefoods shopper's basket of goods, and nine times out of ten it will indeed be more expensive than the typical Safeway shopper's basket of goods. But that says more about the shoppers than the stores. As a matter of verifiable fact, when you compare the prices for the same goods, Wholefoods is just as inexpensive as Safeway.

Safeway and Wholefoods charge exactly the same for bananas. Exactly the same for a carton of cherry or grape tomatoes. Admittedly, Safeway's prices on onions, Irish butter and Cheerios are lower. But Wholefoods charges less for mineral water, Tropicana Premium orange juice and sweet onions. The simple truth is that if you bought a big basket of the *same* goods from Safeway and from Wholefoods, the price tag would probably come out within a dollar or two – and it would be just as likely that Wholefoods was cheaper.

That doesn't quite fit with our common-sense belief that some places are cheap and some places are expensive. But that belief never made much sense. After all, if some places really did predictably charge more for the same product with similar service in a similar location, that would imply that all of their customers were just idiots. Wholefoods is more fun to shop in, but when push comes to shove, it's still just a supermarket, and you wander around filling your own cart just as in Safeway.

Wholefoods is not expensive in the sense that it charges more for the same goods. It is expensive because of where its price-targeting policies are focused: prices for the basics may be competitive, but the selection in Wholefoods is aimed at customers with a different view of what 'basics' are.

For example: Safeway charges more for Tropicana orange juice and for Poland Spring sparkling mineral water than Wholefoods does. For Wholefoods customers Tropicana juice and sparkling water *are* the basics, and so they need to be priced competitively, while Safeway customers might well consider that tap water and concentrated orange juice were perfectly acceptable alternatives. A Safeway customer who buys sparkling water and fresh Tropicana juice is signalling a taste for luxury. A Wholefoods customer may pass by the cheaper option of Tropicana in favour of a more expensive Smoothie made of fresh-squeezed juice at the in-house juice bar.

The basic yellow and sweet onions are priced similarly at both stores. But at Wholefoods, customers have the option to pick fancy varieties: pearl onions, red onions and even organic onions, at a hefty mark-up. The Wholefoods shopper who is looking for decently priced products will find them. The Wholefoods shopper who grabs a bag of the first onions he sees will pay dearly for his lack of price-curiosity.

That is why a basket of goods from Wholefoods can cost so much more than a basket of goods from Safeway. It's not because

Wholefoods is 'expensive' and Wholefoods customers are stupid. It's because Wholefoods offers additional, expensive choices, which Wholefoods shoppers are willing to take because they perceive the quality premium is worth it.

So here's my advice: if you want a bargain, don't try to find a cheap store. Try to *shop* cheaply. Similar products are, very often, priced similarly. An expensive shopping trip is the result of carelessly choosing products with a high mark up, rather than wandering into a store with 'bad value', because price-targeting accounts for much more of the difference between prices than any difference in value between one shop and another.

Mix it up!

Another very common pricing strategy is sale pricing. We're all so used to seeing a store-wide sale with hundreds of items reduced in price that we don't pause and ask ourselves why on earth shops do this. When you think hard about it, it becomes quite a puzzling way of setting prices. The effect of a sale is to lower the average price a store charges. But why knock 30 per cent off many of your prices twice a year, when you could knock 5 per cent off year-round? Varying prices is a lot of hassle for stores because they need to change their labels and their advertising, so why does it make sense for them to go to the trouble of mixing things up?

One explanation is that sales are an effective form of self-targeting. If some customers shop around for a good deal and some customers do not, it's best for stores to have either high prices to prise cash from the loyal (or lazy) customers, or low prices to win business from the bargain hunters. Middle-of-the-road prices are no good: not high enough to exploit loyal customers, not low enough to attract the bargain-hunters. But that's not the end of the story, because if prices were stable, then surely even the most price-insensitive customers would learn where to get particular goods cheaply. So rather than stick to either high or low prices, shops jump between the two extremes.

One common situation is for two supermarkets to be competing for the same customers. As we've discussed, it's hard for one to be systematically more expensive than the other without losing a lot of business, so they will charge similar prices on average, but both will also mix up their prices. That way, both can distinguish the bargain hunters from those in need of specific products, like people shopping to pick up ingredients for a cook-book recipe they are making for a dinner party. Bargain-hunters will pick up whatever is on sale and make something of it. The dinner-party shoppers come to the supermarket to buy specific products and will be less sensitive to prices. The price-targeting strategy only works because the supermarkets always vary the patterns of their special offers, and because it is too much trouble to go to both stores or to order two separate internet deliveries, carefully comparing the price of each good every time we go online. If shoppers could reliably predict what was to be discounted, they could choose recipes ahead of time, and even choose the appropriate supermarket to pick up the ingredients wherever they're least expensive.

In fact, it is just as accurate, and more illuminating, to turn the 'sale' on its head and view prices as premiums on the sale price rather than discounts on the regular price. The random pattern of sales is also a random pattern of price increases – companies find it more profitable to increase prices (above the sale price) by a larger amount on an unpredictable basis than by a small amount in a predictable way. Customers find it troublesome to avoid unpredictable price increases – and may not even notice them for lower-value goods – but easy to avoid predictable ones.

*

Try to spot other odd mix-ups next time you're in the supermarket. Have you noticed that supermarkets often charge ten times as much for fresh chilli peppers in a package as for loose fresh chillies? That's because the typical customer buys such small quantities that he doesn't think to check whether they cost 4p or 40p. Randomly tripling the price of a vegetable is a favourite trick: customers who notice the mark-up just buy a different vegetable that week; customers who don't have self-targeted a whopping price rise.

I once spotted a particularly inspired trick while on a search for crisps. My favourite brand was available on the top shelf in salt and pepper flavour and on the bottom shelf, just a few feet away, in other flavours, all the same size. The top-shelf crisps cost 25 per cent more, and customers who reached for the top shelf demonstrated that they hadn't made a price-comparison between two near-identical products in near-identical locations. They were more interested in snacking.

Admittedly, for some people the difference in flavours is important. Some will notice the higher price for salt and pepper flavour and, irritated, pay anyway. Others will prefer the different flavours and count themselves lucky that they have inexpensive tastes.

But this is an example of a universal truth about supermarkets: they are full of close (or not so close) substitutes, some cheap, some expensive, and with a strong random element to the pricing. The random element is there so that only shoppers who are careful to notice, remember and compare prices will get the best bargains. If you want to outwit the supermarkets, simple observation is your best weapon. And if you can't be bothered to do that, you really don't need to save money.

Reality check number one: does the company really have scarcity power?

It's time for a reality check. When we talk about big companies it is easy to get carried away with notions of how they are infinitely powerful and we are infinitely gullible. Not true.

Remember that no company has power unless it has scarcity, and often that scarcity is something we give them through our own laziness. Nothing is stopping us from walking down the street or driving from one shop to another; certainly nothing is stopping us from a bit of mental arithmetic when buying chillies, or from glancing around for two seconds when buying crisps.

Every shop has a tiny amount of scarcity power, if only because it's an effort to walk out and go next door. But some have more scarcity power than others, which is worth thinking about when estimating the risk of being waylaid by price-targeting strategies.

For instance, what is the answer to the question we posed in the previous chapter: why does popcorn cost so much at cinemas? Is it for the same reason that wine is expensive in restaurants? We know that the first-glance answer in both cases is, 'Because once they get you in the door they can charge whatever they want.' We also know that this first answer is probably not true. Customers may be dumb, but they're not that dumb. People expect to be charged a lot for wine in restaurants and for popcorn and sweets in cinemas *before* they walk in the door.

Now we have a better answer: it's likely to be a price-targeting strategy. Film-goers who are sensitive to price will bring their own snacks from home, or go without. People who are not sensitive to price – perhaps because they're on a date and don't want to look stingy – will simply pay for the overpriced popcorn. Very clever.

This is a much better explanation, since in many towns there is only one cinema, and even in towns with more than one, there is often only one showing the film you want to see. This gives a cinema a lot of scarcity power, and if the manager is clever he'll want to exploit that power to the full.

Yet the same story doesn't ring true for pricey wine at restaurants. The typical restaurant has less scarcity power than a cinema because in most towns there will be a variety of alternatives. Whenever there is little scarcity power, prices need to reflect costs. Yet even the most ordinary restaurants seem to charge a lot for wine. A better explanation is that one of the big costs in a restaurant business is table space. Restaurateurs would therefore like to charge customers for dawdling, but because they cannot do that, they charge higher prices for products that tend to be consumed in longer meals: not just wine but also starters and desserts.

We go to a cinema to see a film and to a restaurant to eat, so is the truth also that we always get gouged on 'options'? Not at all. One option available in both cinemas and in restaurants is the option to use the toilets; this is always an option provided free of charge. Tap water is also free in restaurants. It is not the option that invites the gouging, it's the lack of price sensitivity that allows a business with scarcity power to practise price-targeting.

Reality check number two: can the company plug leaks?

Perhaps you are a company director rubbing your hands with glee as you read this, planning to deploy a range of clever price-targeting strategies in your own business. Before you get too excited, you'll need to deal with the leaks in your price-targeting system.

There are two potentially catastrophic leaks or great holes in an otherwise brilliant marketing scheme. If you don't deal with them, your plans will be in ruins.

The first problem is that supposedly price-insensitive customers may not play the self-targeting game. It's not hard to persuade price-sensitive customers to steer clear of an expensive product, but sometimes it is more difficult to prevent the price-insensitive customers from buying the cheaper one. This is not a problem in the case of small price differences; we have already seen that you can get some customers to pay a modest mark-up in absolute terms (if huge in relative terms), just by wrapping some chillies in a plastic bag, or moving a bag of crisps up onto the top shelf. When it comes to more substantial buying decisions it is not always so easy.

Some of the most extreme examples come from the travel industry: travelling first class by train or air is much more expensive than buying a standard ticket, but since the fundamental effect is to get people from A to B, it may be hard to wring much money out of the wealthier passengers. In order to price-target effectively, firms may have to exaggerate the differences between the best service and the worst. There is really no reason at all why standard train carriages shouldn't have tables, as they typically don't in the UK, for instance, except that potential customers for first class might decide to buy a cheaper ticket when they see how comfortable standard has become. So the standard passengers have to suffer.

The nineteenth-century French economist Emile Dupuit pointed to the early railways as an example:

> It is not because of the few thousand francs which would have to be spent to put a roof over the third-class carriage or to upholster the third-class seats that some company or other has

open carriages with wooden benches ... What the company is trying to do is prevent the passengers who can pay the second-class fare from travelling third class; it hits the poor, not because it wants to hurt them, but to frighten the rich ... And it is again for the same reason that the companies, having proved almost cruel to the third-class passengers and mean to the second-class ones, become lavish in dealing with first-class customers. Having refused the poor what is necessary, they give the rich what is superfluous.

The shoddy quality of most airport departure lounges across the world is surely part of the same phenomenon. If the free departure areas became decent places to spend time – last time I went through Heathrow's brand-new Terminal Five, I couldn't find a working power socket for my laptop – then airlines would no longer be able to sell business-class tickets on the strength of their 'executive' lounges. And it would also explain why flight attendants sometimes physically restrain passengers from the cheap seats from stepping off the plane before the passengers from first and business class. This is a 'service' aimed not at economy-class passengers but at those looking on in pity and disgust from the front of the plane. The message is clear: keep paying for your expensive seats, or next time you might be the wrong side of the flight attendant.

In the supermarkets, we see the same trick: products that seem to be packaged for the express purpose of conveying awful quality. Supermarkets will often produce an own-brand 'value' range, displaying crude designs that don't vary whether the product is lemonade, bread or baked beans. It wouldn't cost much to hire a good designer and print more attractive logos. But that would defeat the object: the packaging is carefully designed to put off customers who are willing to pay more. Even customers who

would be willing to pay five times as much for a bottle of lemonade will buy the bargain product unless the supermarket makes
some effort to discourage them. So, like the lack of tables in standard train carriages and the uncomfortable seats in airport
lounges, the ugly packaging of 'value' products is designed to
make sure that snooty customers self-target price increases on
themselves.

Starbucks offers a splendid example: the world's most famous
coffee company will serve you a better, stronger cappuccino if you
want one, and they will charge you less for it. Ask for it in any
Starbucks and the barista will comply without batting an eye. The
drink in question is the elusive 'short cappuccino' – at eight
ounces, a third smaller than the smallest size on the official menu,
the 'tall', and dwarfed by what Starbucks calls the 'customer-pre-
ferred' size, the 'Venti', which weighs in at twenty ounces and
more than two hundred calories before you add the sugar. The
problem with large cappuccinos is that it's impossible to make the
fine-bubbled milk froth ('microfoam', in the lingo) in large quantities, no matter how skilled the barista. A twenty-ounce
cappuccino is an oxymoron. Having sampled the short cappuccino in a number of Starbucks across the world, I can confirm that
it is a better drink than the buckets of warm milk – topped with
a veneer of froth – that the coffee chain advertises on its menus.

This secret cappuccino is cheaper, too. So why does this
cheaper, better drink – along with its sisters, the short latte and
the short coffee – languish unadvertised? The official line from
Starbucks is that there is no room on the menu board, although
this doesn't explain why the short cappuccino is also unmentioned
on the comprehensive Starbucks website, nor why the baristas will
serve you in a whisper rather than the usual practice of singing
your order to the heavens. Price targeting provides a far more
convincing answer: while some companies make their cheap

products look unattractive, Starbucks simply makes them invisible to those who don't ask around.

The most surprising examples of all come from the world of computers. For instance, IBM's 'LaserWriter E', a low-end laser printer, turned out to be exactly the same piece of equipment as their high-end 'LaserWriter' – except that there was an additional chip in the cheaper version to slow it down. The most effective way for IBM to price-target their printers was to design and mass-produce a single printer, then sell it at two prices. But of course to get anyone to buy the expensive printer they had to slow down the cheap one. It seems wasteful, but presumably it was cheaper for IBM to do this than design and manufacture two completely different printers. Intel, the chip manufacturer, played a similar game by selling two very similar processing chips at different prices. In this case, the inferior chip was actually more expensive to produce: it was made by taking the superior chip and doing extra work to disable one of its features.

Digital SLR cameras have been reported to use much the same tactic: that £600 amateur camera is basically the £1200 professional camera with some of the image processing software disabled. And software packages themselves often have two or more versions: one has full functionality (the 'professional' package), and the other sells to the mass market at a considerably reduced price. What some people don't realise is that the professional version is typically designed first, and certain features are disabled for the mass-market version. Despite the high price of the professional version, it's the cheaper version that actually has an extra up-front cost for the developer, and of course both versions are sold on CDs or supplied through a download, at the same low cost. Computer hardware, and software even more so, has a strange cost structure because of intensive research and development costs, and relatively low manufacturing costs. At the height of the internet bubble, giddy gurus were claiming that the different cost structure changes everything. Now the term of art is 'freemium' – which, of course, is a price targeting strategy in which one of the prices is zero. The internet has revolutionised many businesses, but as we've seen, the basic rules of making money in the digital age are not so different from the rules for train operators or coffee bars.

The first 'leak' in a price-targeting strategy, then, is that rich customers may buy cheap products, unless the products are deliberately sabotaged. The second 'leak' is a particularly difficult one for companies using a group-target strategy to plug: their products may leak from one group to another. The risk is that the customers who are being offered a discount buy the product and then resell it at a profit to the customers who are being charged a higher price. Up until now, we've mostly been discussing services that can't be resold (like a bus trip or a visit to Disney World) or products that are probably too much hassle to resell (such as a sandwich or a cup of coffee). That's not coincidence. Services and convenience products are the most fertile grounds for price-targeting strategies, because they don't leak. The really great pricing tricks take place on airlines, in restaurants and cocktail bars (not many bookshops have a 'happy hour'), in supermarkets and at tourist attractions.

In contrast, some products are inherently leaky: they're expensive, easy to transport and non-perishable. The obvious examples are digital goods – music, video and software – and pharmaceuticals. Companies go to tremendous lengths to plug leaks, which in an age when internet shopping allows us to order products from anywhere in the world are becoming increasingly difficult to prevent. For instance, the DVD industry agreed on a system of regional coding so that DVDs bought in the United States would not work in Europe. But that system is being circumvented by an alliance of customers and DVD-machine suppliers who willingly equip machines to read a DVD from anywhere in the world – and even more so by file-sharing networks.

If your instincts are anything like mine, it all seems like a pretty shabby trick. But the same popular opinion that despises the DVD industry for trying to sell their products at different prices in different markets also believes that the big pharmaceutical companies should supply drugs to poor countries at discounted prices. Confusingly, our moral intuitions seem to be sending us contradictory messages.

Maybe the story is as simple as this: when it's an important product like a treatment for HIV/AIDS, the most important thing is to get it to the poor; when it's as trivial as a DVD, our irritation at being ripped off is the dominant emotion. But that doesn't quite add up: DVDs make it to very poor areas, and surely we should be at least somewhat pleased that the poor get to watch films in bars and village halls across the developing world? Or, conversely, shouldn't we be even more outraged that the pharmaceutical companies are overcharging for crucial treatments in the developed world? An economist cannot solve these ethical conundrums, but economics can unwrap them so that at least the ethical question becomes clearer.

When price-targeting is a good thing

Here is a thought experiment.

Imagine a hypothetical pharmaceutical company called PillCorp, which has developed a uniquely powerful new treatment for HIV/ AIDS. Assume that it doesn't engage in any price-targeting and charges the same price across the globe. PillCorp will set the global price so that the gain in sales from cutting the price exactly balances the loss of margin from a price cut. For example, say that PillCorp cut prices and reduced their margins by half. Unless they doubled sales this would reduce profits. They could raise prices and double their margins, but if sales dropped by more than half that would also reduce profits. PillCorp will maximise profits by pricing at the point where either a price cut or a price increase would slightly damage the bottom line.

The price will be high, because people in rich countries will pay a lot for an effective treatment, and there is no point in losing customers who are paying thousands of pounds or dollars in an effort to pick up customers who are paying a few pence.

That looks like bad news. PillCorp is using its scarcity power to charge a high price for a life-saving drug. As a result, people in poor countries don't get the drug. People are dying because of PillCorp's greed.

Actually, it's only half bad news. People are also *living* because of PillCorp's greed. PillCorp developed the life-saving treatment because it was encouraged to do so by the hope of a lucrative patent. Pharmaceuticals are very expensive to research and develop, and somebody has to pay the bill. The current system is that public and private insurers pay, and since the United States is easily the largest market, innovation is driven by and largely paid for there.

Although PillCorp is making money by selling its drug at a high uniform global price, they could be doing better and so could everybody else. Economists don't just have in mind a shrug-your-shoulders-life's-like-that-sometimes 'could be better'. We mean something more precise: PillCorp could be making more money and serving the world better.

Say that a year's supply of drugs for one customer costs $10 for

PillCorp to produce, and retails at $1000. For rich customers willing to pay – or who have insurance that will pay – that's not really a problem. Each year of treatment transfers $990 from those living with AIDS to those who produced the treatment. But a taxi driver in Cameroon might be willing to pay only $50 a year for treatment; beyond that, he'd rather buy food, or petrol for his taxi. Because of PillCorp's global price policy, the taxi driver loses out on the treatment, and PillCorp loses out on the chance to make some profit. But if PillCorp were able to make a onetime discount to the taxi driver and sell him the treatment for any price between $10 and $50 – say $30 – everybody would be better off. The taxi driver gets treatment for $30 when he was willing to pay $50. PillCorp receives $30 in revenues for a $10 pill – a profit of $20.

That is what economists mean when we say a situation 'could be better'. If we can point to a change that could make at least one person better off, and nobody worse off, we say that the current situation is *inefficient*, or, in everyday language, that it could be better. (We also say that the current situation is *efficient* if every change that could make at least one person better off will also make somebody else worse off. It doesn't mean that an efficient situation can't be improved; it's just that there is no costless way to improve it.)

Now imagine that PillCorp practises price-targeting, continuing to charge $1000 in rich Western countries but supplying people in developing countries, like the Cameroon taxi driver, for $30. Suddenly, a whole new market opens up for PillCorp: the new discount allows the company to acquire millions of new customers at a profit of $20 a year, but at the same time, it still makes all the sales it used to make in rich countries.

This assumes the cheap pills don't 'leak' back, which in practice is a massive concern for pharmaceutical companies. American policymakers wring their hands over the fact that many Americans buy prescription drugs from across the border in Canada – a practice that can be illegal but is typically tolerated. Perhaps it is the Canadian policymakers who should worry: if the leakage becomes unbearable, the risk is that drug companies will simply refuse to offer discounts to Canada any more.

The example should also make us realise that the greater price transparency brought about by the internet and other improvements in communications occasionally has a downside: a company with scarcity power may be discouraged from offering discounted products because they are more likely to leak.

PillCorp's dual-pricing policy creates a much better situation. Customers in rich countries are no worse off. Shareholders in PillCorp are better off. And people living with HIV/AIDS in poor countries are also better off. To use the business-school jargon, this is a win-win situation, or as an economist would say, a clear improvement in efficiency.

This doesn't mean the new situation is perfect; it just means that it is unambiguous progress from the previous situation, where PillCorp's scarcity power was causing a huge inefficiency ... and huge loss of life in poor countries. Perhaps we are outraged to see the poor denied drugs that cost pennies to produce, not because that is unfair (many things are unfair) but because it is also so wasteful of life.

When price-targeting is a bad thing

PillCorp's new price-targeting programme was a win-win affair. But sometimes price-targeting is a losing proposition all round.

Consider another hypothetical organisation, TrainCorp, a

passenger train company. TrainCorp owns a train that always travels full. Some of the seats go at a discount of £50 to leisure travellers who booked in advance, to senior citizens, to students or to families. The other tickets cost the full price of £100 and are bought by commuters and other business travellers. This is a fairly standard group-targeting strategy: by giving away a few low-price tickets, TrainCorp restricts supply and acquires the ability to demand high prices by offering tickets to only the buyers with the highest willingness to pay. (It might be profitable for TrainCorp just to fence off some of the seats and restrict supply that way, but it's even better for them to fill the spare seats if they can.)

We know at once – if we are economists – that this is inefficient. In other words, we can think of something that would make at least one person better off without making anyone else worse off.

That something is to find a commuter who was willing to pay a little less than £100, say £95, and who decided to travel by car instead, and offer him a seat for £90. Where does the seat come from, since the train is full? Well, you take a student who is in no great hurry and was willing to pay a little more than £50, say £55, for the seat and politely throw him off the train. But you refund the price of his ticket, plus an extra £10 for his trouble.

Where do we stand now? The commuter was willing to pay £95 but only paid £90. He's better off by £5. The student was willing to pay £55 for a £50 ticket, so if he'd been allowed to ride, he'd have been only £5 better off. But he has just been given £10, so the student is also happy. And what about TrainCorp? Well, TrainCorp just transformed a £50 ticket into a £90 ticket and made a more profitable sale. Even after paying £10 compensation to the student, the company is £30 ahead. Now everyone's a winner; or they would be if TrainCorp adopted this system instead of its group price-targeting strategy.

But of course, that's not what happens, because if TrainCorp tried it, commuters who were willing to pay £100 would hang around for the £90 tickets, and students who weren't willing to pay £50 would buy tickets anyway and wait to be paid to get off. The whole affair would turn out badly for TrainCorp, who is the one who gets to set the prices.

In case your head is spinning a little, here's the quick-and-dirty summary: the group price-targeting strategy is inefficient because it takes seats away from customers who are willing to pay more, and gives them to customers who are willing to pay less. Yet airlines and railways still use it, because the alternative of individual price-targeting isn't feasible.

OK, so sometimes price-targeting is less efficient than a uniform price, as in the case of the train; sometimes it's more efficient than a uniform price, as in the case of the HIV/AIDS drugs. But we can say more than that. Whenever price-targeting fails to expand the number of sales and merely moves products from people who value them more, like commuters, to people who value them less, like students, as in the case of TrainCorp, it will definitely be less efficient than a uniform price. Whenever price-targeting opens up a new market without affecting the old market, as with PillCorp, it will definitely be more efficient than a uniform price.

And there's a middle position. A lot of group price-targeting does a bit of both: it opens up some new markets but also wastefully moves products away from high-value users to low-value users. For example, this book was published in hardcover at a high price, and then the paperback edition emerged later, at a lower price. The aim is to target a higher price at people impatient to hear what I have to say and at libraries. One good result is that the publisher will be able to sell paperbacks more cheaply, because some costs will be offset by the hardcover sales, and so the book will reach more people. One bad result is that the early version is much more expensive than it would be if there was only a single paperback edition, and some buyers will be put off. That's what life is like in a world of scarcity: when companies with scarcity power try to exploit it, the situation will almost always be inefficient, and – equivalently – we economists will almost always be able to think of something better.

I say 'almost' because a company which is able to practise perfectly individualised price-targeting strategy would never miss a sale: rich or desperate customers would pay a lot, poor or indifferent customers would pay very little, but no customer willing to pay the cost of production would be turned away. The situation would be efficient.

Being realistic, though, it's most unlikely that any company would have so much information about its customers as to be able to make such perfectly efficient sales. The company would need to peer into the heart of every possible customer and find out how badly he or she wanted the product, it would need a supercomputer to operate the cash registers. That just isn't plausible. But perhaps it makes you think. What if you could plug every customer's preferences into a supercomputer? What if you had all the information you needed to never miss a sale? Would the world be a better place?

Something else may have caught your attention. When PillCorp changed its global pricing policy, it did something that was not only profitable but also both efficient and fair. Can we say anything more generally about when private greed will serve the public interest? For the answers to all these questions, and more ... read on.

3

Perfect Markets and the 'World of Truth'

You might not expect Jim Carrey films and economics to have much in common, but in fact there is much we can learn from the rubber-faced comedian. Consider the film *Liar, Liar*, which tells the story of Fletcher Reede. As a result of his son's birthday wish, Fletcher Reede finds that he is compelled to tell the truth for twenty-four hours. This is problematic for Fletcher because he is a lawyer – or a *liar*, as his son understands it – and hilarity predictably ensues as a horrified Fletcher incriminates himself by helplessly blurting out truthful answers to every question he is asked. They don't make as much of a feel-good movie, but free markets are just like Fletcher Reede's son – they force you to tell the truth. Yet while the results were humiliating for Jim Carrey's character, we will discover that a world of truth leads to a perfectly efficient economy, one in which it is impossible to make someone better off without making someone else worse off.

In this chapter we'll see what truth means in economic terms, how it leads to efficiency and why efficiency is good. We'll also explore efficiency's shortcomings: how efficiency isn't always fair, and why we have taxes. As we'll see, taxes are like lies: they interfere with the world of truth. But I'll reveal one way in which taxes can be implemented which is both fair *and* efficient. This could be good news for old people struggling to pay their winter heating bills, but bad news for Tiger Woods.

Imagine if you will that Fletcher's son gets his birthday wish, not just for his smooth-talking dad but for the whole world. So, let's buy a cappuccino in the world of truth. Before frothing up the half-and-half for you, the barista looks you up and down and asks:

'What's the most you're willing to pay for this coffee?'

You'd like to lie and pretend that you don't really want it, but the truth just slips out:

'I'm in caffeine withdrawal. Ten quid.'

With a smirk, the barista prepares to ring up the extortionate sum, but you have a few questions of your own:

'How much did those coffee beans cost?'

'How much did you pay for the plastic lid and the cup?'

'How much does it cost to raise a cow, and how much milk can you get from one?'

'How much did the electricity cost for the refrigeration, heating and light in here?'

Now it is the barista's turn to have a Fletcher Reede moment. No matter how she tries to evade the questions or froth up the cost of the cappuccino, she cannot tell a lie. It turns out that the cappuccino costs not £10, but less than one. The barista tries to haggle, but you have one more killer question:

'Are any other places within thirty yards selling coffee like this?'

'Yes . . .' she moans, her head thudding to the counter in a gesture of abject defeat.

You walk out of the shop with the coffee safely in your possession for the bargain price of 60p.

Prices are optional, which means they reveal information

There's a basic truth incorporated into any system of prices. That truth comes from the fact that stores and consumers do not have to buy or sell at a given price – they can always opt out. If you'd been willing to pay only 50p for the coffee, nobody could have forced you to raise your offer or forced the barista to drop the price. The sale simply would not have occurred.

Of course, you sometimes hear people complaining that if they want something – say, an apartment overlooking Hyde Park – then they have to pay the exorbitant asking price. That's true, but although prices sometimes seem unfairly high, you hardly ever *have* to pay them. You could always use your money to buy a flat in Hackney or a house in Luton or a million cups of coffee instead.

In a free market, people don't buy things that are worth less to them than the asking price. And people don't sell things that are worth more to them than the asking price (or if they do, it's never for long; firms that routinely sell cups of coffee for half of what they cost to produce will go out of business pretty quickly). The reason is simple: nobody is forcing them to, which means that most transactions that happen in a free market improve efficiency, because they make both parties better off – or at least not worse off – and don't harm anyone else.

Now you can begin to see why I say that prices 'tell the truth' and reveal information. In a free market, all the buyers of coffee would prefer to have coffee than the money the coffee cost, which is shorthand for saying they prefer coffee to whatever else they might have spent 60p on. That is, the value of the product to the customer is equal to or higher than the price; and the cost to the producer equal to or lower than the price. Painfully obvious, perhaps, but the implications turn out to be dramatic.

It may seem trivial to say that in a free market we know customers value coffee more than the money they pay for it. Yet it's not quite as trivial as it looks. For a start, this 'trivial' piece of information is already more than we can say about anything that is paid for outside the market – for example, the Olympic Games in London in 2012. The Games will cost around £10 billion, most of which will come from taxpayers. Maybe this is a good use of money, and maybe not. It's not clear how we find out.

When decisions are made inside a market system there's no such controversy. If I pay £25 to see the athletics, nobody questions whether it's worth it; I made my choice, so obviously I thought so. This free choice produces information about my priorities and preferences, and when millions of us make choices, market prices aggregate the priorities and preferences of us all.

Perfect markets: the truth, the whole truth and nothing but the truth

So the trivial piece of information that in a free market customers value cappuccinos more than the money they pay for them is not so trivial after all. But we needn't stop there.

Imagine now that the coffee market is not only free but extremely competitive, that entrepreneurs are always starting new firms with fresh ideas and entering the market in an attempt to undercut the incumbent companies. (Profits in a competitive industry are high enough only to pay workers and persuade entrepreneurs that their money isn't better off in a savings account – no higher.) The competition will force the price of coffee down to the 'marginal cost' – the cost the coffee bar incurs when making one more cappuccino, which we may remember is just under a dollar. In a perfectly competitive market, the price of coffee would equal the marginal cost of coffee. If the price were lower, firms would go out of business until it rose. If the price were higher, new firms would enter or old firms would expand their output until it fell. Suddenly, the price is not conveying a vague fact ('this coffee is worth 60p, or more, to the buyer, and it cost the coffee bar 60p, or less') but a precise truth ('this coffee cost the coffee bar exactly 60p').

What if other industries were also perfectly competitive? That would mean that for every product, the price equalled the marginal cost. Every product would be linked to every other product through an ultra-complex network of prices, so when something changes somewhere in the economy (there's a frost in Brazil, or a craze for iPads in the US) everything else would change – maybe imperceptibly, maybe a lot – to adjust. A frost in Brazil, for example, would damage the coffee crop and reduce the worldwide supply of coffee; this would increase the price coffee roasters have to pay to a level that discourages enough coffee drinking to offset the shortfall. Demand for alternative products, like tea, would rise a little, encouraging higher tea prices and extra supply of tea. Demand for complementary products like coffee creamer would fall a little. In Kenya, coffee farmers would enjoy bumper profits and would invest the money in improvements like aluminium roofing for their houses; the price of aluminium would rise and so some farmers would decide to wait before buying. That means demand for bank accounts and safety deposit boxes would rise, although for unfortunate farmers in Brazil with their failed crops, the opposite may be happening. The free-market supercomputer processes the truth about demands and about costs, and gives people the incentive to respond in astonishingly intricate ways.

That may seem like a ridiculous hypothetical scenario. But economists can measure and have measured some of these effects: when frosts hit Brazil, world coffee prices do indeed rise, Kenyan farmers do buy aluminium roofing, the price of roofing does rise and the farmers do, in fact, time their investment so that they don't pay too much. Even if markets are not perfect, they can convey tremendously complex information.

Governments – or any organisations – find it hard to respond to such complex information. In Tanzania, coffee was not produced in a free market until the early 1990s, and the government, rather than the farmers, received any windfalls from high coffee prices. The government often failed to spend the money sensibly, blowing too much on unsustainable salary rises for civil servants, and failing to realise that the price spike was temporary.

To appreciate why markets do such a good job of processing complex information, first think about the customer. We know that he won't buy a cappuccino unless he values it more than anything else he could buy with the same money. But what else could he buy with the same money? In our world of truth, he could buy *anything* that costs the same as, or less than, a cappuccino. If he chooses the coffee he's saying that of all the things in the world that cost the same as coffee, he would like coffee to be made.

Elsewhere, of course, there are other people spending their money not on coffee but on cinema tickets, bus fares or underwear; and there are others choosing not to spend their money at all and to put it in the bank instead. All of these competing demands pull producers to respond. If people want computers, then manufacturers will build factories, hire workers and buy plastics and metals, which will be diverted from other uses to go into computers. If people want coffee instead of underwear, then more land will be devoted to coffee and less to other uses, like parks or housing or tobacco farming. Lingerie shops will be replaced by coffee shops. Of course, start-up companies will borrow money from banks, and interest rates will rise or fall, depending on the balance between the number of people wanting to save and the number of people wanting to borrow. Interest rates are just another price: the price of spending today instead of next year. (You might have thought that interest rates were set by central bankers like Ben Bernanke at the Federal Reserve or Mervyn King at the Bank of England. Actually, Bernanke and King chair committees that set 'nominal' interest rates. True interest rates are interest rates after inflation – set by the market in response to the central bankers and their monetary operations.)

The changes don't stop there. The ripples in the price system continue outwards. They whip through some parts of the economy at tremendous speed and cause slow but powerful seismic shifts in others, like education or technology. For example, if there aren't enough trained workers to produce computers, suppliers to Dell and Compaq will have to train them, or raise wages to poach them from the suppliers to Apple and Acer. As the wages for skilled workers rise, people will see that it's worth taking time off and paying to go to college. Manufacturers' interest in producing cheaper or better computers will give a boost to research labs and engineering schools. Higher demand for plastics will raise the price of the raw material – crude oil – which will in turn encourage those who use oil for energy to switch to cheaper substitute fuels or to invest in energy-saving technology. And so it continues. Some of these effects will be tiny. Others will be enormous. Some will have an instant effect. Others will not be realised for decades. But in the world of truth – the world of perfect markets – all of them will have an impact.

What is the result of a set of perfectly competitive markets interconnected like this?

Companies are making things the right way. Any company that wastes resources, over-produces or uses the wrong technology will go out of business. Every product is produced in the most efficient way.

Companies are making the right things. The price of a product equals the cost to make it. The price also reflects the terms at which customers can trade off one priority against another. (Two cups of coffee cost the same as one Danish pastry; which would you prefer?) The price is a direct line of communication from what products cost to what customers prefer, and back again.

Things are being made in the right proportions. If too much coffee were being produced, manufacturers would cut prices; and if too little, prices would rise. Either way, the situation would correct itself. In the competitive market, price equals cost; there is no incentive for anyone to produce less (giving up profitable sales) or to produce more (creating products that cost more than anyone is willing to pay). The competitive rule – price equals cost equals value to the consumer – keeps things efficient.

Things are going to the 'right' people. The only people who buy products are the people who are willing to pay the appropriate price. Let's say I confiscate a cappuccino from Axel and give it to Bob. In the world of truth, this is wasteful. Axel was willing to pay for coffee, and Bob was not, which means Axel values coffee more than Bob, and my confiscation is inefficient. Notice that here I am equating 'right' with 'efficient', an assumption we'll examine and challenge shortly.

So: if the right things are being made right in the right quantities and going to the people who value them most, there is no room for any gains in efficiency. To put it another way, *you can't get more efficient than a perfectly competitive market.* And it all follows perfectly naturally from the truth contained in the price system: prices are true representations of cost to firms, and also true representations of value to customers.

Life without markets

Because Western society relies heavily on free markets, we find it difficult to imagine what it would be like if we didn't, or to take a step back and see quite how profound the effect of the market is. Yet any modern democracy provides goods outside the market system, and looking at the way such goods are provided gives us a hint of the strengths and weaknesses of markets. Think of your friendly local police force, which is paid for by a non-market system of taxation. The non-market system has some advantages – for one thing, when you dial 999 nobody asks for your credit card details. The government is supposed to afford the same level of protection to the rich and poor, although it does not always seem that way.

But the non-market system also has some disadvantages. For instance, if a police officer is rude or incompetent, you don't have the option to shop for a different police force. If you think that the level of police protection you receive is excessive, it's not up to you to cut back a bit. Neither can you spend more if you decide that you'd like extra service. No, you have to lobby your local politicians and hope they consider your demands.

Government-provided schooling is another example of a non-market service that many of us use. In both Britain and the United States, most people send their children to government-funded schools. But those schools are different from each other – different atmospheres, different academic emphases. Most importantly, some are good schools, and some are not. The market solution for schools is similar to the market solution for food: the best food goes to the people who are willing – which also implies able – to pay most for it. But within the government sector there are no prices. What happens instead? Parents line up, haggle and protest. They move to districts with better schools. In Britain, government-run religious schools often have the best academic records, so atheists take their children to church every Sunday in order to get good references from priests and get their children into these schools.

As with the police, the non-market system has the cosy advantage of concealing the fact that the poor don't get the same quality of education that the rich do. But again, the non-market system suffers from a serious problem: the truth about values, costs and benefits has disappeared. It is impossible to tell which parents enrol their children in church schools for religious reasons and which parents are just looking for better results. It is also impossible to know how much parents would be willing to pay for more teachers and better materials. In a market system the truth would emerge about how much it costs to provide good schools, and who would be willing to pay for them. The non-market system struggles with these basic questions.

It seems that there is a willingness to pay for good schools, and we see it emerge because house prices are higher in the areas of schools with the best reputation. The non-market system, which gives preference to local children, channels the money that parents are willing to pay for a good school into the hands of property owners near existing good schools. This hardly seems sensible. A market system would simply direct the money to pay for more good schools.

The signalling function of prices

Prices perform two functions, not just one. In a market system, prices provide a way of deciding who gets to enjoy a limited supply of schools: whoever pays most gets to send their children to the best schools, an uncomfortable state of affairs, which the government-school system is designed to prevent. But prices also give the signal to build more schools, hire more teachers or raise their wages if they're in short supply, and buy better materials. In the longer term, a price system will transform a high willingness to pay for good schools into a lot of good schools, just as surely as it will transform a high demand for coffee into a lot of cappuccino.

Don't politicians know that we value good schools already? Should they be making government money available? The difficulty is that politicians hear that we want good schools, but they also hear that we want more police on the streets, a better health service, lots of big roads, excellent welfare benefits, low taxes and a double-shot caramel Venti latte. It's easy for us to demand all of these things, but prices, by forcing us to put money where our mouths are, uncover the truth. Taxes have their advantages, but many don't contribute to truth because we cannot choose whether or not to pay them, depending on whether each penny is spent according to our wishes. Because prices are optional, they reveal information.

None of this amounts to a knockdown argument against providing a police service or a school system with a non-market process. Non-market systems have their advantages, but they also lose something important: information, information about wants, needs and desires, and about inconveniences and costs. Sometimes the loss of information is worthwhile because it is offset by gains in equality or stability. But sometimes the loss of information can leave an economy, and a society, floundering in waste and confusion. We think that the value we get from schools and police are more than what they cost us in taxes, but we don't know for sure. Not so with the cappuccino.

Efficiency versus fairness: can we handle the truth?

A perfectly competitive market is like a giant supercomputer network. With amazing processing power and sensors in every part of the economy – reaching even inside our brains to read our desires – the market is constantly reoptimising production and allocating the results perfectly. Remember that when economists say the economy is inefficient, they mean that there's a way to make somebody better off without harming anybody else. While the perfectly competitive market is perfectly efficient, efficiency is not enough to ensure a fair society, or even a society in which we would want to live. After all, it is efficient if Bill Gates has all the money and everybody else starves to death* ... because there is no way to make anybody better off without making Bill Gates worse off. We need something more than efficiency.

So it's hardly surprising we sometimes prefer the cosy white

---

*I wrote this sentence for the first edition, before Gates left Microsoft to run a colossal charitable foundation. Sorry, Bill.

lies: it is expensive, for example, to heat the house of an elderly lady in Middlesbrough, but we may prefer to subsidise the fuel, not wanting her to face the truth of that expense.

Even more than subsidies, taxes are a common cause of inefficiency: the government taxes market transactions and spends the money on, we hope, good things like police forces and schools. Why are taxes inefficient? Because they destroy the information carried by prices in perfectly competitive, efficient markets: price no longer equals cost, so cost no longer equals value. For example, a sales tax of 10 per cent creates a 'lie' in the following circumstances:

Cost of cappuccino: 60p
- Price of cappuccino in perfectly competitive market: 60p
- Price of cappuccino after tax: 66p
- Willingness to pay for cappuccino: 63p
- Cappuccino sold: *none*
- Tax raised: *zero*

There was a sale that could have created 3p of efficiency gains (cappuccino cost 60p but was valued at 63p) but which never happened because of the tax. What's worse, the tax wasn't even paid. If the government were able to waive the tax in such circumstances, they would be no worse off, but the coffee buyer would be better off: a clear efficiency gain.

It's hard for tax officials to know when to charge the tax (situations where taxes will not change buyers' behaviour) and when to waive the tax (because potential buyers would have avoided it anyway, by not buying coffee). But they try to do so using the kind of price-targeting strategies outlined in Chapter 2. Taxes are often higher when price-sensitivity is low. For example, the government charges high taxes on petrol and cigarettes, not for environmental and health reasons but because people who buy these products need to drive and are addicted to smoking; they won't change their behaviour much even in the face of large taxes. (If you think that taxes on petrol are motivated by environmental concerns, think again: despite the environmental impacts of air travel, electricity and domestic heating, 90 per cent of all 'environmental' taxes in the UK in 2009 were paid by motorists.)

We are faced with a dilemma. We want to avoid inefficiency, because that would leave us passing up an opportunity to make somebody better off at no cost to anyone else. But taxes cause inefficiency, and most of us think we need taxes to redistribute income (to a greater or lesser extent) from the rich to the poor. We seem to be facing two contradictory imperatives: avoid the needless waste that is 'inefficiency', but make sure that wealth is at least somewhat evenly spread. What we need is a way to make our economics both efficient and fair.

Can we enlist markets to help with fairness?

Is it true that we have to choose between the efficiency of perfect markets and the fairness of benevolent government intervention? This seemed to be the conclusion of governments throughout the free world after the experience of the Great Depression and the Second World War. President Roosevelt's 'New Deal' programmes of the 1930s expanded the role of the United States government, in response to the Great Depression. In Britain, Clement Atlee's post-war government took control of much of the health, steel, air travel, petroleum, rail travel and telephone industries. Government-owned businesses took over partly because in the deprived, exhausted yet hopeful years after the war, economists had some confidence in the experts who had masterminded the war effort and thought they might not do a bad job of organising the economy efficiently. Few people foresaw the later collapse of government-run economies, whether vast like the Soviet Union and China, or small like Tanzania or North Korea. But even if they had believed that private markets were more efficient, this was neither here nor there in the 1940s: the post-war Labour government in Britain would have been content to live with some inefficiency if it meant a fairer society.

But the old dilemma between efficiency and fairness was about to be shattered by a young New Yorker called Kenneth Arrow, who knew all about unfairness after watching helplessly as a teenager while his father lost his successful business and all his savings in the Great Depression. The desire for social justice stayed with Arrow, but intellectually he couldn't just ignore the question of efficiency. The young economist set his logical mind to wrestling with the tension between the unerring efficiency of the free market and the imperative that some kind of fairness should prevail. His solution was brilliant, twisting the traditional thinking about competitive markets and efficiency on its head. He proved that not only are all perfect markets efficient, *all efficient outcomes can be achieved using a competitive market, by adjusting the starting position*. Arrow went on to win every plaudit available to an economist, and he remains the youngest man ever to win the Nobel Prize for Economics. But why was his insight so important?

I call it the 'head start theorem'. Instead of focusing on the enormous complexity of a real economy, think of a very simple one-dimensional human challenge: the 100-metre sprint. The fastest sprinter will win the race. If you wanted all the sprinters to cross the line together, you could just change the rules of the race, ordering the fast runners to slow down and everyone to hold hands as they crossed the line. A waste of talent. Or you could move some starting blocks forward and some starting blocks back, so that although each sprinter was running as fast as he could, obeying the usual rules and objectives of sprinting, the fastest had to cover enough extra ground that he would end up breaking the tape neck-and-neck with the slowest.

Arrow demonstrated that the same approach could work when trying to balance the excesses of competitive markets: instead of interfering with the markets themselves, the trick is to adjust the starting blocks by making lump-sum payments and levying one-time taxes.

An example of a lump-sum tax would be the government taxing everybody £500; or alternatively, taxing everyone over the age of sixty-five £500; or alternatively, taxing everybody whose surname on the birth certificate starts with *H* £500. The point is that unlike an income tax or a sales tax on coffee, a lump-sum tax doesn't affect anybody's behaviour, because there is nothing you can do to avoid it. So unlike sales tax, it doesn't lead to an efficiency loss. Similarly, an example of lump-sum redistribution would be to *give* £500 to everybody whose name starts with *H*, a policy for which I would be happy to vote.

In the 100-metre sprint, lump-sum taxation is like moving the starting blocks back a few paces. Income tax and sales tax are like asking the best runners to run backwards. Both would have the effect of ensuring a more equal finish, but moving the starting blocks around doesn't slow anybody down.

In the context of a sprint, it's fairly obvious that one of the ways to get a close result is to give the slower runners a head start. In the context of an economy, with literally billions of different goods, desires, raw materials and talents, the head start theorem is a much bolder claim. But it's true: you can allow the competitive economy to use every skill and every raw material, take advantage of every opportunity to trade, cooperate, educate or invest ... but still get a fair outcome by moving around the starting blocks and letting perfect markets do the rest.

The implication is that in a world of perfect markets, the only thing needed to ensure both fairness and efficiency is a 'head start' strategy: a programme of appropriate lump-sum taxes and subsidies that puts everyone on an equal footing. The perfect markets then find every possible opportunity to make everybody better off from their revised starting points. The question is, can this be done in practice?

Impractical examples

Let's take an example. American political philosopher Robert Nozick deployed a famous argument against taking a view of 'justice as fairness'. In other words, he disputed the notion that one particular allocation of wealth could be deemed the 'best' or 'fair' allocation. Nozick's argument invokes Wilt Chamberlain, a basketball star famous in the 1960s and 1970s, when Nozick was writing. Chamberlain's talents made him wealthy; Nozick felt this was 'just' because Chamberlain's wealth was the outcome of legitimate decisions by fans happy to pay to see him play. The situation may have been 'just' in Nozick's sense of the word, but can any situation that leads to a highly unequal distribution of cash be considered 'fair'?

Perhaps taxing Chamberlain's income heavily would make the situation fairer, but Nozick warns that if Chamberlain did not really enjoy playing basketball *and* he was loaded down with heavy taxes, he might stop playing altogether. So although this situation might seem more 'fair', there would be neither the tax revenue, nor the basketball game: the problem of the cappuccino sales tax all over again. So how is it reasonable to call a distribution of income 'fair' when everybody concerned, both fans and player, would prefer the 'unfair' outcome?

Thanks to Kenneth Arrow, we now know that, when faced with a modern-day sports star like Tiger Woods, the solution is to levy a one-time lump-sum tax of several million dollars on him. He would still have the incentive to earn money by playing golf, since he could not avoid the tax by playing less, as he could do in order to avoid a heavy income tax. He would no doubt earn enough to pay off the tax bill and still retain enough to buy a family car and a nice house somewhere unassuming. In this scenario, there is no waste or inefficiency, but the result is 'fair' in that it produces a much more even allocation of wealth.

The only trouble with this plan is that it's wildly impractical. The problem is not that it's impossible to have taxes that only apply to one individual: President Franklin Roosevelt introduced an income tax rate of 79 per cent, but the threshold was so high that the tax was paid by only John D. Rockefeller. Rather, the problem is more that a true lump-sum tax isn't supposed to change behaviour at all. Ideally it would have been decided before Tiger Woods was born, because if he could have predicted that he would be liable for a tax as a result of his success he might have chosen a different profession.*

This is, of course, quite impossible. But we shouldn't abandon the head start theorem quite yet. While we can't always use lump-sum taxation and redistribution, we can sometimes: and when we can, it's worth considering because it preserves the efficiency and

---

*Such a tax would also have had to predict the fall in Tiger's income after his personal life hit the headlines in late 2009 – his sponsorship earnings reportedly fell by $22 million. I certainly didn't foresee this in the first edition, or I might not have chosen the family car as an example.

the truth of the competitive market while adding a welcome dose of fairness.

A practical example

A more practical application of the head start theorem could be used to prevent elderly people from getting cold in winter, without damaging the environment. In a typical winter in Britain twenty-five thousand old people die as a result of inadequate heating. To address this concern, domestic fuel is subject to lower taxes than many other things. But that's a slightly odd way to deal with the problem – an equivalent to the 'running backwards' solution. If governments need to raise tax revenue – and all of them do, it seems – then a first approximation of an efficient strategy would be to have the same sales tax on everything, because that wouldn't distort people's buying decisions too much. A more refined view would recall the 'price-targeting' of Chapter 2. Because customers cannot easily cut down on fuel consumption, they are not very sensitive to the price of domestic fuel, hence the government should levy a bit more tax on fuel and a bit less on other goods: customers would not change their behaviour much and so the inefficiency would be small. An even more sophisticated view (perhaps acquired from a peek ahead at Chapter 4) would note that domestic fuel is a non-renewable resource and using it causes pollution, so the case for higher tax on domestic fuel becomes even stronger.

The case for lower taxes on domestic fuel and higher taxes on other goods is hard to understand, until we start to worry about the elderly shivering in front of a lifeless gas or oil boiler that they cannot afford to switch on. Is this just one of those hard choices that governments sometimes have to make? Not necessarily.

Instead of levying the wrong rate of tax on everyone else, better to choose a more sensible rate but give the elderly a head start – because of their poverty and because, being frail, they have an additional need for heating. The simple policy remedy is to raise fuel tax but give extra money to the elderly, money that they could use to switch that heating on and stay warm.

We know from the head start theorem that given the money, pensioners will find their way to the efficient outcome – which, incidentally, may not involve more fuel being burned. Not every pensioner feels cold, and those who do may find better solutions to the problem. Some may use the money to move to Spain. Some may insulate their homes. Those who did not feel the cold in the first place can spend the money on other things. Nobody will burn extra fuel unless they need to, and if they need to they'll have the money to meet that need.

The lesson of the head start theorem is that when a problem arises, it's worth asking whether the problem can be addressed by rearranging the starting blocks rather than interfering with the race. This strategy isn't always practical, but because free markets are efficient, it's worth trying to harness that efficiency to meet other goals.

Throughout this chapter, we've been on a flight of fantasy no more plausible than the story of Fletcher Reede. The 'world of truth' is a world where markets are complete, free and competitive. In reality we're about as likely to achieve a world with complete, free and competitive markets as hotshot lawyers are to start telling the truth to everyone.

You might therefore be asking yourself why you've read a chapter, even a brief one, about some bizarre economists' fantasy. The answer is that the fantasy helps us understand why economic problems arise and also helps us to move in the right direction.

We know that a world of perfect markets combined with the head start approach is as good as we're going to get. When real-world economies malfunction, we know to look for the market failures – and to do our best to patch them up.

We've already explored one of those failures: some companies have scarcity power and can set prices that are far above their true cost, which is where they would be in a competitive market. This is why economists believe there's an important difference between being in favour of markets and being in favour of business, especially particular businesses. A politician who is in favour of markets believes in the importance of competition and wants to prevent businesses from getting too much scarcity power. A politician who's too influenced by corporate lobbyists will do exactly the reverse.

Whether abetted by politicians or otherwise, companies with scarcity power are one market failure. There are two others. In the next two chapters, we'll encounter them, leaving the curious world of truth behind us and facing up to the real world once again.

4

Crosstown Traffic

We've just learned that in the world of perfect markets, everything is for the best. We know that perfect markets are completely efficient, delivering outcomes that are flawless in every respect except distribution. We also know from the head start theorem that we can fix any complaints about distribution in advance. Presto, every problem solved, or at least every problem concerning the allocation of goods and services.

That's nice to hear, but then why did I spend two hours stuck in traffic on the way to work this morning? The bumper-to-bumper traffic was a stupid waste. All of us could have been taking buses, or car-pooling, and we would have reached our destinations in fifteen minutes. Where is the perfect market there? The obvious answer is that, of course, there is no market perfect or otherwise for driving around on the streets. What may be less obvious is that there could be.

Economies that work smoothly because they are full of perfect markets are neither interesting nor realistic. But because perfect markets provide such a clear benchmark, economists find it much easier to start from them and work out what is going wrong, rather than start from scratch and work out what is going right. And this method of thinking about the world will lead us to the cure for crosstown traffic.

What's wrong with my world

I am a happy man, but there are things in my life that infuriate me and that I wish could be different. I wish I didn't have to upgrade my computer software every couple of years at great expense. I wish that I could rely on my doctors to give me appropriate medical treatment when I am ill. I wish London's streets were not clogged with traffic and filled with pollution.

These three personal, if common, grumbles correspond to the three key ways in which markets fail to live up to Chapter 3's lofty ideals of perfection. Markets fail to work well in the face of scarcity power, as we saw in Chapter 2. That is one of the problems with buying computer software – the market is dominated by a single company, Microsoft, which has tremendous power to set high prices. Markets also fail to work well if some decision makers lack information. When I lived in Washington DC, I would leave my doctor's surgery with no idea whether he had given me good treatment, while he had no need to take into account the cost of the treatment, and my insurance company had every incentive to refuse to pay, without knowing the true situation. (We'll deal with health care in Chapter 5.) Finally, markets fail to work well if some people make decisions that affect bystanders: when a driver buys petrol from a petrol station, that is all very well for the driver and the petrol station but not for the bystanders, including other drivers, who have to breathe the resulting carbon monoxide.

These three big problems are called 'market failures': scarcity power, which we discussed in Chapters 1 and 2; missing information, which we will discuss in Chapter 5; and the subject of this chapter, decisions that have side effects on bystanders. Economists call the side effect an 'externality' because it lies outside the original decision, for instance, the decision to buy petrol. Whether because of scarcity power, incomplete information or an externality, when the economy fails to live up to the idealised 'world of truth', trouble is in store.

How drivers affect bystanders

London, Washington DC, Tokyo, Paris, Los Angeles and Bangkok, and indeed any of the world's great cities, are full of cars, buses and trucks. Those vehicles seriously damage the happiness of innocent bystanders. They cause severe air pollution. Admittedly, London's current air pollution is not as severe as the 'Great Stink' of the 1850s, in which tens of thousands died of cholera. But still, air pollution from traffic is not trivial: many thousands of people die because other people want to drive. Around seven thousand people a year die prematurely because of traffic pollution in Britain, a little more than one in ten thousand. In the United States, the Environmental Protection Agency estimates that fifteen thousand people die prematurely because of the particulate matter produced from sources such as diesel engines. Within urban areas like London, the cost of delays from congestion are even worse, if you consider the number of hours spent sitting in traffic as being in any way a significant loss of productive or enjoyable life. Then there is the noise, the accidents and the 'barrier effect', which discourages people, and particularly children, from walking to school or the local shops, or even to meet their neighbours across the street.

People are not fools: it's almost certainly true that anyone taking a trip in a car is benefiting from driving. But they are doing so at the expense of everyone else around them – the other drivers stuck in traffic, the parents who dare not let their children walk to school, the pedestrians who risk their lives dashing across the street because they are tired of waiting for the lights to change, the office workers who even in the sweltering summer cannot open their windows because of the roar of the traffic.

Because each driver who gets into his car is creating misery for other people, the free market cannot deliver a solution to the problem of traffic. The external effects of congestion and pollution are important departures from the 'world of truth'. In the 'world of truth' every act of selfish behaviour is turned to the common good. I selfishly buy underwear because I want it, but in doing so channel resources into the hands of underwear manufacturers, and do nobody any harm. Textile workers in China, where the underwear is made, selfishly look for the best job, while manufacturers selfishly look for the most capable employees. All of this works to everyone's benefit: goods are manufactured only if people want them, and they are manufactured only by the most appropriate people to do the job. Self-centred motives are put to work for everybody.

Drivers are in a different situation. They do not offer compensation for the cost they inflict on other people. When I buy underwear, the money I spend is compensation for all of the costs incurred in making it and selling it to me. When I take the car for a drive then I do not even need to think about the costs incurred by the rest of society as I avail myself of the free roads.

Different kinds of prices: marginal and average

It is not quite fair to say that drivers can use the roads for nothing. In the United Kingdom, it's not legal to drive a car, or even to park it on public streets, unless you have paid a sizeable annual tax called 'Vehicle Excise Duty'. Many states in the United States have a similar tax. Petrol and diesel are also taxed heavily enough to cause great resentment. In the autumn of 2000, for example, a series of protests against high fuel prices prevented fuel reaching the country's filling stations, and brought Britain to a standstill. (Later protests were far less disruptive.) In Britain, drivers pay over £30 billion in taxes on cars and fuel every year; in America, the figure is over $100 billion. To ask 'have they paid enough?' is to ask the wrong question. The right question is, 'are they paying for the right things?' The answer is no.

There are two different concepts of price at play here, and the distinction matters. The average price that a driver pays for a journey across a city is quite high if the driver is paying an annual licence fee. But the price that the driver pays for one extra trip across the city is low: the trip doesn't burn much fuel and drivers are not charged for extra trips. Once you've paid for the right to take the car on the street in the first place, you don't get a discount for low mileage: you might as well drive and drive, because it won't put a penny on your tax bill. That is the difference between the average price and the marginal price, which is the price for one extra trip.

To understand why the difference matters, let's turn to alcohol. When I was in college, clubs and societies used to have big parties where some people didn't drink at all and, less surprisingly, most people drank far too much. This was because there were two types of ticket. 'Alcoholic' tickets allowed unlimited boozing after payment of an up-front fee of, say, £10. The other type of ticket was a lot cheaper, and you had to drink rancid orange juice instead and stand in a corner while the drinkers got more and more obnoxious. Turning up and having a couple of beers was a pretty expensive proposition, so most people preferred either to maximise the value of the unlimited drinking opportunity, or opt out of drinking alcohol completely. Of course, the result was chaos, although some people felt it made for pretty good parties.

Since the university felt that the drunkenness represented a problem, they considered dealing with it at the next party by raising the up-front fee to, say, £20. But the likelihood would be that while a few people would switch to being disgruntled orange-juice drinkers or give up on the society altogether, most of the drinkers would decide there wasn't much point in a party without drinking. Grumbling, they would empty the contents of their wallets. Later in the evening, many of them would empty the contents of their stomachs.

The university misunderstood the problem. They understood that people were drinking too much and correctly thought that the solution probably involved raising the price of drinking. The problem is that there are different ways of describing the price of drinking. There's the price of being a drinker: £10. There's the average price of a drink: for the typical student who has twenty drinks, this is 50p. Then there's the *marginal* price of a drink, which is zero. Once you've paid the up-front fee, you might as well keep drinking.

Question: if you were running the university, would you deal with the problem by: (a) raising the up-front fee for drinking?, (b) buying better orange juice? or (c) scrapping the up-front fee and charging people for what they drank?

Better orange juice might be nice, but the Undercover Economist would humbly suggest that the solution to the underlying problem is (c).

Now, back to traffic congestion. If you were advising the Secretary of State for Transport you might suggest an analogy with student parties. Currently, potential drivers have two options: they can cough up a large up-front fee and drive as much as they like; or they can not drive at all. This second option, the 'orange juice' option, requires them to bike, use public transport or walk – although as with the student party, the more people who choose the first option, the less attractive the second option becomes.

You might even propose some policy options: (a) raise the upfront fee for driving; (b) supply better 'orange juice' (more buses, better trains, cycle routes, pedestrian crossings); or (c) scrap the up-front fee and charge people for the trips they drive.

All of these options could be expected to reduce traffic congestion to some extent, perhaps to an important extent. But it is option (c) that attempts to deal with the cause of the problem. Drivers do not live in the 'world of truth'; that is they do not pay the true cost of their actions, including the 'externalities' or side effects that affect bystanders. Option (c) tries to make them pay that cost; we might call it an 'externality charge'.

Currently, every potential driver is being offered the same kind of deal as party-going students: put up a wad of cash in exchange for an unlimited binge, or pay nothing and receive nothing in return. There are no half measures.

Student parties were not livened up excessively by the fact that drinks worked out at 50p on average: they were livened up excessively by the fact that the next drink was always free. Similarly, congestion is not caused by the fact that the tax on a car trip is 50p on average: it is caused by the fact that the next trip is always free.

We must not get obsessed with the question of how much drivers pay on average. Certainly, how much tax any type of person pays on average is an important question of distribution. While distribution is important, however, it doesn't have a big impact on whether our streets are clogged up and our cities are polluted.

What matters much more for congestion is the price drivers pay at the margin; or, to put it another way, the price drivers pay to make one extra trip. Cars don't cause much pollution or congestion, after all: car *trips* are the problem. Universities would encourage appropriate levels of drinking by charging students per drink. Similarly, the Department of Transport would encourage appropriate levels of driving by making drivers pay for each trip.

Pricing should reflect the damage

I've been oversimplifying, as usual. In most European countries, drivers do pay a tax per mile in the form of a high tax on fuel. But the tax on fuel doesn't closely match the costs that drivers inflict on each other and on non-drivers. People in rural areas pay the taxes (typically they spend between a quarter and a third as much again on petrol as those in urban areas), but it is the commuters in the London, New York or Paris rush hours who are causing the most serious congestion, severe air pollution and noise. The same trips made in the small hours of the morning do not cause congestion, although pollution and noise are still a problem. Make a similar trip between two houses in Alaska and you do not cause congestion. The noise is likely to be heard only by the occasional stray caribou. The damage caused by pollutants is much reduced, because many of them will disperse harmlessly. If the idea of a charge on driving is that each driver faces the costs of his actions, the rush-hour New York driver should pay more because he is causing more harm to others. Whatever level of externality charge turns out to be appropriate, if it is to reflect the truth, it should vary according to time and place.

The idea of an externality charge is not to discourage everyone from doing anything that might inconvenience anyone else; it is to get them to take into account the inconvenience they cause to others. To take an extreme example: if I go walking in the Lake District, it is nice to be able to take in the natural beauty of the place in relative solitude, and so it's mildly annoying to find the footpaths cluttered with other people. They may be inconveniencing me, but it would not be efficient to forbid their visit to the area because it gives them so much pleasure and me so little trouble.

Externality charging needs to strike the right balance between pleasure and trouble; it must reflect the cost of the externality . . . but no more. We should aim to make ours a world where people feel free to do things they enjoy, even if others are mildly inconvenienced, but also one where we all refrain from harming other people if the effort involved to avoid harming them is small. We discovered in Chapter 3 that perfect markets deliver this world, at least within the sphere that markets operate. Perfect markets cannot make us smile at passers-by or love our families, but they can make sure that we get a cappuccino if and only if we are willing to pay more than the true cost – which includes the cost in time and trouble of the baristas, the bean pickers, the entrepreneurs, the machine manufacturers and the rest. In other words, perfect markets allow us to feel free to do things that we enjoy only if our enjoyment outweighs the trouble caused to make it all possible.

This is why economists are fairly relaxed when markets seem

to be working well. But we are also vigilant for the many market failures. So how do we make sure that when deciding whether to drive across town, I can be sure that the benefit to me outweighs the cost to everybody else? There's no need to worry about costs and benefits that are part of an efficient market transaction. So, if oil refining and petrol retailing are perfect markets (contrary to popular belief, they are not far off), then the trouble it took to refine and distribute the petrol is fully represented in the price. I will not buy petrol unless the benefit I get from it is greater than the trouble it took to refine and distribute.

Instead, we should worry about costs and benefits missing from the market transaction. The pollution from the petrol causes local poisoning and global warming, and the majority of the pollution damage when I burn a tank of petrol is not caused to me or to the oil company. The trick is to mimic perfect markets by getting drivers to pay all of the costs of their actions: since they have already paid the market costs to the oil company, they also need to pay, on top of that, the externality costs. These externality costs are the costs inflicted on others but not borne by the driver or the oil company.

We now have all the elements in place to design an externality charge. We know that there may be costs and benefits that spill over from an individual choice or a market exchange, and if so, this will be inefficient (translation: we could do better, making at least one person better off and nobody worse off). We also know that if we want to change behaviour to correct the inefficiency, we need to address prices at the margin, not average prices. Third, we do not need to worry about costs, which have been incorporated into a well-functioning market transaction, only externality costs, which have been left out. Fourth, our marginal pricing should reflect those externality costs accurately. It's not enough simply to ban any behaviour we don't like. Instead, we should be focusing on cases where the active person gains small benefits but causes large costs for others.

Two objections to externality charges

A charge for externalities is effectively a government tax, and all government taxes are controversial. Externality charges are often attacked from two opposing ranges of moral high ground. On one flank comes the objection that the externality charge is an unfair tax aimed at a disadvantaged group. Consider the idea of charging drivers to drive at congested times. To such proposals (and they have been widespread, although only a few have become a

How much do people spend on fuel?

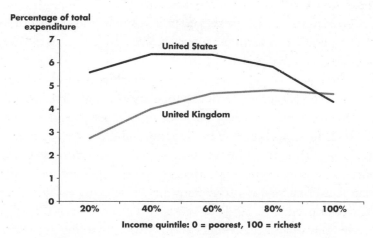

Source: US Bureau of Labor Statistics, Consumer Expenditure Survey 2008; UK Office for National Statistics, Family Spending report 2008.

reality) the pro-car lobby argues that drivers pay enough, and it is not fair to price poor drivers off the road. On the other flank come those who strongly object to the activity that is to be taxed on the grounds that after the externality charge has been imposed, the rich will still be able to do whatever it was that was objectionable. In the case of traffic, the anti-car lobby claims that it is outrageous that rich drivers can afford to drive around as much as they like, given the environmental damage caused by cars.

Are externality charges unfairly redistributive? They are not aimed at poor people but at voluntary activities: if you decide to stop causing trouble for others, you don't have to pay an externality charge. It is true that the rich can afford to drive more than the poor, but it is just as true that the rich can afford to eat more than the poor. This is unfair too, but if you accept the workings of the price system for typical goods like food, why not road space or clean air? We recognise that food, clothes and houses cannot be free or we would quickly run out of them. It is because roads are free that we have run out of spare road space.

Furthermore, since the rich do more of most things, externality charges often redistribute money in a desirable way. In the case of congestion charging, the truth is striking: in the United Kingdom, poor people do not drive – they bicycle, walk or take the bus. The poorest tenth of the population spends almost seven times less on fuel than the richest tenth, as a percentage of their much smaller income. The total spending on fuel by the richest 10 per cent is at least thirty times more than by the poorest 10 per cent. The conclusion is that congestion charging not only improves efficiency, it also redistributes money by raising more tax from the rich.

That's nice for the defenders of congestion charging in Britain, but useless in the United States, where the poor still drive a lot and so pay larger amounts of tax as a percentage of their incomes.

But this needn't be an impossible objection, because externality charges can be designed not to redistribute very much. In the case of roads, the government could scrap the vehicle excise duty, which is a large up-front tax, while starting to levy congestion charges on each trip. This would capture the efficiency benefits of a congestion charge without having major effects on distribution. It is possible to neutralise much of the redistribution caused by the externality charge, while keeping its efficiency-boosting effects. This is a variant of the lump-sum tax on Tiger Woods proposed in Chapter 3: we can use lump-sum taxes to redistribute without destroying efficiency.

Having met the attack from the redistributive flank, the economist must face the other way and deal with the enthusiastic charge from the moral high ground of environmentalism. Not every environmentalist opposes pollution and congestion charges, but some do. The reason is that they feel that pollution should simply be illegal, rather than illegal for the poor and affordable for the rich. Why should the rich be allowed to pollute? More generally, some pressure groups protest against externality charges on the grounds that they allow people to pay and thus continue doing whatever objectionable thing it was that they were doing.

A partial response is to say that even the rich do not pollute for fun. It is true that the rich are more likely to be able to pay a congestion charge, but they will not ignore it. Perhaps they will be careful to make one trip to the store rather than two, or even walk to the local shop rather than drive to somewhere further away. Externality charges make other alternatives look more attractive, both to rich and to poor.

More fundamentally, we must not confuse the strictness of the externality regulation with the method of the regulation. A congestion charge can be set at £1 a day, or £10 a day or £1000 a day.

What we know is that whatever society decides about the seriousness of the externality, externality charges are the most efficient way to deal with it. Well-designed congestion charges, for instance, are the most efficient way to achieve any given reduction of road use. How much of a reduction is desirable is an open question, but congestion charging can deliver no matter what the answer is.

There are alternatives to congestion charging which stop short of the extreme of an outright ban on driving. The trouble is, they don't work as well. For instance, the government could give everybody vouchers, which allow them to drive up to twenty miles per week. The immediate result of such a plan is that some people, mostly poor, would want to sell their vouchers to others, mostly rich: the poor would rather have the money, the rich would rather have the right to drive. If the government allows vouchers to be traded, they have simply imposed a congestion charge by another means and probably a slightly less efficient one, given the hassle of trading. (The charge is whatever the market value of the vouchers turns out to be.) And if the government bans voucher trading, the plan is clearly inefficient, because people who wish to trade are being prevented from doing so.

Other alternatives such as high parking charges are probably less efficient still, although it is harder to prove this in a paragraph. For instance, high parking charges do discourage some drivers; but the relationship between driving and parking is rather indirect. Some drivers spend extra time on the streets, looking for free spaces. Speed bumps also discourage driving and increase maintenance costs – but isn't it better to charge drivers directly and spend the revenue on something useful?

Some interest groups will always complain that externality charges are not tough enough, while others squeal that they are draconian. The economists' defence is that however tough we agree to be, an externality charge is the most efficient way to be tough. For any other policy, the economist can propose an alternative, using an externality charge, which would make some people better off and nobody worse off.

How much is your life worth?

The previous section makes it very clear that the level of any externality charge is bound to be a matter for controversy. For the Undercover Economist, seeking to re-create the 'world of truth', the ideal externality charge addresses all the real external costs and *only* the real external costs.

It's worth thinking about what the ideal system would look like for the externalities surrounding driving. Any driver making a trip which emitted pollutants that damaged the local area would be charged for the pollution if he drove in a densely populated area. There would be a different charge, which would be imposed for every trip, for emitting carbon dioxide, because it contributes to climate change no matter where on the surface of the planet it is emitted. In each case, the price of the trip would also depend on how clean the vehicle emissions were. Drivers would face additional charges for trips in congested areas at congested times. Older buses, which emit the worst pollutants, would be heavily taxed, and this is likely to lead to an upgrading of their engines. Heavy vehicles would incur a charge for trips on fragile roads and bridges. SUVs would be taxed because they are more likely to kill other road users in an accident.

That sounds complicated. Could it possibly work? It's easy to imagine each car having a little computer linked to a global positioning system to track congestion; the computer would also monitor the vehicle's exhaust. A display on the dashboard would flash up the rate at which the charge was being incurred, perhaps with helpful tips. 'Tim, your trip is currently costing you 9p per minute. Did you know that you could halve this if you got your engine tuned?'

The technology will come; much of it is already available. But there is another difficulty: working out what the costs of the externalities really are. The computer can measure congestion and pollution, but what is the cost of wasting other people's time in a traffic jam? What is the cost of poisoning people with particulates or benzene? Many other externalities involve real external costs and benefits that are very hard to measure: time, health, peace, even death.

For the sake of clarity, it may help to focus on the specific example of pricing the externalities caused by driving. It is hard enough to measure physical facts: how much road damage does one more vehicle do? How much noise does one more vehicle cause? How many accidents? How much delay to other vehicles? How much pollution? What ill-health does that pollution cause? But it is harder still to measure psychological consequences. How much do people care about various annoyances: foul air, noise, delay and stress – even illness and death? Not to mention that every individual values these things differently.

It is very tempting to give up in the face of these problems. Surely it is not possible to set a value on noise or delay, and certainly it seems impossible to set a value on human life. But we're kidding ourselves if we think we can opt out of these decisions. Every policy the government adopts, and every individual choice you make, implies that a valuation has been made, even if nobody has been honest enough to own up to it or even admit it to themselves.

Individually, we constantly make decisions that put a value on our own environment, our own time and even our own lives. If you pay more to avoid a noisy area when you rent a flat or a hotel room, then you have implicitly put a value on peace and quiet. If you decide to wait for the bus rather than flagging down a cab, you are implicitly putting a value on your time. If you decide you can't be bothered buying a smoke alarm, you have traded off saved time and expense against an increased chance that you will die. However, when you make any of these decisions, you probably don't come clean to anyone, even yourself, about the price you've put on quiet, time or life.

Governments, too, make decisions that imply that they have worked out how much our lives are worth. Should the government install extra street signs and markings, or spend more money on speed cameras, or improve health care or fund cancer research – or indeed not do any of these things but cut taxes, improve the quality of universities or spruce up national parks? Such decisions have to be made; when they are made, embedded within them are assumptions about subjective values, including the value of human life. Estimating externality charges is simply more awkward because, if done properly, it requires that those assumptions be justified and made explicit. Leaving them implicit and unjustified leaves us at best at the mercy of the random drift of political processes, and at worst acquiescing to the self-serving demands of interest groups.

One of the best ways of estimating these subjective values is to look at what people actually do. Economists have a theory of 'revealed preference', which is that people's preferences are revealed by the choices that they make as consumers. You bought apples when you could have afforded pears: therefore you preferred apples to pears. For an economist, preference is not just deduced but actually defined by such choices. It is a short step to conclude that people are also rational consumers when it comes to less tangible factors, even when it comes to their health and safety. If you are not willing to pay £5 to catch a cab and save twenty minutes, then the Undercover Economist concludes that you would rather spend the £5 on something else. This is not a very dramatic conclusion, but some people find it controversial. He also concludes that peace and quiet is worth an extra £15 a week to you, on the basis of your rental decision; and observing that you have no smoke alarm, he presumes that you are not willing to spend an hour and pay £20 to reduce your chance of death by one in a million.

Two important sources of information about people's preferences are house prices and wages. House prices contain embedded information about the value people place on all kinds of amenities: shops, greenery, low crime, quiet, the sun through the window in the morning and so on. Some of these can be quite accurately measured: for instance, the price of two identical houses facing each other across the same street will probably reveal how much people prefer a house that faces the sun. Meanwhile wages can reveal information if there is a salary differential for jobs with very similar skill requirements but different levels of danger.

There are flaws in this method: in particular, what if the peace and quiet comes hand-in-hand with a cul-de-sac which is safe for your children to play in, and insulation, which will save your heating bills? How much of the £15 a week is really a payment for quiet surroundings? What if the well-paid but dangerous job on the oil rig also requires you to not drink for six weeks at a time and spend all your spare time indoors? Perhaps the payment is nothing to do with danger, and everything to do with inconvenience. It will always be hard to disentangle these different factors, and it is impossible to know how well you have succeeded. But with enough information, economists can have what they think is a decent try.

A second problem is that when you bought your smoke alarm, perhaps you thought that it would reduce your chance of death by only one in fifty million, not one in a million. So before we leap to conclusions about how much you value your own life, we really need to find out how likely you thought the smoke alarm was to save it, and recognise that you may quite rationally not bother to invest too much time in finding out.

Controversial and imperfect as these methods are, they reflect an important presumption of mainstream economics: nobody has your best interests at heart quite as much as you do yourself.

Two different gaps in our knowledge

The use of externality pricing does rely on shaky information about how much it is really worth to us to reduce externalities such as noise, accidents, pollution and congestion. But this is not the only gap in our knowledge; we also do not know the cheapest way of reducing noise, accidents, pollution and congestion. It is with this second gap that externality pricing comes into its own.

Externality pricing is no worse than any other policy when it comes to facing up to the first kind of shaky information. We now know that any policy – of regulation, pricing, command and control, tax or 'laissez-faire' – contains implicit or explicit assumptions about the scientific evidence on externalities like pollution and congestion, and the subjective preferences of people about their time, convenience and health. No policy can be more successful than the accuracy of its assumptions.

The real advantage of externality pricing is that it circumvents the second gap in our knowledge. Nobody knows the cheapest way of solving our traffic problems – yet. But externality pricing brings pollution, congestion and the rest inside the world of truth which markets create for us. As long as individuals have to face the truth, or at least our best estimate of the costs of their actions, they will find a way to reduce those costs. The longer they have to respond, the more surprising and innovative the responses can be, as we are about to see.

The New Orleans effect

A visit to New Orleans tells us how profoundly people can react to price signals. New Orleans displays a unique architectural style – the 'Camelback' house – based on avoiding tax. In the late nineteenth century, houses were taxed according to the number of storeys at the front, so the Camelback design had one storey at the front and more at the back. They are charming, but if it was a practical design for a house it would have caught on elsewhere. There is a similar story in Britain, which is full of dingy houses in response to the policy, in force from 1696 to 1851, of taxing people according to the number of windows their homes had.

Advocates of congestion charging believe that it must be easier to persuade people to find a way to make fewer trips by car than it is to persuade people to build their houses in an architecturally innovative but wasteful style. Their expectation is that things wouldn't change much for a few weeks, but over the months and years, we would be living in a society where we could all get around safely and quickly.

Congestion charging can change the small decisions we make every week about whether to drive to a supermarket, or catch the bus, or walk to a local store or buy food on the internet. But it will also weigh in the balance with the big decisions. Each year, one in three people change jobs and one in seven people move; every time that happens, there is a clear opportunity to reconsider travel choices in the light of congestion charging.

There's also a domino effect here, as changes in behaviour reinforce each other. If more people begin taking buses, there will be more room on the streets and buses will move more quickly ... and can cost-effectively run more frequently. If more people join car pools, each person will find potential pool members more quickly and with more similar trips. If more people try to save the congestion charge by working at home a couple of days a week or commuting at a different time of day, more companies will find ways of accommodating them. People may try to live closer to their jobs; or companies may move to more rural areas to allow staff to commute without paying a high congestion charge.

We simply do not know. The attractive thing about externality pricing is that it attacks the problem but makes no assumption about the solution. The congestion charge gives drivers a signal: by bringing your car into town in the rush hour, you are imposing a cost on everybody else. The drivers then have a choice: pay compensation, or find a way to avoid imposing the cost. There are many, many ways to avoid that cost, and markets can produce the ingenuity needed to uncover them. When no externalities are present, markets automatically take account of costs and provide incentives for producers to reduce them. When externalities are present, those costs are invisible to the market, but systems such as externality charging provide the missing signal that the cost exists.

When London introduced a congestion-charging zone in early 2003 (charging £5 per day to drive into the city centre at first, and more recently £8 per day) people responded far more quickly than many critics had expected. After a year, car journeys fell by nearly a third. Trips that were exempt from the charge became more popular: there were 15 per cent more bus journeys, 20 per cent more motorcycle journeys, and 30 per cent more trips by bicycle. Drivers who no longer enter the charging zone have chosen a variety of responses: one quarter drive around it, 55 per cent have switched to public transportation and 20 per cent use alternatives like bicycles, car pools or working from home on some days. While the number of trips by car fell, the total delays caused by congestion fell by much more, which suggests that the congestion charge allowed the streets to be much more efficiently used. However, the scheme has not been an unqualified success: while London's commuter culture continues to change, with far more cyclists on the roads, traffic levels have been creeping steadily back up. A case for another increase in the congestion charge?

Battling pollution on the cheap

In the 1990s the Environmental Protection Agency (EPA) in the United States discovered how cost-effectively an externality charge could fight pollution when it decided to attack acid rain. The EPA wanted to reduce sulphur pollution from power stations. It seemed likely that some reduction would be efficient, but reducing pollution has costs as well as benefits. So the regulators were unsure by how much they should demand that pollution be reduced.

The trouble is that polluters will lie to regulators about what the cost of abatement really is. After all, even breathing emits a pollutant, carbon dioxide. But regulators could hardly demand that we all stop breathing to prevent pollution. So which pollution should be reduced? And how? By switching to different methods of power generation? Or reducing power consumption?

Or something else? Ask the polluters and they will all tell you that reducing their pollution is like stopping breathing – it would be very expensive to stop, and so somebody else should make the changes.

But it's not really hard to find out the truth. Regulators can find out how much it costs to reduce pollution by telling people either to change their ways or pay a charge. Watch which decision they make. Judge them by their actions.

The EPA tried this in the case of sulphur emissions. They set up an auction for the right to emit sulphur dioxide, which causes acid rain. Polluters were given a quota of emission permits and could either buy more permits in the auction or reduce their emissions by shutting down, installing sulphur scrubbers or buying cleaner coal. When the EPA simply tried to tell them to install sulphur scrubbers, the power generators argued that it would be very expensive to do so, and they lobbied hard to stop the mandatory regulation. Even the EPA estimated that the cost of reducing sulphur dioxide emissions by one ton would probably be in the range of $250 to $700 and might be as high as $1500. But when the EPA conducted the auction in 1993, very few polluters made high bids. The companies had been exaggerating their costs. By 1996 permit prices had fallen to $70 a ton, and even at that price many polluters were buying cleaner coal or installing scrubbers rather than buying permits to continue polluting.

The regulators discovered that getting rid of sulphur dioxide was so cheap that few people were willing to pay much for the right to keep producing it. In the end, the only people willing to pay high prices for permits were student environmental groups buying single permits in an attempt to win fifteen minutes of fame. The clever thing about the auction was not that the sulphur emissions were reduced – that could have been required by law –

but that legislators all over the world found out how much sulphur scrubbers *really* cost. It created a basis for further legislation: not making rules in the dark but in full knowledge of the (modest) cost. And it has set an example to the world; for instance, China has been running pilot programmes in sulphur dioxide trading, although it is fair to say that they have suffered from some serious teething problems.

Now economists are designing the same kind of auction for carbon dioxide emissions in the hope of reducing the effects of climate change. There is massive controversy about how much emission reduction will cost, but an auction of permits to extract oil, coal and gas would soon start to tell us. An auction could start gently: in 2012, auctioning permits to extract the same number of tons of carbon as were extracted in 2011. This would require that economic growth take place without any growth in carbon emissions. If many environmentalists are to be believed, the auction wouldn't even sell all the permits, because basic energy efficiency measures cost nothing. We'd soon find out.

Then over the next few years, we would auction fewer and fewer permits. Carbon emissions would probably fall faster than the number of permits, because carbon speculators would be buying the permits and hoarding them. This would cause no problems: the same emissions take place in the end but are delayed. If it turned out that the permits were expensive, then we would have the information for an informed debate. We could ask if the costs of climate change were worse than the cost of emission reduction. But many economists believe that, like sulphur permits in California, the carbon permits would quickly reveal that decarbonisation is cheaper than we expected, and we will wonder why we took so long to start.

Is the environment too important to be a moral issue?

'How did you travel here today?'
'I'm sorry?'

I'm puzzled. Here I am, going to a panel discussion organised by an environmental charity, and a very earnest young member of staff is grilling me before I even get past the door of the lecture hall.

'How did you travel here today? We need to know for our carbon offset programme.'
'What's a carbon offset programme?'
'We want all our meetings to be carbon-neutral. We ask everyone who attends to let us know how far they came and on what mode of transportation, and then we work out how much carbon dioxide was emitted and plant trees to offset the emissions.'

The Undercover Economist is about to blow his cover.

'I see. In that case, I came here in an anthracite powered steamer from Australia.'
'Sorry . . . how do you spell anthracite?'
'It's just a kind of coal – very dirty, lots of sulphur. OW!'

The Undercover Economist's wife gives him a sharp dig in the ribs.

'Ignore him. We both cycled here.'
'Oh.'

Apart from being a good example of how irritating an Undercover Economist can be, this true story should, I hope, provoke a few questions. Why would an environmental charity organise a carbon-neutral meeting? The obvious answer is 'so that it can engage in debate without contributing to climate change'. And that is true, but misleading.

The Undercover Economist in me was looking at things from the point of view of efficiency. If planting trees is a good way to deal with climate change, why not forget about the meetings and plant as many as possible? (In which case, everybody should say they came by steamship.) If the awareness-raising debate is the important thing, why not forget about the trees and organise extra debates?

In other words, why be 'carbon-neutral' when you can be 'carbon-optimal', especially since the meeting was not benzene-neutral, lead-neutral, particulate-neutral, ozone-neutral, sulphur-neutral, congestion-neutral, noise-neutral or accident-neutral? Instead of working out whether to improve the environment directly (by planting trees), or indirectly (by promoting discussion), the charity was spending considerable energy keeping itself precisely 'neutral' – and not even precisely neutral on all externalities, nor even a modest range of environmental toxins, but preserving its neutrality on a single, high-profile pollutant: carbon dioxide. And it was doing so in a very public way.

A kind view would be that the charity was setting a 'good example', if acting nonsensically can ever be a good example. An unkind view would be that it was indulging in moral posturing.

This line of reasoning may make economists look too smug for their own good, but it is an important illustration of a wider point. The ethical grandstanding of an environmental charity can be directly connected to the fact that public policies do not make evident the environmental costs of our actions. If they did, environmentalists could argue their points from an economic standpoint; much of the moral tone would drain out of the environmental debate, but the environment itself would be much more effectively dealt with.

In a world where environmentalism is merely a moral issue, even the environmentalists themselves cannot work out the environmental impact of everyday decisions. Which is worse: disposable nappies (which clog up landfill sites) or washable nappies (where the washing process uses electricity and releases polluting detergents)? Even with the best will in the world, it is hard to know how to make the right choice.

More importantly, the nappy problem, like any other environmental issue large or small, will certainly not be solved by a tiny minority arguing inconclusively over the morally appropriate individual action. While the Green minority lacks the right signals about environmental damage to act appropriately, the majority of people would not inconvenience themselves even if they understood environmental problems. Both information and incentives are necessary, and as we discovered in Chapter 3, markets can provide both.

Economists have long been in the forefront of analysing environmental problems, and this double difficulty is why they advocate externality pricing. Economists care about the environment but dream of a world where it is no longer an issue that invites moral posturing, but is properly integrated into markets and the world of truth, which would provide both the information and the incentives necessary to persuade ordinary people to behave in an environmentally responsible way. In such a world, we would all have clear signals about the costs of our actions within a market price. Plastics might well be taxed, because they do not biodegrade and so fill landfill sites. This would discourage the use of plastic packaging, disposable plastic bags and plastic nappy liners. People would use only the more expensive plastics if the convenience it provided was worth the extra money – as it probably is in the case of nappies but might well not be in the case of plastic packaging. Electricity generation that contributed to climate change would be taxed, too, which would raise electricity prices unless we could develop cleaner fuels. Nappy-washers, and everybody else too, would have an incentive to buy more efficient washing machines and cut down on energy use generally.

Instead of fretting about the environmental impact of our decisions, we would be well aware that if we were willing to pay the externality charge on a product such as a nappy, we would be compensating others for the harm done by our actions, and at the same time we would be confident that that harm was less than our own convenience. We might even find that there are easier ways to improve our environment than by messing around with nappies. They're messy enough already.

Being positive

We've spent a lot of space on what economists call 'negative externalities' – unpleasant side effects of actions people get away with scot-free.

Once you start to think about the idea of 'negative externalities', you quickly realise that there must be 'positive externalities', too. These are *pleasant* side effects of things people do, for which they are not rewarded. If Abraham paints the front of his house and sorts out his garden, the whole street looks better as a result, but nobody will offer to pay for his paint or pruning shears. If Belinda opens an attractive pavement café, the streets are more pleasant to walk along, but her clients will be willing to pay only for their own pleasure, not for the pleasure of bystanders. And if Craig decides to vaccinate his son for measles, mumps and rubella, this means other children are less likely to catch the diseases, but the government can only go so far in encouraging Craig to do this.

'Positive externalities' all seem very agreeable, until you realise that Abraham may decide he can't be bothered to paint his house, Belinda, fearing bankruptcy, may not set up her café and Craig may be too panicked by scare stories to take his son to the doctor, even though doing so would make other children safer. The rest of us would have benefited if they had gone ahead, but they each decided that on balance it wasn't worthwhile. Just as negative externalities will tend to lead to too much pollution or congestion, positive externalities will leave us undervaccinated with scruffy neighbours and a dearth of pleasant cafés. And while negative externalities attract all the attention, positive externalities may be even more important: so many of the things that make life worth living are, in fact, subject to positive externalities and are underprovided: freedom from disease, honesty in public life, vibrant neighbourhoods and technological innovation.

Once we realise the importance of positive externalities, the obvious solution is the mirror image of the policies we considered to deal with negative externalities: instead of an externality charge, an externality subsidy. Vaccinations, for example, are often subsidised by governments or by aid agencies; scientific research, too, usually gets a big dose of government funding. But we need to be realistic about how far all this should go, because although externality charges and subsidies seem a great fix for externalities, there may be an unexpected hiccup.

Too much of a good thing? Solving externalities without the government

When is an externality not an externality? Here's an example. I may complain about my neighbour's tree damaging my wall, but if it really bothers me I can pay him to let me cut it down. If he refuses the offer then I have to conclude that he gets more pleasure out of the tree than I get nuisance, and in fairness it should stay up. Or perhaps I have the right in law to force my neighbour to cut down the tree. But in that case he can pay me not to exercise that right, and I can spend some of the money fixing my wall. If I have the right to decide then I end up richer; if he has the right to decide he ends up richer. But either way the tree stays up if it's worth more to him and it comes down if it's more irritating to me.

Externalities simply aren't externalities if people can easily get together and negotiate. Remember that they were called 'externalities' because they stood outside market transactions. But some of the things that we imagine to stand outside the market can easily be brought into it.

Since these pseudo-externalities can in fact be dealt with very well by the private sector, if the government also steps in with an externality charge, we may find ourselves 'solving' the externality twice. This would be just as undesirable as not solving it at all: instead of having too much pollution from power generation, we exaggerate the cost and overcompensate by switching off our freezers and streetlights and walking to restaurants every evening, in the dark.

How would you get this kind of 'overdose' of a remedy for externalities? When mentioning the case of Abraham painting the front of his house, I glibly said that the neighbours wouldn't compensate him for his paint, but in fact such things have been known to happen. It's particularly common for landlords to buy paint for tenants to deal with a positive externality: if the tenants repaint, they get a more pleasant flat, but the landlord will also find it easier to rent it out in the future. Taking into account the advantage to both landlord and tenants, the flat is worth painting, but without cash from the landlord, the tenants may decide it's not worth the bother. By providing paint the landlord shares the cost as he will also enjoy the benefit. It might well be that in this case what appeared to be an externality has been 'internalised' by bargaining over sharing the costs.

But what if the government has been thinking about subsidies for positive externalities? Imagine that the policy wonks wrongly believe that wherever a flat is being rented, landlords and tenants will renovate too infrequently and let the place fall apart. It isn't worth it either for the tenants or for the landlord to refurbish more often, but if either of them were taking the other's interests into account, they would agree to do the work. Seeing this positive externality, the government starts dishing out externality subsidies of £500 to tenants who renovate their flats.

(If you find this implausible, remember that governments certainly grant subsidies for improvements to the energy-efficiency of homes, which produce a positive externality.)

Imagine that the redecorating effort is worth £300 of cleaner living to the tenants and £500 of higher future rents to the landlord, but that it costs £1000. The government has identified the externality perfectly: £500 of benefits (higher rents) to the landlord that the tenants do not take into account. But note that since £300 plus £500 is less than £1000, the subsidy is not enough to persuade the tenants to redecorate: nor should it be, because the redecorating is clearly more trouble than it is worth to both landlord and tenants.

Unfortunately, the tenants have every incentive to pocket the

£500 subsidy and ask the landlord to chip in another, say, £350. Then they are doing very nicely, enjoying a £1000 renovation for only £150 – because 85 per cent is paid for by the landlord or the government – and which is worth £300 to them. The landlord is willing to play along, because he pays £350 for a renovation which is worth £500 to him. But the redecoration should never have happened: after all, the government has spent £500 but managed to make tenants and landlord only £150 each better off: not a very effective way to give money away.

Why does the problem arise? Because the positive externality has been dealt with twice over, once by a government subsidy and once by a process of bargaining. Either solution alone represents an efficient way for a society to deal with externalities and to come to the right conclusion, which in this case is that the positive externality is not large enough to justify the decoration work. Both solutions together mean that there is too much subsidy of positive externalities. The same thing could happen for negative externalities too. If the government taxes my neighbour's dirty petrol-driven lawnmower and I also offer to pay him to get rid of it because I dislike the noise and smell, the combination of the taxes and my own offer may persuade him to ditch the monster, even though the fun and convenience he gets from the thing outweigh any damage to anybody else and he really should be keeping it.

Yet many externalities are very real. Outside the cosy (if cracked) walls of our gardens or our unpainted flats, we still have clogged, choking streets. Traffic congestion is not easily solved by sitting down over a cup of coffee and making a deal. There are too many people involved, enforcing the agreement would be impossible and there would always be a temptation for many tenants to avoid the costly negotiations but hope to enjoy the benefits for free.

Government-imposed externality charging is far more likely to be appropriate in situations where a negotiation over the externality will not work, as in the case of the noise from low-flying aircraft . The more likely people are to be able to sit down round the table and work something out, the more likely government intervention is to screw things up: first, because governments can be swayed by interest groups and so they do not always act in the public interest; second, because of the 'overdose' problem; and last, because people know the truth about their costs and benefits better than any government ever could. Externality pricing will work very well for problems such as congestion and climate change, for which individual negotiation is nearly impossible. For smaller-scale situations we must ask whether the government-imposed cures are worse than the disease.

Epilogue: what is economics really about?

This chapter has proposed ways of dealing with some of the major blights on our society: pollution, congestion and fights with neighbours. We've learned that an externality charge on waste or on driving in congested areas, or a subsidy for research or for vaccinations, is the most efficient way of dealing with many of the problems that the market leaves to one side. Externality charges give people both the information to make the right choices and the incentives to do so. Such charges do not automatically answer the question of how tough regulation should be, or what should be regulated, but once our political processes have produced a view about what we want, they provide the most cost-effective way of getting there.

Yet you will often hear so-called experts complaining that taxes on driving or on pollution would be bad for the economy. That sounds worrying. But what is 'the economy'? If you spend enough time watching Bloomberg television or reading the *Wall Street Journal* you may come to the mistaken impression that 'the economy' is a bunch of rather dull statistics with names like GDP (gross domestic product). GDP measures the total cost of producing everything in the economy in one year – for instance, one extra cappuccino would add £1.85 to GDP, or a little less if some of the ingredients were imported.

And if you think this is 'the economy', then the experts may be right. A pollution tax might well make a number like GDP smaller. But who cares? Certainly not economists. We know that GDP measures lots of things that are harmful (sales of weapons, shoddy building work with subsequent expensive repairs, expenditures on commuting) and misses lots of things that are important, such as looking after your children or going for a walk in the mountains.

Most economics has very little to do with GDP. Economics is about who gets what and why. Clean air and smooth-flowing traffic are part of the 'economy' in this sense. It's possible that congestion charging would increase GDP because people would get to work more quickly and produce more, and prices in shops would be lower because of more efficient distribution. But it's perfectly possible that congestion charging would reduce GDP. This does not, in fact, matter in the slightest. We know for certain that it would make us better off in a much more meaningful sense: that we would have many new choices open to us about where we go and what we do. There is much more to life than what gets measured in accounts. Even economists know that.

5

The Inside Story

Jerome K. Jerome's nineteenth-century comic travelogue *Three Men in a Boat* begins with Mr Jerome flipping through a medical dictionary in the British Museum:

I came to typhoid fever – read the symptoms – discovered that I had typhoid fever, must have had it for months without knowing it – wondered what else I had got; turned up St Vitus's Dance – found, as I expected, that I had that too – began to get interested in my case, and determined to sift it to the bottom, and so started alphabetically – read up ague, and learnt that I was sickening for it, and that the acute stage would commence in about another fortnight. Bright's disease, I was relieved to find, I had only in a modified form, and, so far as that was concerned, I might live for years. Cholera I had, with severe complications; and diphtheria I seemed to have been born with. I plodded conscientiously though the twenty-six letters, and the only malady I could conclude I had not got was house-maid's knee.

If you were Mr Jerome, what would you do? He decided to go for a trip up the river, but then he was not an economist. My advice in such a situation would be to pick up the phone and buy yourself some really generous medical insurance. After all, since you know for sure that you will be making expensive claims, why not pay the premium for the best possible care?

Yet this raises a question. If people like Mr Jerome could rush to buy health insurance if and only if they knew they were ill, who would want to insure them?

Inside information

This is more than an idle question. Economists have known for a while that if one party to a deal has inside information and the other does not, then markets may not work as well as we would hope. That makes intuitive sense. But it wasn't until an American economist named George Akerlof published a revolutionary paper in 1970 that the profession realised quite how profound and dramatic the problem might be.

Akerlof chose as his example the market for used cars and showed that even if the market is highly competitive, it simply cannot work if sellers know a lot about the quality of their cars and buyers do not. To take a stark example, let's say that half the used cars on sale are 'peaches' and half are 'lemons'. The peaches are worth more to prospective buyers than to sellers – otherwise the buyers wouldn't be buyers – say, £5000 to prospective buyers and £4000 to sellers. The lemons are worthless pieces of junk. Sellers know whether the car they're selling is a lemon or a peach. Buyers have to guess.

A buyer who doesn't mind taking a fair gamble might think that anything between £2000 and £2500 would be a reasonable price for a car that has a 50-per-cent chance of being a peach, and a 50-per-cent chance of being a lemon. The seller would also think this was a fair deal for a 50/50 prospect, but the seller doesn't face a 50/50 prospect: the seller knows for certain whether the car is a peach or a lemon. The problem is that a seller with a lemon would bite your hand off if offered £2500, but a seller with a peach would find it rather insulting. Wandering around offering £2500 for a car, you quickly discover that only lemons are for sale at that price. Of course, if you offered £4001 you would also see the peaches on the market – but the lemons won't go away, and £4001 is not an attractive price for a car that only has a 50-per-cent chance of running properly.

This isn't just a trivial problem around the fringes of the market. In this scenario, there *is no market*. No seller is willing to sell a peach for less than £4000, but no buyer is willing to offer that much on a car that has a 50-per-cent chance of being a lemon. Sellers don't offer peaches for sale, buyers know that they won't and in the end the only cars that are traded are worthless lemons, which get passed around for next to nothing. Less extreme assumptions about the problem lead to less extreme breakdowns of the market, but the conclusions are similar: if some people know more than others about the quality of a product, then some high-quality products may not be traded at all, or not be traded very much.

Anyone who has ever tried to buy a second-hand car will appreciate that Akerlof was on to something. The market doesn't work nearly as well as it should; second-hand cars tend to be cheap and of poor quality. Sellers with good cars want to hold out for a good price, but because they cannot *prove* that a good car really is a peach, they cannot get that price and prefer to keep the car for themselves. You might expect that the sellers would benefit from their inside information, but in fact there are no winners: smart buyers simply don't show up to play a rigged game.

Let's be clear about how dramatic and how worrying this problem is. What Akerlof described is not a market where some people get ripped off; it's much more serious than that. He described a market that should exist and simply doesn't because of the corrosive force of inside information. Sellers with good cars should be trading with buyers – each trade produces £1000 of value, because that's the difference between the value to the seller and the value to the buyer. If the price is close to £4000, the buyer gets more of that value, and if it is close to £5000, the seller gets more. But Akerlof showed that none of those value-creating trades happen because the buyers will not buy without proof, and the sellers cannot offer proof.

The market for used cars is not the only one affected by inside information. Think about furniture in a rented flat – why is it never built to last? Akerlof's model provides an answer. Flats have many noticeable, even obvious, attributes that can influence our decision whether or not to rent – size, location, interior design and so on. But there are also qualities that are difficult to observe – for instance, whether the furniture is durable. The landlord has little incentive to provide expensive, hard-wearing furniture, since this is not one of the features that potential tenants can recognise before they move in, and so not one for which they are willing to pay. (Of course, the landlord might also go for cheap, fragile furniture because he expects the tenants to trash whatever he puts in the flat. But that fear is equally an argument to get in more durable stuff.) As a result, there is a market for rented flats with flimsy furniture but not a market for rented flats with durable furniture.

Inside information also means that it is hard to get a decent meal in a tourist trap like London's Leicester Square, Times

Square in Manhattan or the Plaka in Athens. With few exceptions, the hungry visitor will pay a lot for mediocre cuisine. Tourists are willing to pay high prices because they have no sense of where better alternatives, even just a few streets away, might be found. (Perhaps smart phones are beginning to change this, providing restaurant reviews on the run.) But the tourist-trap phenomenon is not just about high prices. If it was, we would see a wide range of restaurants, charming little bistros and down-market pasta or burger joints, all kinds of food from superb to disastrous, all charging a premium. Instead, we see a truncated market – high-quality places, whether the good food is fried chicken or fine dining, are simply not to be found. I think the reason is simple enough; tourists will only be making a single visit and will find it hard to pick out the great food from the bad. Good restaurants all locate where they are more likely to be appreciated by more informed locals. The bad ones remain ... the 'lemons' of the restaurant trade.

It's worth emphasising that Akerlof is not describing universal ignorance but a situation where one side knows more than the other. If buyers and sellers were both ignorant about whether a car was a lemon or a peach there would be no problem: buyers would be willing to pay up to £2500 for a car that had a 50/50 chance of being a peach; sellers, equally ignorant, would be willing to accept any offer over £2000. Of course they will strike a deal. It's only when one negotiator knows too much and the other too little that agreement becomes impossible. Because the problem is caused by an uneven grasp on the facts, economists tend to call it 'asymmetric information'. Ripping the 'world of truth' apart, this imbalance in information can completely destroy perfect markets.

Inside information and health insurance

Akerlof's 'lemons' problem would be troublesome enough if it applied only to second-hand cars, furnished accommodation and dubious restaurants in the world's beauty spots. Unfortunately, it also damages the market for more important goods – most notably, health insurance.

Health insurance is important because illnesses are extremely unpredictable and sometimes cost a lot to treat. Not only can some medical treatment be very expensive, it is often impossible to postpone it until a more convenient moment. It can also coincide with periods of low income because people are more likely to need medical care after retirement, and because those who need medical care may also be too ill to work.

So health insurance is a valuable product. If the health insurance market doesn't work well, the results will be excessively high premiums and a large number of uninsured people. This will sound very familiar to readers in the United States, where markets do not, in fact, do a good job of providing medical insurance, precisely because of Akerlof's 'lemons' problem.

Let's say that people who are likely prone to sickness are 'lemons'; people who are likely to stay healthy are 'peaches'. If, like Jerome K. Jerome, I suspect myself to be a lemon, I'd be well advised to buy all the medical insurance going. On the other hand, if you feel fine and all your ancestors lived to be a hundred, then perhaps you will buy medical insurance only if it is extremely cheap. After all, you hardly expect to need it.

Thanks to Akerlof's proof that markets whose players have asymmetric information are doomed, we know that the insurance market may disappear just as the market for good-quality used cars did. You, whose body is a succulent peach, will not find the typical insurance package a good deal; while Mr Jerome and I, whose bodies are bitter little lemons, will embrace the typical insurance package with open arms. The result is that the insurance company only sells insurance to people who are confident they will use it. As a result, the insurer loses clients who are unlikely to make claims and acquires the unwanted clients who are likely to make costly claims, and then the insurer has to cut back on benefits and raise premiums. People of middling health now find the insurance is too expensive and cancel it, forcing the insurance company to raise premiums even higher to stay in business. More and more people cancel their policies, and in the end only the most sickly of the lemons will buy insurance and at a price that will be nearly impossible to afford.

The insurance companies will, of course, try to repair the insurance market by finding out more information about their customers. Do they smoke? How old are they? Did their parents die of hereditary diseases at the age of thirty-five, or in sports car accidents at the age of a hundred? With more genetic information becoming available, insurance companies will be able to gain an increasingly accurate picture of the costs of providing medical insurance to particular individuals. Previously the insurance market was constrained by the presence of inside information: insurers knew less than those they were insuring. But if insurance companies can continue to close that information gap, they will be willing to provide insurance to more people.

This might sound like the price-targeting used by Starbucks and Wholefoods in Chapter 2, but in fact it's a different game. When Starbucks tries to price-target, it knows its own costs and is simply trying to find out whether it can get away with a higher price for some customers. The health insurance companies face a more fundamental task: they don't know how much it will cost to cover the claims of each customer, and if they can't work this out with more accuracy than the customer can, they will simply go bust under the burden of claims. The effects are different, too: price-targeting is a way of getting a larger slice of the pie by squeezing more money from customers, while finding out about insurance customers can create a new pie by making trades possible when previously there were none.

Unfortunately, the insurance market would be saved at some cost: what we would find is that lemons, like Mr Jerome and me, would be able to buy insurance only at enormous rates. Peaches like you could pick it up for a nominal sum. Both premiums would reflect an actuarially fair rate, which means a rate that covers no more and no less than the likely medical expenses. If companies had really accurate information, perhaps obtainable from the genetic tests of the future, then someone who was likely to get ill would pay hundreds of thousands of pounds in premiums; but this would hardly be insurance at all.

By assessing our individual backgrounds and predicting the cost of providing benefits to each of us, the insurance industry manages to stay afloat; if companies did not raise prices for lemons like me and Mr Jerome, they would soon go out of business. The problem is that people who expect to have expensive medical needs – the elderly and the chronically ill, for example – will find that their insurance company does not really give them much insurance at all. Because their premiums are adjusted to take these expenses into account, they will pay more for insurance than they would for the out-of-pocket medical costs they would face without insurance.

The curious conclusion, which is obvious in retrospect, is that an insurance policy depends on mutual ignorance. An insurance company can only insure me against an event like a burglary, a fire or a medical bill if neither of us has any idea whether it will happen. If we could predict the future, insurance would be meaningless. If my insurance company could predict fires much better than I could, it would sell me insurance only if I didn't need it. And if I knew that my house would burn down, the insurance company should be calling the police rather than selling me fire insurance. Since insurance depends on mutual ignorance, then any advance in medical science which pushes back the boundaries of ignorance, whether for the insurers, the insured or both, will weaken the basis of insurance. The more we know, the less we can insure. This is a worrying prospect if we want to give people a chance to protect themselves against the high costs of bad luck.

Making lemonade

A slightly vexing aphorism recommends, 'If life deals you lemons, make lemonade.' How can we make lemonade out of Akerlof's lemons? To return to Akerlof's original example of the market for second-hand cars, both buyers and sellers have an incentive to try to fix the problem: sellers want to get a decent price for their peaches, and buyers want to buy peaches. If inside information is wrecking the chance of a mutually beneficial deal, both sides will want to find a way to bridge the information gap.

Akerlof won the Nobel Prize in 2001 for his work on the problem of asymmetric information; he shared it with two economists who proposed partial solutions. Michael Spence argued that the person with the information might be able to communicate it in a way that the person without the information could trust. Joe Stiglitz looked at the problem in reverse and explored ways in which the person without the information might uncover it.

Spence realised that it wasn't enough for a seller of peaches simply to say, 'All my cars are peaches', because talk is cheap. A seller of lemons can also say, 'All my cars are peaches.' The buyer wouldn't know who was telling the truth, so the claim itself doesn't carry any information. Spence realised that a real signal of quality would be one that a lemon-seller could not make, or at least, could not afford to make.

An example would be buying an expensive car showroom, an investment affordable only by a businessman who plans to stick around for the long term. A peach-seller expects satisfied customers to return, and to tell their friends about his reliable, trustworthy cars. Over the years the sales would pay for the showroom. A lemon-seller couldn't operate like that; instead, he would sell a few overhyped lemons and then have to move to a place where his reputation for dishonesty could not follow.

It's for this reason that banks always used to build such impressive buildings. In the days before governments began to insure banking deposits and simply let banks collapse – such days seem a long time ago now – depositors needed to think hard about where to place their money. If they deposited their savings with a fly-by-night operation, nobody would come to their aid when the bank collapsed. Customers realise that crooks planning to run off with the money or gamble it away do not first clad their branches with bronze and marble: they're in for the long haul instead. This is one reason, too, why you will pay more at an established shop than at a market stall if you buy a product about which you lack inside information about quality and durability. The established shop will still be there to refund your money in the case of a complaint, and that very possibility gives you an assurance that a complaint is less likely to be necessary.

Other economists have used Spence's theory to explain enormously expensive advertising campaigns with no informational content. What, after all, is the information contained within a soft-drink advertisement? 'Coca-Cola. Real.' Pardon? The only information that potential customers can glean from such an advertisement is that it was expensive to make, and that therefore the Coca-Cola company plans to stick around with the same commitment to high-quality products that it always had.

Spence himself first used his insight to show why students might choose to pursue a degree in philosophy, which is difficult but does not lead to specific career opportunities, like an economics degree or a marketing degree. Assume that employers would like to hire smart, diligent workers but can't tell from an interview who is smart or diligent. Assume also that everyone has to work hard to obtain a philosophy degree, but lazy, dumb people find it particularly troublesome.

Spence then shows that smart, diligent people can prove they're smart and diligent by going to the trouble of getting a philosophy degree. It's not that lazy, dumb people can't get that degree but that they wouldn't want to: employers will pay philosophy graduates enough to compensate them for the trouble but not enough to persuade lazy, dumb people to bother. The employers are willing to do this despite the fact that the philosophy degree itself does not improve the candidate's productivity at all. It is merely a credible signal, because a philosophy degree is too much trouble for lazy, dumb people to acquire. Since Spence himself majored in philosophy at Princeton, perhaps there is something in his idea.

Spence proved that one way to bridge the information gap in markets previously hindered by inside information is for trustworthy vendors to find ways to signal their reliability. High-quality job applicants, banks, used-car salesmen and soft-drink manufacturers may find it worthwhile to spend excessive amounts of time and money (by pursuing a degree that does not really add to one's qualifications, paying for lavish decorations, buildings and advertising) simply to distinguish themselves from low-quality job applicants, banks, used-car salesmen or soft-drink manufacturers.

Spence's ideas suggest that the lemons problem is not insoluble, but they are not particularly reassuring. In some variations of Spence's model, everyone would be better off if the wasteful signal were impossible. If studying philosophy were banned, employers would be unable to distinguish between lazy workers and smart workers and would pay both the same wages, an average of their expected productivity. The lazy workers would be better off; the smart workers might also be better off if the new, lower, wage is more than the old wage minus the cost of getting a philosophy degree. And the employers don't mind; they employ worse workers on average but also have to pay less for them. Akerlof showed that inside information could reduce people's ability to find trades that made both sides better off. Spence showed a way of making those trades possible but also found that the social cost of doing so can be too high.

While Spence asked what the informed side could do to credibly signal information, Stiglitz studied what the uninformed side could do to uncover it. He explicitly considered markets for insurance and concluded that the uninformed insurer was not completely helpless in the face of customers who could predict the likelihood of needing to file insurance claims. The insurer could offer different deals: for instance, reducing the premium but increasing the excess. This has the effect of reducing the level of insurance: the low premium makes the insurance cheaper, but the higher excess, which is the amount by which any claim is reduced, means that any claim would pay out less. Low-risk customers would be attracted by that kind of deal, because the insurance is cheaper and they don't expect to claim very often anyway, but high-risk customers would rather pay the higher premium because they expect to claim frequently, so a high excess will cost them a lot. So insurers could persuade different types of customer to reveal their inside information. This is a little like the self-targeting strategy used by coffee bars in Chapter 2. One of the reasons why Starbucks offers frills like whipped cream and flavoured syrup is to persuade customers to reveal whether or not they are price conscious. Aetna Insurance offers nine different packages to Californians, with excesses ranging between $2500 and $8000; in Washington DC there are eleven packages on offer, with a choice of excesses between nothing and $7500. All this is designed to entice policy buyers to reveal their predictions for how many insurance claims they will file. But again, Stiglitz did not conclude that Akerlof's lemons problem could be costlessly solved. On the contrary, he showed that in response to inside information, banks might deny loans to whole sections of society, firms might prefer to pay high wages to privileged insiders rather than lower wages to more workers and insurance companies would prefer to exclude high-risk individuals. Spence and Stiglitz both showed that you can make lemonade from Akerlof's lemons – but that you cannot get rid of the bitter aftertaste.

Lemons, health care and the United States

The difficulty of solving the lemons problem may explain why the American health-care system is malfunctioning so badly. The United States relies upon private health insurance to provide much of the financing for medical costs. This is unusual: in Britain, Canada and Spain, for example, health-care costs are largely paid for by the government. In Austria, Belgium, France, Germany and the Netherlands, medical costs are paid for by a system of 'social insurance': it is compulsory for most people to buy insurance, but insurance premiums are tied by law to income rather than to the risk of a claim.

The United States system makes it voluntary to buy insurance, and premiums are linked to risk, not to income. But these market-based principles, beloved of many Americans, do not seem to be delivering health care that makes them happy. A recent survey revealed that only 17 per cent of respondents in the United States were content with their health-care system and thought no substantial reforms were necessary. Why the discontent?

The superficial reasons are simple enough to describe: the system is hugely expensive, very bureaucratic and extremely patchy. The expense first: US health care costs a third more, per person, than that of the closest rival, super-rich Switzerland, and twice what many European countries spend. The United States government alone spends more per person than the combination of public and private expenditure in Britain, despite the fact that the British government provides free health care for all residents, while the American government spending programme covers only the elderly (Medicare) and some of the marginalised (Medicaid). Most Americans worry about health-care costs and would be stunned to discover that the British government spends less per person than the American government but still manages to provide free health care for everyone. In fact, if you factor in the costs of providing health insurance to government employees and providing tax breaks to encourage private health care, the US government spending on health care, per person, is the highest in the world.

Bureaucracy next. Researchers at the Harvard Medical School found that the administrative costs of the US system, public and private, exceed $1000 per person. In other words, when you count all the taxes, premiums and out-of-pocket expenses, the typical

American spends as much on doctor's receptionists and the like as citizens of Singapore and the Czech Republic spend on their entire medical care. Both places are countries with health outcomes very similar to those in the United States: life expectancy and 'healthy life' expectancy (a statistic that distinguishes a long healthy life from a long life plagued by years of severe disability) are a shade lower in the Czech Republic than in the United States; and in Singapore they are a little higher than in the United States. The cost of US bureaucracy is also more than three times the $307 cost per person for the administration of the Canadian health system, which produces noticeably superior health outcomes.

Then there is the patchy coverage of the system. Health insurance is usually packaged together with a job, which reduces the efficiency of the labour market; workers are hesitant to quit their jobs without lining another job up first for fear of being uninsured. Worse, 15 per cent of citizens have no insurance coverage of any kind which should be a stunning statistic for the world's richest economy, but probably isn't because it has been lamented

The US spends most on medical care

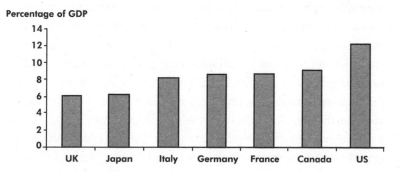

Percentage of GDP

Source: Cutler 2002.

for so many years. Compare it with Germany, where 0.2 per cent of the population has no coverage, or with Canada or Britain, where everyone is provided for by the government. (The situation in the US is changing, as we shall see shortly.)

Given what we have learned from George Akerlof and his lemons, the troubles of the US health-care system should be no surprise. We should expect a voluntary private insurance system to be patchy. A few people who have more pressing costs than health insurance (for example, the young poor, who have little money and rightly expect that they are unlikely to become seriously ill) will drop out of the system. As a result, health insurance companies, needing to cover their costs, will raise the premiums for the average client, driving out more and more people. Unlike the very stark lemons model, the market does not completely collapse; this is partly because many people find that the risks of having to pay for medical treatment are so worrying that they're willing to pay substantially more than an actuarially fair premium. As a result, the process of unravelling stops, but not before many people have been excluded from the system.

Thanks to Spence and Stiglitz, we should also expect insurance companies to devise ways to get around this lemons problem, but that although the solutions may be effective they will probably also be wasteful. The huge bureaucratic burden of the US system is one of the results, as insurance companies struggle to monitor the risks, behaviour and expenses of their customers. The clunky linkage of health insurance with jobs is another result: at first sight, there is no reason why a job should come with health insurance, any more than it should come with a house or free food. Employees are frequently forced to buy the health insurance that is packaged with their job. This packaging compels the healthiest members of society to buy insurance packages and so helps prevent the unravelling of the market. But this solution doesn't come cheap: health-care plans are not chosen by their beneficiaries, who would aim to get the ideal coverage for the right price, but by human resource managers with other priorities, such as making their own lives easy with a 'one-size-fits-all' bulk purchase. The result is likely to be further wasteful spending.

Not every drawback of the US health-care system should be blamed on Akerlof's lemons problem. Even without the difficulty of inside information, the system of insurance is problematic, because patients are not always able to choose their treatment. With the insurance company picking up the bill, choosing the appropriate treatment is always going to be something of a matter of negotiation. When you ask somebody else to pay for your health care, don't be surprised if you don't get exactly what you would have chosen yourself.

Nevertheless, it is striking that partial coverage, inefficiency and high costs are not only the defining characteristics of private health insurance, they are also exactly what we would have predicted armed only with the theoretical models of Akerlof, Spence and Stiglitz.

I am not sure if President Obama was inspired by the first edition of this book, but it is interesting to observe that many of the chief elements of 'Obamacare', the Patient Protection and Affordable Care Act, are designed to combat the lemons problem. Insurance companies are prohibited from cancelling coverage or raising premiums for customers who have pre-existing conditions. This provision alone would seem to make access to healthcare more universal. However, it will also increase the implicit cross-subsidies in the system and encourage healthy people to opt out. So there's a second rule, which is that with a few exceptions, insurance is compulsory: refuse to buy health insurance and you're liable for a tax bill of at least $695, or 2.5 per cent of income, whichever is greater. That is the logic of the lemons problem.

These measures should help to deal with adverse selection, and they will certainly expand healthcare coverage. But by making sure almost everyone is insured, they may encourage the over-consumption of expensive medical tests and thus worsen another problem of inside information: one called 'moral hazard', to which we will now turn.

Imperfect information – the whole story

The lemons problem ('adverse selection' in the economists' jargon), when inside information guts a market because ignorant buyers are unwilling to pay for quality they cannot observe, is one example of the broader problem of inside information ('asymmetric information' in the jargon). 'Moral hazard' is another facet of the information problem. The concept is simple: if you compensate people when bad things happen to them, they may get careless.

Moral hazard can sometimes take extreme forms. According to the Florida newspaper the *St Petersburg Times*, in the late 1950s and early 1960s, more than two-thirds of insurance claims for the loss of a limb originated in the Florida Panhandle. At the epicentre, 'Nub City' – the tiny town of Vernon, Florida – almost 10 per cent of the adult population had lost a limb. One man was said to be insured by dozens of companies when he lost his foot; fortunately he had been carrying a tourniquet at the time of the accident. He pocketed a million dollars. Another man shot his foot off – 'while aiming at a squirrel' – just twelve hours after buying insurance. Now that's careless – and that's moral hazard in spades.

But moral hazard is usually more humdrum. If my car is insured against theft, I will park wherever I find a space, even on a deserted street that doesn't seem entirely safe. If my insurance doesn't cover theft I may choose to pay a little extra to park in a car park with an attendant. If I lose my job and the government pays unemployment benefit, I may not hurry to find a new job quite as quickly as I would if I had no income whatsoever. If the money in my bank account is insured against a bank failure, why should I bother to check that the bank is financially sound?

(When I wrote that last sentence for the first edition, it may have seemed like the sort of curious thing only an economist would worry about. The credit crisis has shown sharply why it matters. Banks in Iceland – a tiny economy – offered tempting interest rates to depositors in the UK, who rushed to place their money with institutions they'd never heard of. Shortly after the crunch began it became clear that the banks were bust and Iceland wouldn't be able to prop them up. The depositors themselves were bailed out by the British government. At least the possibility of moral hazard was recognised in the case of depositors, who were explicitly protected by governments. Much more serious and alarming, the credit crisis showed that major commercial investors in banks were also implicitly insured by governments, at tremendous cost. If governments had been able to distance themselves from banks a decade ago, then banks would have been forced to be more cautious in order to attract investors. But once implicit government backing became taken for granted by commercial investors, it was impossible to withdraw it without collapsing the whole financial system.)

While it is impossible for insurance companies (or anyone else) to avoid moral hazard altogether, they can take steps to reduce it. For example, they do not offer insurance against being fired or becoming pregnant, which is a shame, because it would be great to have that kind of insurance. The reason is easy to see: it is easy to arrange to be fired or to get pregnant. There are many people who would like to leave their jobs and many others who would like to have children, and such people would be particularly eager to buy an insurance policy that would pay them handsomely for putting their plans into action. As a result, moral hazard destroys the market for private unemployment insurance.

On the other hand, public unemployment insurance still exists, in spite of moral hazard. It is not polite to say so, but it is obvious that paying people to be unemployed encourages unemployment. Yet if a government scrapped unemployment benefit, there would still be jobless people, and supporting the jobless is something that every civilised society should do. The truth is that we have a trade-off: it is bad to encourage unemployment but good to support those without incomes.

Both governments and private insurers will try to protect themselves against moral hazard. One of the most common ways insurance companies do this is by modifying the insurance policy to provide incomplete insurance, in the form of an excess. If my car insurance excess is £200, the fear of losing that money probably won't persuade me to take extravagant safety precautions, but it should be enough to make me check that my car is locked.

Another way insurance companies can fight moral hazard is by gaining access to the inside information. Health insurers will want to know whether I am a smoker before they set my premiums. Of course, I could lie, but it wouldn't be too hard for insurers to expose my lie; a simple medical examination would reveal that I smoke. When most governments pay unemployment benefits, they do so on the condition that recipients are actively looking for work. Because the government cannot monitor people's job searches perfectly, it pays out only meagre unemployment benefits. Yet if the government could really tell how hard unemployed people were looking for jobs, then it would be possible to pay more generous benefits to genuinely deserving recipients.

The problems of imperfect information include adverse selection (lemons) and moral hazard, but there are other, broader and vaguer issues. For example, my boss would like to pay me extra if I try harder to do a good job, but because he has only a vague idea how hard I am trying, my performance bonus is only a small part of my salary. If my boss could observe my skill and effort perfectly, he could make my entire salary performance related. Another example: let's say I would like to eat at the best-value restaurant in town; I don't know what it is, so I look for a familiar brand name, where I know I can't go wrong. Knowing that customers won't bother trying to find the cheapest place around, established restaurants are able to charge more than they should.

Do these information problems destroy markets completely? They certainly don't help, but it would be wrong to exaggerate the problems. In spite of asymmetric information, markets do often work well, because people produce ingenious solutions to improve the quality of information – or to reduce the damage caused by imperfect information.

When I buy complicated equipment like a camera, I talk to friends and consult websites and consumer magazines, which I hope will give me useful information about the products I am trying to choose between. Expert reviews providing 'inside information' can be particularly helpful when we are ignorant about what we're buying. I rely on them all the time in another market, which suffers from severe information problems: the market for holidays. I'm the kind of person who likes to visit new places, but often I have no idea where to go or what will be fun, where is tacky and who offers a good deal, where is beautiful and where is dangerous. If the problem were insoluble we wouldn't bother to take holidays at all. (Or we might demand that governments provided them, which in my mind conjures up images of being on a waiting list for years before enjoying organised team games and artificial cheer in an overcast concrete resort.) Instead, we simply buy decent guidebooks and try to learn more on our own.

Health-care provision, yet again, provides a particularly acute example of the problem. It's one thing to check a guidebook to find out what to do on holiday. It's quite another to consult a guidebook to find a heart surgeon. Yet the basic information problem is the same as the one faced by holidaymakers. Heart surgery patients try to learn more about which doctors have good reputations, which procedures have the highest success rate and which hospitals provide the best recovery care. Still, most patients would admit that they don't have much idea just how good their doctor really is.

Market failure versus government failure

This is not exactly comforting. A health-care system based on private insurance will be, as we have discovered, patchy, costly and bureaucratic. What's more, it will offer patients choices, such as the choice of heart surgeon, that they are not very well qualified to make. So could the government do better? After all, every chapter of this book so far – with the exception of Chapter 3 – has lamented the causes and costs of market failures. It's tempting to look to the government to sort things out.

Unfortunately, while markets can fail, governments can fail too. Politicians and bureaucrats have their own motivations. Scarcity power, externalities and imperfect information do not magically disappear when the economy is run or regulated by governments. When market failure and government failure are both present, the choice is often between the lesser of two evils.

An intriguing case in point is Britain's National Health Service (NHS), which offers health care to all citizens. It is almost completely free, although people with jobs need to pay a token amount for prescription drugs. It provides universal coverage: if you walk into any doctor's surgery or any hospital in the country, you will be treated free of charge.

As you would expect, the system gets overcrowded, people often have to wait and patient choice is not a major feature of the system – although researchers at the London School of Economics did discover higher standards where there were an unusually large number of competing hospitals. (Recognising the iron law of British politics that nobody ever closes down a hospital in a closely fought political battleground, the researchers used constituency boundaries to conduct a kind of natural experiment exploring whether more competition raises management standards. It does.) Overall, the medical outcomes in the NHS are not bad, but the waiting lines for treatment have been a major bone of contention for many years. The same survey, which found 17 per cent of American citizens approved of the US health-care system, reports that only 25 per cent of the British are happy with their own system – better, but hardly a resounding endorsement.

If you were going blind in Britain a few years ago, you would have been well aware of the difficulties faced by such a system. The Royal National Institute of Blind People, along with other organisations representing people with vision problems, campaigned vigorously against a ruling by the National Institute for Health and Clinical Excellence (NICE), an agency that evaluates treatments and decides whether the National Health Service should pay for them. Heart surgery, for example, is on the approved list; nose jobs are not.

The controversy stemmed from NICE's half-hearted endorsement of a treatment called photodynamic therapy. The therapy uses a drug called Visudyne or verteporfin, combined with a low-intensity laser treatment, to destroy lesions under the surface of the eye's retina, usually without damaging the retina itself. If the lesions are not treated they can irreversibly damage the centre of the retina, called the macula. The resultant condition, age-related macular degeneration (ARMD), destroys central vision so that the victim cannot recognise faces, read or drive. It is the leading cause of blindness in the United Kingdom.

In 2002 NICE filed a report recommending photodynamic therapy only in more extreme cases, only when both eyes are affected, and only in the eye that is less seriously damaged. The implication is that even treated patients will lose their sight in one eye, while others whose sight might be improved are denied treatment altogether.*

It is easy to condemn NICE without appreciating its methods and the situation it was in. The basic challenge confronting the National Health Service is that it has a limited amount of money to spend and an unlimited number of ways of spending it. It is no good asking patients, who pay little or nothing for treatment and will as a result demand more of everything. So NICE must resolve the inevitable dilemmas, determining who will get what type of health care and who will be left to fend for himself.

How can medical spending be decided under such conditions? What would *you* do if you were in charge of NICE? It's a near-impossible task, but you would probably work out the costs and

---

*This particular controversy has now faded: in 2008, NICE recommended a new drug, ranibizumab, for some forms of macular degeneration. But each new NICE recommendation has the same potential to create a moral and political minefield.

the effects of each treatment, and then you'd compare them with each other. Sometimes this is quite simple: a treatment with a 20-per-cent chance of preventing another heart attack is better than a treatment with a 10-per-cent chance of preventing another heart attack. Under pressure to make decisions, you might go further and say the first treatment is twice as good, and should be used if it is less than twice as expensive. Even to go that far would be a stretch. How, then, would you compare a treatment that increases the chance of walking again after an accident, with a treatment that reduces the likelihood of going blind? Impossible! But if you were running NICE you would have to try.

The way NICE does it is to calculate the impact of each treatment in 'Quality-Adjusted Life Years', or QUALYs. A treatment that saves ten years of life is better than a treatment that saves five years of life; a treatment that gives somebody ten years of able-bodied life is better than a treatment that gives somebody ten years alive but in a coma. Evidently, the value-judgements involved are extraordinarily difficult. Yet they must be made in a system that provides health care free of charge.

As an example, think of the problems involved in judging the QUALY impact of photodynamic therapy, which reduces the chance of blindness. The best way for the Royal National Institute of Blind People to get a higher priority for photodynamic therapy would be to argue that a year alive but blind is worth much less than a year alive and fully sighted. If NICE accepts this view, treatments curing blindness will become very valuable on the QUALY measure, which places years alive and fully sighted high above years alive but blind.

But hang on. The strict logic of the view that 'it's bad to be blind' would suggest that while that claim places a high priority on vision treatments, it places a low priority on treating people for *other* illnesses if they are already blind. If two people, one blind and one sighted, simultaneously turn up in a hospital in coronary arrest and there is time to treat only one, the QUALY methodology offers a truly unpalatable conclusion; that it is more worthwhile to help the person who can see rather than the blind patient.

We could backtrack and argue that in fact there is no difference in the value of life for the blind compared with the sighted. That is certainly more comfortable. Unfortunately, in conjunction with the QUALY methodology, this produces the conclusion that there is no point in spending anything at all on photodynamic therapy – or indeed on a pair of glasses. If treatments do not improve the value of people's lives then they are not worth spending money on, particularly when there are many causes, such as treatment for cancer, which certainly do improve the value of people's lives.

It is no wonder that the Royal National Institute of Blind People steered well clear of even mentioning QUALYs in its campaign. It simply argued that photodynamic therapy is proven to improve vision and so should be comprehensively available. I do not blame the RNIB. But given the problem NICE is trying to solve – allocating finite resources among an unlimited range of medical treatments – it is easy to understand the position NICE takes: in particular the apparently heartless ruling that treatment should be applied in only one eye, leaving the other to go blind. The dispassionate perspective of QUALY analysis argues that the difference between having two good eyes and one good eye is less significant than the difference between having one good eye and none at all. Small wonder that the calculations tend to churn out embarrassing recommendations. But a free service will always be in demand, and it is hard to see a better way of rationing it.

Fixing health care with keyhole economics

Keyhole surgery techniques allow surgeons to operate without making large incisions, minimising the risk of complications and side effects. Economists often advocate a similar strategy when trying to fix a policy problem: target the problem as closely as possible rather than attempting something a little more drastic.

How, then, can we fix health care? The insurance-based market solution is misfiring badly in the United States, in large part because of the problem identified by Akerlof's lemons model. The result: expensive, bureaucratic care ... and even that, only for some.

The British approach has been to sweep away the market completely and replace it with a system governed by the decisions of bureaucrats like NICE rather than directed by market prices, as though part of the old Soviet Union had been transplanted into the hospitals and surgeries of the English shires. Fortunately, political and bureaucratic decisions are much more accountable in the United Kingdom than in the USSR, so the system works fairly well. But this is a colossal and wide-reaching response to the serious but rather specific problem of inside information. We owe it to ourselves to ask: is there a 'keyhole' solution, which could fix health care without sacrificing the ability of patients to decide how much they value their own eyes?

Keyhole economics would first identify the specific market failures, which fall into three categories: scarcity power, externalities and imperfect information, plus the issue of fairness. Scarcity power is a potential problem, but for most treatments not a significant one. In the United Kingdom, for example, there are roughly fifteen hundred patients per general practitioner (the doctor who is the first port of call for most patients using the National Health Service). So, a small town of nine thousand people can support six doctors, probably more than enough to encourage real competition, in a country where 90 per cent of people live in urban areas. Some special treatments will wield greater scarcity power – people fly from Australia and New Zealand to Hawaii for treatment with the Leksell Gamma Knife, a device for treating brain tumours. There are only three hundred Gamma Knives in the world. So there are some situations, but few, where scarcity power is a concern.

Externalities, too, are important only in select cases: for instance, for public health projects to restrict communicable diseases. (If everybody else had been using condoms to protect themselves from HIV/AIDS, I would not have needed to bother.) Yet neither externalities nor scarcity power are so severe or widespread that government provision becomes an attractive alternative. The keyhole solution would be some light-touch regulatory oversight to prevent the exploitation of scarcity power, coupled with focused subsidies to boost inoculation programmes.

Fairness is not, strictly speaking, a market failure; it is something that even perfect markets do not necessarily provide. But we care deeply about fairness when it comes to medical care, both because we do not want the poor to be deprived, and because the cost of health care can vary dramatically, depending on the luck of each individual. In a civilised society we will want to make sure that everyone can afford some standard of medical care. The best way to do this is to tackle the general problem of poverty (think back to the 'head start theorem' discussed in Chapter 3) using redistributive taxes. After all, why spend so much to provide free medical care to poor people while ignoring the fact that they cannot afford healthy food or a safe house to live in?

That leaves inside information as the big obstacle to a well-functioning health-care system. The economic analysis we've done suggests that government provision is ineffective because decision making is out of patients' hands and resources are rationed by political processes. Meanwhile, the overwhelming problem for the market provision of medical care is inside information, and more specifically its tendency to destroy insurance markets.

This diagnosis suggests a two-part keyhole treatment. The first part is to ensure the widespread availability of information: it should be easy to get a second opinion, easy to call a help-line, and easy to get information from libraries, clinics, the internet, even supermarkets. In the United Kingdom, people do not pay much attention to this information because doctors make the decisions. If we were asked to take responsibility for our own medical care we would pay much closer attention, and many more resources (public and private) would respond to our demands to know more.

The second part is to give patients an opportunity to use this information. In a privatised, insurance-based system the insurance company tends to make a lot of choices; in a government-provided system the government makes the choices. In a market-based system without insurance, the patient makes the choices. Much better. But the patient also has to pay for unpredictable and potentially catastrophic health-care costs.

How to give patients choice and responsibility without putting an unbearable burden on them? The best system would be one that compels patients to pay for many of the costs, thus providing an incentive to inform themselves and to make choices that are both in their interests and reasonably cost-effective but which leaves the most severe costs to the government or insurance. This might work, because most medical bills are not catastrophic and so do not need insurance.

How might such a system work, in more detail? The aim would be to give maximum responsibility and choice to patients, therefore requiring them to spend their own money rather than that of governments or insurers, but to make sure that nobody faced catastrophic medical bills and to make sure that even the poor had enough money to buy medical care.

These requirements suggest: people should pay for all medical care; but insurance should cover the largest bills; and that everyone should have a savings account dedicated to medical expenses, to which the government would contribute in the case of the poor or the chronically ill.

Catastrophe insurance, which pays out only when a particular course of treatment is very expensive, is fairly cheap. The savings are no problem either: simply reduce each person's tax bill by, say, £1000 a year – this is very roughly the cost, in taxes, of both the UK and the US public health systems – and make them put the money in a savings account. For people who pay less than £1000 in tax a year, the government would contribute money to make up the shortfall. Since the system is compulsory, no adverse selection takes place.

If you participated in such a programme, how would it work for you? Your health-care savings would automatically go into a high-interest bank account. They would build up gradually throughout your life. For most people, medical bills are low in their younger years. So you could expect to have £20,000 in your account when you turn forty; more, if you've managed to keep your spending low and watched the money earn interest. Twenty thousand pounds buys a lot of medical care. Of course, it could all be consumed by a single expensive procedure, except that catastrophe insurance restricts your expenses.

If you reach retirement age with money still in your medical savings account beyond some minimum, you can put the excess towards your pension. When you die, you can pass the savings to other people's savings accounts (usually your spouse or children).

So at every point in your life, you would have an incentive to spend money only on health care that you feel is absolutely necessary. If you felt that the right treatment for you was a bit of preventive maintenance – a course of shiatsu, say – then that would be your choice. You might well consider giving up smoking, given how much it would cost you in medical bills over the years. The catastrophe insurance would still pay for your lung transplant, of course, but no humane system can avoid moral hazard completely.

If one day your optician told you that you were suffering from age-related macular degeneration, but that a treatment with photodynamic therapy would increase your chances of maintaining your sight for a few more years ... well, the choice would be yours. The photodynamic therapy drug, Visudyne, cost $1288 a treatment when I last checked. It would increase your chance of keeping good sight from about 40 per cent to 60 per cent. No need to start talking about QUALYs: it's your money, and your choice. (Or you could try a number of new drugs – including Avastin, which costs just $65. The RNIB is, at the time of writing, concerned about a lack of evidence as to whether Avastin has side effects or not.)

The exception would be if you had a catastrophic expense, in which case the insurance company would prefer to pay for the cheapest treatment while you would want the best – a difficult problem, but no different from the conflict of interest faced for every single treatment in our medical systems today. The new system simply means that that inherent conflict of interest happens far more rarely.

It is common to provide goods and services via the private market, but one of the main alternatives – certainly, the main ideological alternative – has been to provide them using a political market instead. Medical goods and services are among the most difficult to distribute. We have tried using political markets, but they have let us down badly, and for obvious reasons.

At first sight, the private market failures, exemplified by the US system, are also obvious. But when we closely examine the market failures, it's the lack of information that is most serious, and the insurance market suffers the most serious consequences. American citizens receive much of their medical care through the intermediation of this badly malfunctioning market.

With some imagination, and some economics, we can step back from the troubles of our current systems and think about how to fix them. In Singapore, the system sketched in the last few pages has been successful for almost two decades. The typical Singaporean lives to the age of eighty, and the cost of the system (both public and private) is a thousand dollars per person – less than the cost of the bureaucracy alone in the United States. Each year, the typical Singaporean pays about seven hundred dollars privately (the average American pays twenty-five hundred dollars privately) and the government spends three hundred dollars per person (five times less than the British government and seven times less than the American government). Keyhole economics works.

The reason why Singapore's success is uncommon is probably that policy debates get stuck with one side claiming that we should rely on the market and the other side asserting that the government would do a better job. So, government or market? We've learned that the question doesn't make any sense in isolation. To answer it we need to understand why markets might work, and how and why they fail.

We learned in Chapter 3 exactly why markets work: because our choice as consumers between competing producers gives them both the right incentives and the right information to produce the right amount of exactly what we want. And we've also learned that scarcity power, externalities and inside information can each ruin the way markets do this.

In the case of health care, the market works poorly because while we want the reassurance of knowing they can afford expensive medical bills, inside information eats away at the insurance by driving away low-risk customers and forcing premiums to rise. Private companies have developed ways to get around the problem, but they are expensive and bureaucratic. Singapore's government had the power to tackle the problem head on, by using forced saving and catastrophe insurance to make sure costs were manageable but keeping the power of patient choice at the heart of the system. Governments can replace markets, but they will often do better to try to fix them. They are unlikely to succeed unless they appreciate exactly what the problem is in the first place.

6

Rotten Investments and Rotten Eggs

In the first edition of *The Undercover Economist*, this chapter detailed the dot-com bubble and bust of the late 1990s and early 2000s: in a wave of excitement about the internet's potential to transform business models, shares in red-hot high-tech start-ups were traded up to absurd levels before inevitably crashing back to earth again. After that first edition was published, however, the banking crisis that began in 2007 made the dot-com crash look like a minor inconvenience.

We'll come back to the dot-com crash in due course, but it would be impossible to produce this second edition without going undercover again to see if we can explain just what went so hideously wrong with the banks. And this is quite a challenge, because as well as being deeply serious, the banking crisis was also mind-bogglingly complicated. So in an attempt to understand it, let's start with something altogether simpler: a carton of eggs.

In Cumbria, in the north of England, early in 2010, a lady named Fiona Exon bought a carton of six eggs and discovered that all six of them had double yolks. Newspapers reported this as beating odds of 1,000,000,000,000,000,000 to one. (Some of them also reported this as 'a trillion to one'. That's old school. These days we'd call a number with eighteen zeroes a 'quintillion'.) The mathematics seemed straightforward. According to the egg-watchers to whom the newspapers spoke (the British Egg Information Service – who knew?), the chance of any given egg having two yolks is one in a thousand. The chance of any two given eggs both having double yolks would therefore appear to be, from multiplying the two probabilities together, one in a million. Three in a row would be a one in a billion chance; four would be a trillion, five a quadrillion, and six double-yolked eggs in a row would be a one in a quintillion chance. If that calculation is right, then if each and every person in the world bought six eggs each morning, we'd expect to see a carton of double-yolk eggs being sold somewhere on earth roughly every four centuries.

The trouble is, after Mrs Exon's apparently astonishing discovery was reported in the media, lots more people popped up to announce that the same thing had happened to them. I was invited onto national radio to explain the mathematics, and a number of listeners phoned in to say they'd also once bought a carton of eggs that turned out to have six double-yolks. It seemed they were rare, but not *that* rare.

What had gone wrong with the calculation? Perhaps double-yolk eggs are more common than the British Egg Information Service thinks. But let's be charitable to the British Egg Information Service and assume that it provides accurate information about British eggs. (It would be a minor tragedy if it did not.) The problem is that the newspapers made an insidious assumption: that double-yolk eggs do not come in clusters. Allowing for the fact that they might, we get a very different equation. In an extreme case, where double-yolk eggs *always* come clustered with other double-yolk eggs, you will either see no double-yolk eggs in a carton (with probability 999 in 1000) or you will see six double-yolk eggs. Even though the chance of a single double-yolk egg hasn't changed, the chance of seeing six together has increased a million billion fold, simply because the eggs tend to come in clusters.

All this would be simply a curiosity unless large amounts of money were riding on it. So imagine that Fiona Exon's friendly local egg retailer had come up with a clever marketing wheeze and offered a million-pound jackpot to any customer who bought a carton full of double-yolk eggs. Sitting with his calculator, and working from odds of a thousand to one per egg, he would have concluded there was effectively no chance that he'd ever have to pay out. If the offer enticed in a few more egg buyers a week, it was easy money.

Unless his calculations were wrong, of course, and the eggs came in clusters. Then it would be only a matter of time before the retailer bankrupted himself.

How might double-yolk eggs come in clusters? As it turns out, there's a human explanation. A caller to the radio show I was on explained that they used to work in an egg packing plant. They and their colleagues could easily identify double-yolk eggs by holding them up to the light. They used to put several double-yolk eggs in a carton together to take home for breakfast. And if each of them had all the eggs they could stomach, the double-yolk carton would be placed back on the production line to be shipped to the likes of Fiona Exon – to the horror of our imaginary cal-culator-wielding retailer.

All this is roughly – very roughly – what happened in the finan-cial crisis. Bear with me, and we'll discover how.

Rotten eggs and rotten investments

Essentially, the banking crisis came about because banks and other financial institutions were taking very big bets on the chance of events that, like Fiona Exon's discovery, seemed too unlikely to contemplate. They were wrong, because they had made the wrong assumptions about the process producing these events.

The financial egg cartons were called mortgage-backed securities, and the rotten eggs that filled them were the now-infamous subprime loans. Banks bought these risky – or 'subprime' – mortgages from 'originators', companies who initially made the loans. Then the banks repackaged them into financial products, which provided the rights to a stream of mortgage repayments and the risks that mortgage would not be repaid. The repackaging was often repeated many times. (The first package was called a residential mortgage-backed security, or RMBS. The repackaged versions were called collateralised debt obligations, or CDOs, then CDOs-squared and CDOs-cubed.)

These RMBSs, CDOs and the rest were tremendously complex products, but their aim was simple enough: to create financial assets that promised a safe and predictable income, rather like the one our fictional egg retailer thought he'd come up with. This predictable income could then be traded between banks, pension funds and other financial institutions. If the underlying risks had been misunderstood, however, the value of these financial assets would collapse, threatening the companies that owned them with bankruptcy.

So how did these strange mortgage-backed products work? Let's switch the analogy from double-yolk eggs to rotten ones. Imagine that a bunch of mortgages is simply a basket full of eggs, some of which are rotten – say 5 per cent. The bank repackages the eggs into cartons of six, keeping one egg and selling the rest. The price of those other eggs reflects the risk of who gets the rotten eggs. It turns out that, assuming the rotten eggs don't cluster, the chance that at least one egg will turn out to be rotten is 27 per cent. If the first egg is rotten, the bank is first in line and takes the hit. But it's a risk they're happy to take, because they've sold the rest of the carton at a profit.

The buyer of the second egg – the 'junior investor' – is next in line if there's another rotten egg. Do the sums, and the chance of a second bad egg comes out at just over 3 per cent. The junior investor gets a decent discount on the price of the egg for taking this fairly small but still meaningful risk. Senior investors buy the remaining eggs, and as the chance of any further bad eggs is very low – only about 0.2 per cent – they pay top dollar. They're expecting a safe and predictable income; in the very unlikely event that there's a third rotten egg, they'll get a nasty surprise.

The repackaging makes some sense, because some investors prefer to pay for a guarantee of safety while others would prefer to get a cheap egg and take a risk. But why repackage two or three or four times, creating CDOs-squared, CDOs-cubed and so on? There is a reason. The first egg is quite likely to be rotten – not very interesting for repackaging purposes. The final four eggs are almost certainly fresh and don't need any repackaging. But the second egg is more interesting. It is fairly safe but not that safe. So a bank could take six 'second eggs' and repackage them into another carton. The bank would take the first rotten egg, new senior investors would queue up for the four guaranteed-fresh eggs, and there would be another 'second egg' which might or might not be rotten. This process can be – and was – repeated many times. In each case, it all seemed at the time like a perfectly rational way to ensure that investors with different preferences could pay a fair price for the different levels of risk they were taking on.

Now, here comes the catch with this repackaging. If the banks had got their sums wrong – no prizes at this stage for guessing whether they had – then each level of repackaging dramatically amplified the effect of that mistake.

Remember we assumed that the risk of a rotten egg picked at random from the basket of eggs was 5 per cent,. This turned out to imply that, in the first carton of eggs, the chance of a second rotten egg is just 3 per cent. The CDO, then, is made of eggs with a probability of being bad of 3 per cent. The chance that any one of these eggs is bad turns out to be about 18 per cent, and the chance that a second egg in the CDO is off is about 1.5 per cent. The CDO-squared is made of eggs with a probability of being rotten of 1.5 per cent, and the chance that the second egg in the CDO-squared is bad is less than one third of one per cent. That's a very small risk.

What happens if the chance of a rotten egg isn't 5 per cent at all, but really 10 per cent? Crunch the numbers and it turns out that the chance the second egg in the RMBS is rotten hasn't fallen from 5 to 3 per cent, it's *risen* from 10 to 11.5 per cent. The fact that it's risen is more important than how much it's risen – because now each successive repackaging will further increase the risk. The second egg in the CDO now has a 15 per cent chance of being bad, rather than a 1.5 per cent chance. It's ten times as risky. The second egg in the CDO-cubed becomes almost 2500 times riskier. The risk seemed laughable; suddenly, it's no joke.

Much the same analysis applies if the eggs come in clusters (although the mathematics are harder). Why did the banks' mathematicians assume that mortgage defaults wouldn't cluster together as much as they did? Well, one borrower might go through a divorce, another lose her job, and a third fall ill. But one person's divorce is nothing to do with a stranger's health, so mortgage defaults caused by these problems should come in ones and two, not clusters. As long as that assumption held true, the re-re-re-packaged loans were extremely safe, for much the same reason that Fiona Exon apparently faced a one in a quintillion chance of picking up a carton with six double-yolk eggs in it.

But if the mortgage defaults come in clusters, disaster looms. Every egg could end up stinking; the safest-seeming mortgage products could end up suffering awful losses. The banks' mathematicians realised, of course, that some degree of clustering was possible. But clustering is a difficult thing to measure,* and they apparently based their estimates on a limited run of data from a time when house prices were rising across the United States. And they therefore seem to have missed the scenario in which mortgage defaults would cluster together ferociously: a national slump in the price of housing.

With hindsight, it is blindingly obvious why such a slump would lead to mortgage defaults. Subprime mortgages depended – in a way no other mortgage in history ever had – on the value of houses continuing to rise. Subprime mortgages were typically offered with generously low introductory interest rates

---

*Here's an example from the financial analyst and commentator, Paul Wilmott. Imagine that you're trying to measure the clustering (more formally, the correlation) between the price of shares in two rival companies, Nike and Adidas. At first they're not very closely correlated. Then imagine that one of Adidas's sponsorship deals goes wrong and the brand is tarnished by association with some wayward celebrity. Adidas shares would fall and Nike shares would rise as they picked up market share – a negative correlation. Then imagine there's a craze for branded sportswear thanks to a great World Cup. The price of shares in both companies rises. So the correlation could be small or large, positive or negative, depending on what's happening in the world. If you looked only at the two share prices moving, you would have very little idea what to make of it all. And if you looked only at data for a limited period of time, you might leap to entirely the wrong conclusion.

for a fixed period, after which both borrower and lender assumed that they would be cancelled and replaced with a new mortgage. The idea was that, as the house would by then be worth more, lenders would be happy to offer a range of follow-up mortgages secured against the value of the house. But if the value of the house was lower by the time the loan came up for refinancing, no lender would want to take the risk of offering a new mortgage. The borrower would be stuck with the ballooning repayments on the original loan. They would likely default, leaving the lender with a house worth less than they'd loaned for it. And if a few people defaulted on their mortgages because house prices were falling, it was highly likely that an avalanche of defaults was on the way.

And the very system of intricate CDO repackaging that was supposed to protect investors from the small chance of getting a bad egg instead hugely exaggerated the problem. Because the sums were wrong, each repackaging of the second egg actually *concentrated* the risk instead of reducing it. We ended up in a Looking-Glass world where investments that had been thought to be preposterously safe turned out to be preposterously dangerous.

The products and the calculations were far more baffling even than I've suggested, so all this is a simplification. But it is not an exaggeration. To give you a sense of just how badly wrong the sums of the financial mathematicians became in reality, ponder the words of David Viniar, the Chief Financial Officer of Goldman Sachs. At the beginning of the credit crunch, he explained the sudden loss of 30 per cent of the value of a Goldman Sachs spin-off fund by saying, 'We were seeing things that were 25-standard deviation moves, several days in a row.'

Viniar meant that Goldman Sachs had been unlucky. But just how unlucky, exactly? The financial economist Kevin Dowd has calculated that (given some reasonable assumptions) we'd expect to see three 25-standard deviation days in a row roughly once every 28,900,000,000,000,000,000,000,000,000,000,000,000, 000,000,000,000,000,000,000,000,000,000,000,000,000,000, 000,000,000,000,000,000,000,000,000,000,000,000,000,000, 000,000,000,000,000,000,000,000,000,000,000,000,000,000, 000,000,000,000,000,000,000,000,000,000,000,000,000,000, 000,000,000,000,000,000,000,000,000,000,000,000,000,000, 000,000,000,000,000,000,000,000,000,000,000,000,000,000, 000,000,000,000,000,000,000,000,000,000,000,000,000,000, 000,000,000,000,000,000,000,000,000,000,000,000,000,000, 000,000,000,000,000,000,000,000,000,000,000,000,000,000, 000,000,000,000,000,000,000,000,000, 000,000,000,000,000, 000,000,000,000,000,000,000,000,000,000,000,000,000,000, 000,000,000,000,000,000 years. For reference, the universe is about 13,000,000,000 years old. Bad luck is not really an explanation. Somewhere, somehow, Goldman Sachs had got its sums wrong and then the inexorable complexity of the financial instruments it was dealing with magnified the error almost beyond comprehension.

Of course, we can always add layers of explanation for the banking crisis. Why did lenders make those subprime loans? There was a flood of cheap money they were keen to lend to someone. Why was there a flood of cheap money? Opinion is divided: some blame western central banks, some blame the Chinese government, which kept lending money to the US at rock-bottom rates. Why didn't regulators spot that subprime loans were storing up trouble? The regulators were far too confident that the banks knew what they were doing. Not only that, there was an implicit subsidy of banks by governments – the banks were sure governments would never let them go bust, which encouraged them to take on too much risk. Why were the underlying risks underestimated? Because it was in the interests of many people – some borrowers, some originators, and some bank analysts – to conceal just how dubious some of the underlying mortgages were.

Why didn't the banks take steps to protect themselves from risk? They did. They devised a clever form of insurance called 'credit default swaps', which essentially involved them covering each other's liabilities, or unloading them to insurers such as AIG, a once-boring insurance company that found itself at the heart of the crisis after insuring far more bad loans than it could possibly afford. The credit default swaps made banks even more careless about taking on too much risk. If catastrophic losses to an individual bank are vanishingly unlikely, the swaps look like a sensible precaution. If catastrophic losses to multiple banks are sooner or later inevitable, they are an unwittingly suicidal way to ensure that apparently separate companies are all bound together and will all be dragged down together – which is exactly what happened.

Despite all these layers of explanation, if I had to point to one single innovation that sparked the crisis, it would be those endlessly repackaged cartons of rotten subprime eggs. It was an accident waiting to happen – indeed, bound to happen – as soon as the global economic equivalent of Fiona Exon came along.

Cheap bailout, costly crisis

Soon enough, Lehman Brothers had gone under and more and more banks were teetering on the edge of collapse. The rest is folklore: although the banks had been greedy and stupid, governments couldn't afford to let the financial system collapse so they began desperately to throw taxpayers' money at them. This incurred debts for which ordinary people are even now suffering through hefty tax rises and painful cuts in public services.

Or did it? There is truth in that analysis, but the story is not quite so simple.

The banking crisis has, indeed, cost citizens and taxpayers dearly. And in some countries – such as Ireland – the cost of bailing out the banks was directly responsible for crippling levels of public debt. No wonder: the banks were large relative to the size of the economy and made astonishing losses. The official estimate in late 2010 was that Anglo Irish – 'probably the world's worst bank,' says the hedge fund manager Theo Phanos – had managed to lose €30 billion despite making only €72 billion of loans. This is an almost inconceivable rate of losses. It is also almost a quarter of Irish national income – from just a single bank.

For comparison, the stricken British bank, Royal Bank of Scotland, lost similar sums of money: £24 billion in 2008 alone, and £3.6 billion in 2009. But RBS was a far bigger bank and the UK economy is well over ten times the size of Ireland's. RBS's losses were a few per cent of its loans; Anglo Irish's losses were approaching 50 per cent.

While it's easy to draw a straight line between the government bailout of Ireland's banks and the Irish's government's debt problem, in other countries the story of the bailout is a subtler one.

In the UK, for instance, Gordon Brown's Labour government ended up borrowing gigantic sums of money. The budget deficit reached around £150 billion a year, the equivalent of £2500 of yearly borrowing on behalf of every man, woman and child in the country. But very little of this was to do with the banking bailout itself. While British taxpayers did indeed bail out British banks, the taxpayer is likely to get most of the money back. Some of the intervention took the form of guarantees for the banks, reassuring creditors that they could continue to lend money to any

British bank. This was invaluable, but in the end the banks did not use the guarantee, so fortunately it turned out to cost nothing. The Treasury even turned a profit, because the banks paid fees for these guarantees. Other money was spent injecting capital into the banks; in exchange for this, the British government received shares in the banks; this transaction may also make a profit.

It's difficult to tell exactly what the UK bailout will end up costing the taxpayer directly. The budget of June 2010 estimated that the likely cost would eventually be £2 billion. That's a very uncertain figure. The final outcome could be a lot more, or tax-payers could make money on the deal: the cost was estimated at £20 billion–£50 billion in 2009 and £6 billion in March 2010, so it is heading in the right direction. £2 billion sounds a lot – it is a lot – but that is roughly what the government was borrowing every four days in the tax year 2010–11. 'The fact is that in most crises – this one and previous ones – the taxpayer is typically paid back,' says Andy Haldane, the Bank of England's executive direc-tor for financial stability. The bailout itself does not explain the huge government deficits that were accumulated. What does?

The real cost was the damage done to the British economy. As the banks teetered on the brink of collapse, they tried to suck up as much cash as possible to prevent their bankruptcy. That meant that every loan and every overdraft facility in the country was sud-denly under scrutiny. Businesses suddenly found their access to credit drying up; consumers spent less, feeling the same pressures. Potentially healthy businesses were crushed by the financial tur-moil. Andy Haldane reckons the crisis could have lowered the UK's national income by about 10 per cent – and put it on a per-manently lower trajectory. The loss 'occurs year by year by year. We know from past financial crises that they leave a permanent scar.'

The total damage? Haldane reckons it could easily be

£1700 billion – and plausibly £8000 billion–£9000 billion. As he concludes, 'those are big sums'. It's because the economy has shrunk so much that taxes must rise and government spending must fall if the government's books are to balance – not because the government threw money at bailing out the banks.

Indeed, it is worth contemplating how much worse things might have been if they hadn't.

When Lehman Brothers went bust, the money that it was holding immediately froze up. On the small scale it meant that the phone company, electricity company, and companies employing the cooks, cleaners and security guards were all suddenly not being paid until the bankruptcy experts figured out how much money there was to go around and who might get a share. That happens in any bankruptcy and it can take a long time to sort out, with much misery all round.

But what was different about Lehman – about any large bank – was the fact that it was also holding vast sums of money from other financial institutions, money it was investing on their behalf. And it also had billions of dollars of financial contracts open with other banks – promises to pay money (or be paid) depending on what happened to the price of oil, or gold, or the debt of the government of Japan, or whatever. Suddenly all these bets were off in a mess of confusion – and in a market where milliseconds can matter, investors were facing the prospect of not seeing their money for months or even years.

The clear danger was that other banks failed too, perhaps dragged down by their connections to Lehman Brothers, or perhaps because they were suffering similar problems. Given the interconnections between these institutions, there was a serious risk that if one failed – or maybe not one, but two, or three, or four – then they would all fail, and with them the infrastructure that modern everyday life depends on.

Under normal circumstances, the payment systems in most developed countries seem very robust. In the UK, for instance, as well as having the usual back-ups you might expect, additional security comes from the fact that the system that deposits your salary (BACS), and the system linking cash machines to banks (LINK) and the various systems that deal with debit and credit cards at shops, are all separate. Even if the cash machine network went down for a bit, you'd still be able to get cashback at the supermarket; or if the supermarket's system temporarily stopped accepting debit cards, you could always go to the ATM and buy your groceries with cash instead. But there is one scenario in which all these systems would fail simultaneously: if the banks that stood behind them collapsed.

What then? Imagine waiting for your salary to arrive in your bank account, and it never does – not because your employer is bankrupt, but because your employer's bank is. Imagine going to the cash machine and getting no cash, because the cash machine company doesn't believe your bank is good for the money. You go to the supermarket with your debit card and meet with exactly the same response. It's not much of an exaggeration to say we'd be looking at the end of western civilisation.

No wonder so many governments took the view that, although it was the banks that had got us into this mess, they effectively had no choice but to dump tens of billions of pounds of taxpayers' money on the banks to keep them running. If the banks had collapsed like a row of dominoes, disaster might just about have been averted – but it would have required some quick and decisive action. Someone – a regulator, perhaps – would have had to find a way of parking the unholy mess, all the arguments about who owed what to whom, somewhere out of the way. And while the mess was being sorted out, all the basics – the borrowing and the lending, paying salaries and getting cash out of the hole in the wall – would have needed to be kept running smoothly somehow.

Such a trick would not be impossible – but it would take careful preparation and a solid legal footing, both of which were lacking in the crisis of 2008. It would make sense to be prepared for next time; whether we will be is open to question.*

So by all means blame the banks for the behaviour that required a bailout – but don't blame governments for the bailouts. Though if it seems unsatisfying to be giving pats on the back to politicians for decisive action, fear not – there is still plenty of blame to go around. While governments probably had to bail out the banks, they didn't have to be so extraordinarily generous about the way they did it.

Pietro Veronesi and Luigi Zingales, two economists at the University of Chicago, studied the effect of the US bailout that saw Treasury Secretary Henry 'Hank' Paulson call bank bosses to a meeting on 13 October 2008, shortly after the collapse of Lehman Brothers. Paulson stumped up $125 billion of US taxpayers' money in exchange for shares in nine US banks. Some banks, such as Citigroup and JP Morgan, received as much as $25 billion each. The Treasury also guaranteed new issues of bank debt.

Veronesi and Zingales concluded that Paulson's move cost taxpayers $20 billion–$45 billion. That's a lot – although the US budget deficit that fiscal year was over $1400 billion, so as far as US government overspending or undertaxing was concerned, it was pretty much an average week. But they also concluded that shareholders and bondholders in the banks were about $130 billion better off as a result of Paulson's gift. In short, every tax dollar

*In my book, *Adapt: Why Success Always Starts with Failure*, I discuss some ways in which governments might be able to let banks fail while letting all those vital basics continue smoothly.

spent created between $3 and $5 of wealth. There are very few government policies in history that can claim such a spectacular return on investment.

Why such a large effect? Veronesi and Zingales believe the gift prevented runs on the banks, the risk of which was depressing bond and share prices. A bank run is a situation where a bank can be bankrupted simply on the strength of the fear that it might happen. If a government guarantee can relieve such panic, it can create great value at little cost. And, indeed, the banks that gained most from Paulson's gift are also the banks that were in imminent danger of a run.

Sadly, that wealth accrued entirely to investors in banks – galling for taxpayers who had no desire to write a cheque to bank bondholders. Three weeks before Paulson's gift, the world's most successful investor, Warren Buffett, had injected capital into Goldman Sachs, and he had secured more generous terms. Veronesi and Zingales reckon that if Paulson had successfully demanded Buffett's terms, the taxpayer would have made more than $40 billion, a roughly even split with the banks' creditors.

The bailout was well worth doing. It's just a shame that Mr Paulson didn't drive a harder bargain.

The 'Greenspan doctrine' and efficient markets

Once commentators took stock of the crisis, two high-profile tenets of faith in the investment world were widely deemed to be casualties – one justifiably, the other less so.

The first was the 'Greenspan doctrine', arguably *the* basic regulatory mistake that allowed the crisis to happen. This doctrine held that self-interest was the best guardian of banks' balance sheets. Consumers would need protecting from mis-selling, and fraudsters had to be spotted and jailed; but if there was one thing the regulators didn't need to lose much sleep over, it was the possibility that banks would simply make decisions so bad that they bankrupted themselves. So thought Alan Greenspan, Chairman of the Federal Reserve for nearly two decades in the build-up to the crisis.

A few weeks after the collapse of Lehman Brothers had become the defining moment of the crisis, Mr Greenspan admitted that he had been wrong. He told Congress, 'Those of us who have looked to the self-interest of lending institutions to protect shareholders' equity – myself especially – are in a state of shocked disbelief.'

It may have been wrong to believe the banks would look after their own best interests, but it wasn't absurd. It's understandable that Greenspan was surprised by the self-destruction of the bankers. Many people were – it took months for it to dawn on most commentators that the crisis wasn't about the banks selling junk to other people, but hoarding the junk for themselves. Greenspan's error was not in overestimating the banks' self-interest. It was in overestimating the quality of their management.

Many commentators also hastened to declare the collapse of the 'efficient markets hypothesis'. David Wighton of *The Times* commented in January 2009, 'The theory was officially declared dead yesterday at the World Economic Forum in Davos. There were no mourners.' In June of that year, Roger Lowenstein wrote in *The Washington Post*, 'The upside of the current Great Recession is that it could drive a stake through the heart of the academic nostrum known as the efficient-market hypothesis.'

But it's not at all clear why the efficient markets hypothesis should be blamed for the crisis – nor that the crisis told us anything we didn't know about the flaws in the idea. To see why, let's first explore what the hypothesis actually means.

The efficient markets hypothesis essentially states that anything which can be predicted by rational, well-informed investors will already be reflected in the price of assets. Rational people would buy shares today if it was obvious that those shares would go up tomorrow, and sell them if it was obvious that they would fall. But this means that any forecast that shares will obviously rise tomorrow will be wrong: shares will rise *today* instead, because people will buy them, and keep buying them until they are no longer so cheap that they will obviously rise tomorrow.*

Paradoxically, this hypothesis predicts that if investors are all rational and well-informed, the behaviour of asset prices should be completely random – because when all the predictable trends are anticipated, the only thing left to drive market moves is unpredictable news. Stock prices should take what mathematicians call 'a random walk' – equally likely on any day to rise as to fall. (More correctly, the stock market should exhibit a 'random walk with a trend', meaning that it should on average edge up over the long term – even though, on any given day, this long-term trend will be dwarfed by random movements.)

This is a paradox because if the behaviour of asset prices was truly unpredictable, there would be no incentive for investors to remain well-informed. They might as well buy shares completely at random. But then, if everyone bought shares at random, that would open up opportunities for investors to outperform the randomness by becoming more well-informed. Somewhere in the

---

*Strictly speaking, I have described the 'semi-strong form' of the efficient markets hypothesis. The 'weak form' says that investors cannot predict future share price movements by looking at past share price movements, but accepts that they might profit from a more fundamental approach, analysing corporate balance sheets and underlying trends. The 'strong form' of the hypothesis says that even insider traders can't make money, because their private information will leak out so quickly.

middle is a balancing point: a nearly random market with enough quirks to reward the informed investors who keep it nearly random.

You can see the same phenomenon at work in the more mundane setting of the supermarket checkout. Which queue is the quickest? The efficient markets hypothesis suggests it's not worth worrying about: if it was obvious which queue was the quickest, people would already have joined it, so you may as well just stand in the first queue you see. Anyone who has been in a hurry in a supermarket will know that's not quite right: some queues will obviously be slow, as they contain someone with a cart brimful of small items or clutching a sheaf of money-off coupons. Yet we also know it's right enough: you don't bother to analyse in detail which queue is likely to be fastest, because you're never surprised when the queue you stand in turns out to be agonisingly slower than expected.

There's plenty of evidence that the same is true of investing in the stock market. The efficient markets hypothesis says there are no obvious bargains, no easy forecasts, no get-rich-quick schemes. It tells us to ignore the blandishments of expert fund managers charging large commissions, ignore the prognostications of city economists, don't even bother trying to buy low and sell high – which in practice has always meant rushing in during booms and panic selling during busts. We should instead merely gently invest in a wide variety of shares, with no expectation of making a killing – we should diversify, keep charges low and avoid trying to be too clever. And in the past, investors who have done just this have indeed outperformed those who overrated their own stock-picking skills.

So I do think the pundits who have written off the efficient markets hypothesis have done so too sweepingly. It remains a useful guide to humble, practical investing, even if it failed so badly to prevent the banking crisis. (The egg-carton products were being sold to investors with the claim that they were both cheap and almost risk-free. Any fan of efficient markets should simply have asked, 'What's the catch?' It seems that the only investors who did were the ones betting *against* the subprime mortgage market. There's a telling scene in Michael Lewis's book, *The Big Short*, in which Greg Lippmann – a banker who effec tively functions like a bookie, collecting bets for and against the subprime mortgage market – organises a dinner in which poten- tial investors on opposite sides of the bet can meet each other. The smart, sceptical minority who'd been thinking of betting against subprime had held back because they thought there must be a catch: it was so obvious to them that the subprime egg cartons stank, they were sure they must have missed something. Then they met the guys buying the subprime egg cartons, and concluded they really were that stupid.)

I'm also puzzled by why the banking crisis should have caused anyone to lose a faith they'd previously held in the efficient mar- kets hypothesis, given that we'd already had plenty of obvious and fresh evidence of its limitations: recall the dot-com bubble, a story told in the first edition of *The Undercover Economist*. Just as wiser commentators before the banking crisis called a bubble in the housing market and warned that subprime mortgages were stor- ing up trouble for the banks, sage investment managers in the late 1990s clearly saw the dot-com bubble as a bubble. Investment managers such as the late Tony Dye called it at an early stage and shunned dot-com shares. He was, eventually, proved absolutely right.

But not before he'd had to find himself a new job. By the time Tony Dye was proved right, his clients had missed out on hand- some profits because the bubble had gone on inflating much further before it burst. Dye left the investment firm at which he was working, amid speculation that he'd been forced out. His problem was that while he was right that the stock market was overvalued, that wasn't enough to keep his clients happy while they watched others ride the dot-com bubble. Even the savviest investors, such as Tony Dye, cannot predict precisely when a critical mass of other investors will realise that shares are overvalued and rush to sell them.

Both the hi-tech shares on the Nasdaq stock exchange and the subprime mortgage-backed securities were badly mispriced. In the dot-com crash it was all too easy for investors simply to assume that the pioneers of new-fangled internet business models must have known what they were doing, and the same overconfidence afflicted investors when it came to the mind-bogglingly complex CDOs-squared and cubed and so forth. The difference is that the consequences of the banking crisis were far greater than those of the dot-com bubble – with a far longer and deeper recession and far greater need for government assistance. By the time it became clear that the banks' financial whizkids had got their sums catastrophically wrong, deep and lasting damage to the global economy was already inevitable.

7

The Men Who Knew the Value of Nothing

> Someone who knows the price of everything and
> the value of nothing.
>
> Oscar Wilde's definition of a cynic,
> now commonly applied to economists

Imagine hiring an economist to sell your house. He designs a clever-looking kind of auction, which he assures you should raise the £300,000 you think your house is worth. The bids come in, and to your horror and the economist's embarrassment you somehow end up with less than £3000. You're left homeless and nearly penniless, your wife divorces you and you spend the rest of your days in a dank basement.

Meanwhile, your next-door neighbour also decides to sell his house and engages a different economist, who also designs a clever-looking kind of auction. Your neighbour also expects £300,000, but the bidding just keeps on going up and he ends up with £2.3 million.

Far-fetched? Not at all. Something very similar actually happened, not to home-owners but to governments. The real estate in this situation was constituted not of bricks and mortar but of thin air, wavelengths of radio spectrum, to be exact, which mobile-phone companies use to operate their networks. Over the past few years, governments across the world have been selling the rights to use this spectrum to telecom companies. There is a limited amount of the spectrum available, and as we have learned, where there is scarcity there is money to be made. Unfortunately, not all of the economists who were hired as consultants knew how to set up the auction so that it was likely to produce a good price. One auction really did raise less than 1 per cent of what was hoped for, while another raised ten times as much as expected.

This wasn't down to luck but to cleverness in some cases and blundering in others. Auctioning air, like playing poker, is a game of great skill – and one that was played for very high stakes indeed.

Love, war and poker

Many of those who knew the mathematician John von Neumann regarded him as the 'best brain in the world', and they had a chance to compare him with some stiff competition, given that one of von Neumann's colleagues at Princeton was Albert Einstein. Von Neumann was a genius around whom grew a mythology of almost superhuman intelligence. According to one story, Von Neumann was asked to assist with the design of a new supercomputer, required to solve a new and important mathematical problem which was beyond the capacities of existing supercomputers. He asked to have the problem explained to him, solved it in moments with pen and paper and then turned down the request.

Von Neumann made dramatic strides in logic, set theory, geometry, meteorology and other fields of mathematics, and he took a central role in developing quantum mechanics, nuclear weapons and the computer. But it's his role as the founder of game theory that interests us here.

A game, to a game theorist, is any activity in which your prediction of what another person will do affects what you decide to do. Such games include poker, nuclear war, love or bidding for thin air in an auction. Game theory can seem deceptively simple: for instance, the game 'driving' is thoroughly straightforward.

In 'driving', I receive an acceptable payoff if I drive on the right and so do you. I also receive an acceptable payoff if I drive on the left side, and you do too. If one of us chooses to behave otherwise, I receive a very bad payoff – a ride in an ambulance. (You also receive a bad payoff if we have a head-on collision, but in game theory I don't usually care about your payoff for its own sake. I care about your payoffs only because they help me predict your behaviour.)

Games are often described in just that way, using little stories or anecdotes, but these stories conceal the fact that for a game theorist, games are mathematical objects. The great game theorists are brilliant mathematicians, such as von Neumann himself, or Nobel Prize winner John Nash, the subject of *A Beautiful Mind*. As in the case of all game theory, Nash's revolutionary new way to predict a game's outcome was an inspired application of well-understood mathematics.

Von Neumann was fascinated by poker, and as he turned his mind to the game he developed mathematical tools that are handy not only for economists but for people trying to understand everything from dating to evolutionary biology or the cold war.

The fundamentals of poker are simple: players conceal their cards until the final showdown, when the player with the best cards wins the pot, full of all the accumulated bets. Each player has to keep betting to stay in the game, but some will give up along the way, preferring to forfeit a little money rather than risk losing much more in the showdown. If all the other players give up, you can win the pot without ever showing your cards.

If you were playing poker, your basic challenge would be to work out whether it was worth paying to stay in the game. Probability theory won't get you very far. It is not enough to calculate the odds that the hand you hold is better than the other hands hidden around the table. You need to analyse your opponents' moves. Is a small bet a sign of weakness, or a trick to tempt you to raise the stakes against hidden strength? And do big bets mean a big hand – or a bluff? At the same time you must recognise that your opponents will be trying to interpret your own bets, and you must be careful not to be predictable.

Poker is full of spirals of second-guessing: 'If he thinks that I think that he thinks that I have four kings, then ...' Poker is a game both of luck and of skill, and most importantly, it is a game of secrets: each player has access to information hidden to the others. In chess, a game of pure skill, the battle takes place in plain sight of everyone. In poker, no player can see the whole truth.

This is where game theory comes in. Von Neumann believed that if he could analyse poker using mathematics, he could shine a spotlight onto all kinds of human interactions. Poker is a game where a small number of players try to outwit each other in an environment of luck, secrets and skilled calculation. But poker is not the only situation to fit that description. Think of generals fighting a war, or even – if you're a cynic like me – men and women playing the great game of love itself. Many human interactions can be interpreted as battles of wits, like poker. All these interactions came to be described by theorists as 'games' and explored using game theory.

Economic life is no exception. Von Neumann teamed up with the economist Oskar Morgenstern to write the bible of game theory, *Theory of Games and Economic Behaviour*, which was published just before the end of World War II. Ever since, game theory and economics have had a close relationship: game theory is taught to most students studying economics, and several game theorists have been awarded the Nobel Prize for Economic Sciences.

If you want examples of real-life 'economic games', think of bargaining between landlord and tenant, between government and trade union, between used-car salesman and used-car buyer. Think of oil-producing nations deciding whether to adhere to OPEC rules to help drive up oil prices, or produce flat out and take advantage of the high prices that others have created.

Or, to take the example we'll explore in most depth in this chapter, think of a collection of eager telecom companies trying to acquire radio-spectrum licences from a government with a limited number to offer. Every bidder has some idea of how profitable it would be to own a licence (and so how valuable a licence is), but nobody knows precisely how profitable. The government's challenge is to find out some secrets: to determine which of the telecom companies can best use the licences, and how much the licences are worth to them. Ideally the government would want to assign the licences to the firms who will use them best. Since the government is to be divvying up a valuable public asset, they also want to get the best value for the taxpayer.

Poker and the spectrum licence problem are both games in von Neumann's sense. There is an even closer similarity: in both cases, it's important to put large sums of money at the heart of the process. Without stakes, poker makes no sense. To a gambler, any game may be regarded as 'more interesting' if there is money riding on it, but in poker, money is central to the play of the game. This is because bets communicate strength and weakness in poker – if players are not betting with real money, the 'communication' is meaningless. As we know well by now, talk is cheap. Bluffing only has consequences if real money is at stake.

The same is true of spectrum licences. Economists specialising in game theory argued that the allocation of public assets, from the right to drill oil to the right to use radio spectrum, ought to be determined by methods similar to those that determine a game of poker. In order to sift out competing companies' cheap talk and empty promises, the government had to impose high stakes and, to use an old phrase, force each negotiator to 'put his money where his mouth is'.

Games within games: how to sell a £300,000 house for £3000

The US government employed game theorists to help sell spectrum rights throughout the second half of the 1990s. This was not an easy task: a company bidding for a Los Angeles licence and a San Diego licence might want both of them, or neither, because it is cheaper to run adjacent networks. But how to bid sensibly on Los Angeles before knowing who will get San Diego? This is a complex problem represented by a complex piece of game theory. The theorists duly designed a complex set of parallel auctions.

The first sales were highly successful (and very lucrative for the government), but after a few auctions things went wrong. The theorists had got the complex things right but made some simple mistakes, like publishing the bids without rounding them to the nearest few thousand dollars. Firms took advantage by making bids which contained area codes. This allowed them to signal which licences they'd prefer, and so carve up the US telecom market without having to bid aggressively against each other.

This scheme didn't even require an (illegal) agreement, because the auction allowed such clear signals. It looked like cheating, but nobody could prove it. Three years after the first auctions, an auction in April 1997 raised less than 1 per cent of the expected revenue because, claimed many commentators, firms had learned to cheat by avoiding competition with each other.

This is the equivalent of selling your £300,000 house for less than £3000. It seems hard to understand how this might happen, but it's simple. If there are only a small number of potential buyers for your house, they could agree among themselves not to bid against each other. The one who buys the house cheaply needs to find some way to compensate the others. The most obvious form of compensation would be to agree not to bid against them in future auctions. In the same way, telecom firms seemed to work out a way of agreeing not to bid against each other for spectrum licences in different regions. It was a humiliation for game theory, only slightly better than having given away the licences for nothing.

An alternative way of seeing the problems of the American auctions is that the game theorists failed to see that what they had analysed was only part of a wider game. The government was like the poker player blissfully unaware of hidden cameras in the room; oblivious to the fact that the other players, by a series of nods and winks, are taking turns winning his money. The game he thinks he's playing isn't the real game at all.

Game theory for dummies

Whether applied to colluding at auctions or cheating at cards, it must be clear by now that game theory is as much art as it is mathematics. All games need some simplifying assumptions before they can be modelled; if the theorists use the wrong assumptions (for example, that bidders won't use area codes to coordinate a carve-up) then they will produce perfect solutions to the wrong problems.

One of the most difficult challenges of all is rooted in the very origins of game theory: it was developed by men of nearly super-human intellect like Nash and von Neumann. That is both its great strength and its great weakness, because for game theory to be successful, it has to provide insight into what mere mortals do. Game theory expresses the way people would act as the solution to a mathematical equation. It presumes hyperrational players who are able instantly to solve very tough problems, and this description starts to look unrealistic if game theory is to be a prac-tical tool for explaining how real people actually behave. Nash and von Neumann really could solve such problems instantly. The rest of us cannot.

For instance, game theory tells us that chess is not worth play-ing because in theory its outcome is predetermined: one player can force a result. However, we do not know whether it is black or white that can force the result, we do not know whether the forced result is a win or a draw and we certainly do not know how the game would be played. We only know that in theory, the forced result is possible. In practice even the strongest players (computer or human) do not know this optimal strategy, and in practice the outcome of a game of chess is far from being prede-termined. So what use is a theory that tells us that chess would be trivial, if only we were all smart enough to know how to play it?

Not all of us think like a genius. Most of us would try to bluff at poker with a halfway good hand; von Neumann showed that the correct play is to bluff with the worst possible hand. Chris 'Jesus' Ferguson, a disciple of von Neumann, proved it when he won the World Series of Poker in 2000. But poker with your buddies in the garage is not the World Series; what can game theory say about players who get drunk and bluff badly?

This is not a knockdown objection to game theory. It is possible to model mistakes, forgetfulness, misinformation and any other kind of failure on the part of the players to live up to the impossibly high standards of John von Neumann. The trouble is that the more mistakes that need to be taken into account, the more complicated and the less useful game theory becomes. It is always useful for the game theorist to draw on experience as well as pure theory, because if the game becomes too complex for the players to understand, then the theory becomes nearly useless for practical purposes since it tells us nothing about what they will actually do.

Enter the auctioneers

In late 1996, I saw one of the UK's leading auction theorists illustrating this point – in passing – in a seminar on applying game theory to auctions. As part of his talk, Paul Klemperer confiscated the wallets of two members of the audience, counted the money they contained and then offered to sell that (unknown) sum of money back to whichever of the victims would bid highest. The two members of the audience, put on the spot, were quite unable to work out what the optimal strategy was for bidding in the auction.

The difficulty – which is a challenge for bidders in many auctions, including spectrum auctions – is that the two victims just didn't know the value of what they were bidding for. They knew part of the value, of course, because they knew how much money had been in their own wallet. But each knew nothing about the contents of the other's wallet. In a spectrum auction, the problem is similar: each bidder has his own forecasts and technology plans, but each knows that other bidders will probably have different insights. The optimal strategy would take advantage of any information revealed by other players' bids – but this is not easy. (In the wallet game, one solution is for each player to keep bidding until he reaches twice the sum in his own wallet. The player with the fatter wallet would win but pay less than the combined contents of the wallets. Bidding more aggressively risks paying too much.)

The failure of the two dumbfounded 'volunteers' to work out how to bid in the auction was more remarkable because they were Ken Binmore and Tilman Börgers, themselves experts in the game theory of auctions. Klemperer, Binmore and Börgers were about to become members of the team of academics who designed the mechanism for distributing the licences in the UK for 'third generation' (3G) mobile-phone services.

They had two serious difficulties to wrestle with. First, to avoid being outmanoeuvred by cheating bidders as the US authorities had been. Second, even if they couldn't find the optimal strategy for each other's auctions on the spot, how could they expect a collection of businessmen to behave as game theory predicts? And if those businessmen behaved unpredictably, who was to say what might happen?

John Maynard Keynes, the most influential economist of the twentieth century, longed for a day when economists were no longer arch-theorists but instead, 'rather like dentists', consulted to solve everyday problems and give straightforward advice. Economics is not there yet, and any economist who wishes to be even half as helpful as a dentist must temper economic theories with heavy doses of the hard lessons of real life: players cheat; bidders make mistakes; appearances matter. Auctions, like games of poker and chess, do not always unfold in the way the game theorist would predict.

The New Zealand government, which auctioned radio spectrum as early as 1990 with advice from some economists who seemed to have a slender grasp on reality, learned such lessons the hard way. The auctions were held without making sure that there was any interest from bidders, without minimum prices and using a theoretical curiosity called a 'Vickrey auction', which led to considerable embarrassment. (The auction was named after its inventor, Nobel laureate William Vickrey, who made major early advances in applying game theory to auctions.)

The Vickrey auction is a second-price sealed-bid auction. The 'sealed bid' means that each bidder writes down a single bid and seals it in an envelope. When the envelopes are opened, the highest bidder wins. 'Second-price' is the curious rule that the winner pays not his bid but that of the second-highest bidder. The elegant reasoning behind this auction is that no bidder ever has an incentive to shave his bid in an effort to make more profit; making a lower bid affects his chance of winning but not the price. To a theorist, this doesn't seem odd at all: after all, in a traditional auction at Sotheby's or Christie's, the price is also set by the second-highest bidder, because bidding stops when the second-highest bidder drops out. To the press and many others, this Vickrey auction looked nothing short of crazy. The problem with the Vickrey auction is not substantive but stylistic: in a traditional auction nobody ever finds out the maximum price the highest bidder would have been willing to pay, but in a Vickrey auction that fact is made public. Justifiably, New Zealanders wanted to know why a bidder who had offered NZ$100,000 for a licence only had to pay NZ$6 or why one who had offered NZ$7 million was only coughing up NZ$5000. These figures were embarrassing. The theorists knew that on average, Vickrey auctions make just as much money as other auctions because, by not demanding payment of the highest bid, they encourage all bidders to offer more. But what the theorists knew did not matter to the press and to the public: the harsh reality is that Vickrey auctions were seen as a failure of the New Zealand government.

Game theory can help predict some problems, such as cheating in the US auction. Others, such as the public reaction in New Zealand, simply don't show up in the theoretical analysis. Economists who aspire to dentistry have to think carefully and learn from mistakes: new ones will continue to be discovered the hard way.

Why use an auction?

When the UK government started to consider using an auction to sell spectrum rights, they were taking a bold step. After initial success, the US auctions had fallen apart because the game theory used to construct them had been far too narrowly conceived. The New Zealand government had made itself a laughing stock. And they weren't the only ones: Australia had also run auctions for TV licences and left loopholes in the bidding rules, which had been so badly exploited that the minister responsible lost his job. Why did Britain even consider using an auction, given the risks?

Like the US government, the UK government wanted to sell the licences to the companies that could use them best and to raise money while doing so. Of course, there was an additional unstated aim: to avoid embarrassment for bureaucrats and politicians alike. For the taxpayers of New Zealand and the United States, an auction that raised some money was better than simply giving the licences away, but for a politician, giving away public assets is a great way to make friends and allies. Auction theorists therefore had to make a strong case for auctions.

That case relies on game theory, which clearly demonstrates the power of simple auctions. One of the trickiest problems is making sure that the licences end up in the right hands. With a limited number of licences it would be a criminal waste if one of them went to timharford.com, a funky start-up with no relevant experience and no capability to use the valuable asset. The licences should go, instead, to companies that will use them to deliver the best-quality services at the lowest cost. Competition between licence holders will then set prices.

So what is the best way to identify the most capable companies? One possibility is simply to ask them, but companies will boast and bluster. Some will point to their experience, others to the latest technology. But would any really tell the truth? Talk is cheap.

Another idea that might seem more promising is to appoint experts to decide which companies are most deserving. But in the fast-moving world of mobile telephony, most experts would have some financial interest in one company or another – who is expert yet totally detached from the industry? Even if a truly impartial expert could be found, he would still have little success in penetrating trade secrets and judging the true potential of rival technologies.

Game theory shows how a simple auction can cut through all the complexity and solve the problem elegantly. For simplicity, imagine a straightforward auction of a single licence, which is like a traditional auction where bidders yell out higher and higher offers, with one difference: anyone who stays in the room is presumed to be willing to pay the current high bid. Anyone who drops out must leave the room and not re-enter. This slightly different auction is easier for game theory to analyse, but also closely reflects many of the actual auctions used to sell licences.

Each bidder must now make a straightforward judgement about what the licence is worth. The better their innovative ideas and the cheaper their technology, the more money they will make if they win a licence. Of course, none of the companies can perfectly forecast what profits they would make with a licence, but each is in a better position than any external expert to make the judgement.

When the auction starts and the price begins to rise, bidders will start to drop out once the asking price for the licence exceeds their own estimate of its value to them. Companies without confidence in their business plans and technologies will be the first to go. If the price rises a long way without anyone leaving the room, each bidder learns that the others are confident about the prospects for the market as a whole. (This provides the distinction between this auction and a traditional auction at Sotheby's – while a Sotheby's auction is in progress you never know who is still a potential bidder and who is just watching.) If some bidders leave surprisingly early, the rest should take note and revise their own assumptions. The auction neatly summarises the collective wisdom of all the bidders.

Meanwhile, nobody is in a position to lie. Talk is cheap, but bidding is expensive. No company will drop out while the price is still lower than their prediction of the licence's value, and no company will keep bidding once the price rises too high. In a sense, the auction is like von Neumann's game of poker: because money is at stake, the bids have to be taken very seriously. In another sense, it is not like poker at all, because the auction makes it absolutely impossible to bluff.

The auction forces each bidder to tell the truth about his own estimate of the licence's value. At the same time, the auction broadcasts the collective view to all the bidders, so that they can update their own opinions accordingly. What's more, it collects cash while it does so.

Game theory also shows that this simple auction is generally a better cash-generating machine than the alternative ways of nego tiating a sale. This is not obvious. One alternative would be for the seller to run an auction but to set a reserve price (open or secret) below which he will not sell. Another would be to nego-tiate in secret with several buyers in parallel and lie about how the negotiations were going. Or the seller could make a one-shot, 'take-it-or-leave-it' offer to each buyer in turn. Or something else. Given the perplexing array of possibilities, how can a seller choose the most lucrative way of making a sale?

Game theory slices through to the core of the problem. In the mid-1990s, Klemperer and Jeremy Bulow (who became another member of the auction design team) published a paper showing if the simplicity of the auction attracted just one extra serious bidder, that straightforward auction would raise more money than any other kind of negotiating set-up.

In addition to the central claim that auctions really do raise more cash, the paper finally focused the attention of auction the-orists on what should have been obvious: if you want a successful auction, you need plenty of serious bidders.

The UK auction in action

The UK auction design team certainly went all-out to make sure those serious bidders turned up. By March 2000, the UK auction was ready to go with thirteen registered bidders who had paid

£50-million deposits and were hooked up to the internet to submit their bids remotely. The team had been advertising the auction for more than a year in advance and had made sure they were the first European nation to hold an auction for third-generation phone licences. The result promised to be a highly competitive auction.

The team had been focusing obsessively on the details. They'd tested the auction design using computer simulations and test-runs with London students playing the role of telecom executives. They crawled over the fine print of the auction, trying to eliminate loopholes. They even gave themselves options to postpone the auction if something suspicious appeared to be going on. But despite all this preparation, nobody really knew if the auction would work, or whether it would be yet another bungle by the economists.

The auction was set to run in short rounds – lasting half an hour or so – during which the bidders had to submit new bids or withdraw. Those who chose not to enter a valid bid had to drop out of the auction; each bidder was allowed to 'pass' three times before finally withdrawing. There would be a couple of rounds every day, maybe more once the bidders became comfortable with the bidding process. Each of the rounds would be posted promptly on the internet; this auction was to take place in full view of the world.

The initial expectations were that the auction might raise a lot of money: £2–3 billion, enough to knock a penny off the UK income tax for the year. While the team was obviously nervous, they were thrilled to have nine new companies join the four established players in the bidding, and they expected the auction to be a success.

They attributed the interest from new companies in part to the fact that five licences were available. Originally, the engineers had believed that the airwaves could accommodate four licences, operating on adjacent wavelengths of radio spectrum and each covering the entire country. But with four established companies, an auction for four licences would have had obvious winners and the new entrants would not have bothered turning up simply to get beaten. The economists on the project were therefore very relieved when the engineers worked out that there was enough radio spectrum available for one extra licence. This licence, called 'licence A', was reserved for new companies who were not currently operating in the UK mobile-phone market.

The idea of the auction was that competition for licence A would drive up the prices of the other four licences. Any firm not currently in the lead for a licence had to keep bidding or withdraw; but as long as firms kept making legal bids, they could switch bids from one licence to another. The firms would obviously choose to bid on whichever licence appeared to offer the best value at the time. This meant that the hot competition for licence A kept the auctions for the other licences simmering nicely – every time the price of A rose above the rest, the other licences looked like bargains. Entrants would peel away and challenge the established companies for the licences they had staked out for themselves. When the established firms raised the price, the underdogs flipped back to bidding for licence A.

Although the simultaneous auction of five licences is complex to explain, it is quite simple for a bidder to understand the best strategy. Because bidders never know when the auction is going to end, they need to make sure they are always comfortable in their current position. The best strategy is to look at all the licences and submit a new high bid on whichever licence looks like the best value. If none looks like good value at that time, then the right move is to withdraw. The simplicity of the auction may help to explain why so many companies decided to bid, and unlike

World Series Poker or the wallet game, it is close to being idiot-proof.

Imagine selling your house in a prolonged auction that goes on for weeks and weeks. You've heard the stories about other auctions, and you're afraid that instead of getting the £300,000 you expect, you'll end up like your unfortunate neighbour, divorced and penniless. The first week is agony. But the price slowly starts to rise, and your blood pressure starts to fall. Eventually the bidding gets to £250,000 – you realise that, whatever happens, you're not going to do too badly. A few days later the bidding reaches £300,000 and you're smiling. From here on everything is a bonus; maybe you'll get £310,000, or £320,000, or even £350,000. Who knows? Then the price keeps going up. It hits £320,000. It reaches £350,000. £400,000. £500,000. What's happening? You can scarcely believe it.

This unexpected turn of events is similar to what happened in the UK spectrum auction, except the stakes were ten thousand times higher: not £300,000 but £3 billion. For a week, the bidding went smoothly; the rules about continuous bidding kept the total revenue rising steadily. After about twenty-five rounds of bidding, bidders were committed to around £400 million for each licence. After fifty rounds of bidding the total stood at £3 billion: what the government had been hoping to raise. (In comparison, the deposits, even though they had been raised to £100 million, were starting to look a little trivial.) But something extraordinary was happening. Bidders were staying in the auction. All thirteen companies continued submitting bids regularly and the prices of the licences kept rising without any sign of slowing down.

As the auction rolled on, the press started to take interest. Photographs of the design team began appearing in the newspapers. Journalists struggled to explain exactly what the team had done, but everybody started to realise that something remarkable was happening.

The bidding moved through round sixty (total revenue: £4 billion). Round seventy (£5 billion). Round eighty (£7 billion). The end of March came and went. The price was still rising.

The auction designers were keeping quiet about what they thought of all this, but behind closed doors they were both excited and nervous. The auction was becoming a victim of its own success: it was lasting too long. There were jitters on the US stock market – what if a stock-market crash spread to the UK, destroyed the confidence of the bidders and brought the whole auction to a sudden stop? The deposit was obviously too small to deter bidders from walking away if they had a change of heart. Perhaps the bidding should be speeded up? It turned out that there was no need to worry.

On the morning of 3 April, almost a month after the first bid had been cast, with more than £10 billion (£200 per person in the UK) raised, something finally happened. After round ninety-four had finished, it was announced that one of the bidders, Crescent, had dropped out. The auction then started to change quickly. That afternoon, in round ninety-five, a second bidder, the 3G-UK consortium, dropped out. The next morning, in round ninety-seven, a third bidder, Spectrum, also quit. Some other bidders were stalling for time by playing their 'waivers' to stay in without raising a bid. In round ninety-eight Epsilon withdrew. The next day, at lunchtime on 5 April, One-Tel quit.

After ninety-three rounds of bidding without any withdrawals, the auction had lost five bidders in eight rounds over the course of three days. Now only eight bidders remained. Why was the bidding stuttering so suddenly? Perhaps it was pride: nobody wanted to be the first to drop out, but once Crescent quit, others who had been waiting for the chance also quit soon after.

Game theorists have an alternative explanation: bidders were learning from each other's bids about what the 3G licences were likely to be worth. This was one of the advantages of the auction's transparent design. A commonly used alternative would simply have been to run a 'sealed-bid' auction where everyone handed in an envelope containing a single bid. But such an auction would have left every bidder guessing in the dark, probably leading to much more conservative bidding and a much less profitable outcome for the government. With an open auction, even when the bidding rose higher than anyone had expected, each bidder could see that its twelve competitors were making equally large offers and shared confidence that the licences would prove hugely valuable. Each company had its own business plan, its own technology partners, its own sales projections. All of these were speculative, but the transparent auction gathered signals of these plans together and put the information at the disposal of all the bidders. (The auction also put the information at the disposal of the government and collected revenue on that basis at the same time – all very neat.)

Crescent's withdrawal sent a signal to the other bidders that the company felt the licences were not worth a higher bid. Taking into account Crescent's doubts, other bidders who were also having second thoughts were tipped into withdrawing. Crescent set off a spiral: each new withdrawal reinforced the news that the bidding was getting too high.

Of course, the companies who dropped out were just sticking with the herd, but remember that herds run together for good reasons. The transparent auction was designed to spread information around, so it was hardly surprising that bidders looked at the same facts and came to the same conclusions.

The auction had seen a sudden run of withdrawals but it was far from over. By the middle of April the total revenue of the auction topped £29 billion. The government's profit was almost enough to halve the basic rate of income tax for a year. What actually happened was that the British chancellor, Gordon Brown, launched a generous round of spending in the run-up to the election without a large increase in taxes or borrowing. The British public was given an enormous free lunch, courtesy of the telecom boom and the painstaking determination of the auction design ers to take advantage of it.

The last three withdrawals happened gradually over the course of April. Just after breakfast on 27 April, NTL Mobile announced that it would be withdrawing, and suddenly all the excitement was over. A company called TIW was the new name in mobile telephony, having paid £4,384,700,000 for licence A. Vodafone had won its bloody struggle with British Telecom and was the proud holder of licence B, at a price of almost £6 billion. British Telecom settled for a smaller licence. The auction raised £22.5 billion and in the process had become the biggest auction in modern history.

If you had been selling your £300,000 house at an auction which exceeded expectations like this one, you would eventually have closed the deal at £2.25 million – and you'd have had to pinch yourself the next morning to check that you weren't dreaming.

Remember: strength from scarcity

Critics of the auctions assumed that because the telecoms had paid so much for the licences, they would in turn charge consumers very high prices for 3G services. But did the auctions ruin 3G? Consider the following sentence:

If 3G licences are very expensive, then firms will charge customers more.

It seems persuasive, but think like an economist for a moment: if 3G licences are very cheap, will firms charge customers less? What if the government gave the licences away for nothing, would firms charge customers nothing? And if the government paid telecom companies to take the licences off its hands, would firms give each customer a cash bonus along with her free wireless service?

We learned way back in Chapters 1 and 2 that firms will charge the maximum they possibly can, under any circumstances. We also know that their ability to do this is limited by their scarcity power.

For the UK, the crucial determinant is that there are five licences. Five licences are few enough to give each company enough scarcity power to be able to charge quite high prices. If only two licences were available, then the scarcity power would be greater and the prices would be higher. If twenty licences were available, the scarcity power would be less and the prices would be lower. It is the scarcity power, and not the price of the licences, which determines the price for customers.

In the UK there was scarcity built into the amount of radio spectrum available: five licences were the most the technicians could offer. It does not make any difference to the customer how much the licences cost, but it does matter to the taxpayers, who would like the government to get a lot of money for this valuable public resource, and the telecoms' shareholders, who would like their companies to dish out as little as possible.

In the wake of the dot-com crash, some commentators complained that the high 3G prices were crippling telecoms operators and slowing down the rate at which new 3G services were rolled out. There is little reason to believe this is true: the most seriously affected firms were US firms who did not participate in the European auctions, or troubled cable companies such as NTL and Telewest, who withdrew from the 3G auctions without spending anything. The 3G licence winners, such as Vodafone, remain successful firms, sadder and wiser after the telecom bubble, perhaps, but still perfectly viable. Nor is there any evidence that 3G rollout was affected by the auctions. France and Germany had much the same prevalence of 3G by 2006, despite the fact that France had given licences away without an auction, while Germany had raised a vast minimum. The UK, as it happened, had a strong market for 3G.

The whole experience seems to have encouraged governments to continue to auction scarce rights to use radiospectrum. Germany held a 4G spectrum auction in the spring of 2010, but the sums raised were disappointing, perhaps because the incumbent firms dominated the bidding and the government imposed rules about rural rollout that were likely to have discouraged new bidders. The UK plans to hold a 4G auction in 2012. India held a 3G auction in May 2010 and raised about twice what most analysts expected: a total of $14.6 billion.

Telecom executives may curse the spectrum auctions but the public should celebrate them. All the companies involved were convinced that the 3G licences offered tremendous scarcity value, and these auctions successfully secured a fair price for that apparent value. John von Neumann's successors used game theory to achieve one of the most spectacular, if controversial, policy triumphs that economics had ever seen. The men who knew the 'value of nothing' had shown that economists, like dentists, could finally earn their keep.

The crisis auction

Shortly after the collapse of the British bank Northern Rock in mid-September 2007, the Bank of England ran four auctions designed to inject cash into the banking sector. The auctions were not a success, and the Bank of England – in fact, the Governor of the Bank of England, Mervyn King – called Paul Klemperer for advice.

The Bank of England's aim was easily stated: how to lend the right amount of money to the right banks? But the details were difficult. Many banks had lots of valuable assets, but trust in the banking system had evaporated to such an extent that banks wouldn't lend each other the cash that they needed to conduct the simplest operations. The lack of access to cash from other banks had already pole-axed Northern Rock.

The Bank of England wanted to fix this problem by lending money to the banks. But they didn't want to lend any amount of money to any old bank: they wanted to lend only to banks that were fundamentally sound, and that meant asking for collateral. Collateral is a basic idea in borrowing and lending; a mortgage is a loan with a house as collateral, while a credit card balance is a loan with no collateral at all. Loans with better collateral should be cheaper, because they are more secure.

The total amount that the Bank of England lent out was also important: too much cheap credit would give bankers unnecessarily cheap loans to gamble with, while too little would risk another collapse.

The challenge seemed formidable. Previously, the Bank of England had lent money to banks based only on the very best collateral, and set the interest rate by holding an auction. The banks willing to pay the highest interest rate secured the cash.

But now the Bank wanted to hold an auction that allowed two different types of collateral – high-quality stuff, such as German government bonds, and riskier assets with less certain values. And ideally, both the amount of money lent out, and the interest rates for high- and low-quality collateral, would be determined by the auction itself. If the Bank tried to guess at any of these numbers, it risked lending too little or too much. If it made the wrong guess about the difference between the interest rates, it would bias the flow of cash entirely towards one form of collateral or another. At best all that would be wasteful; at worse, the Bank's guestimates might spark panic in the market.

An alternative would have been to hold two separate auctions. But the two products on offer – borrowing with strong collateral versus borrowing with weak collateral – are very close substitutes. Banks would find it hard to bid in the first auction without knowing what would happen in the second auction. And by splitting the auction into two, the Bank of England would make each auction less competitive and less efficient.

And there was one further challenge. When offering liquidity to banks – when the state of the banking system would have affected the auction, and the state of the auction would have affected the banking system   speed is essential. Unlike the prolonged spectacle of the 3G auction, this one had to be concluded almost instantly.

Proxy bids, instant auction

Klemperer's proposal exploited a long tradition in auctions: that of proxy bidding. The simplest proxy bid in a standard auction – say, an eBay auction or a traditional open-cry auction at Sotheby's – works in a straightforward way. The real bidder gives his bid to the proxy – which may be an actual person, a piece of software or simply a note on the auctioneer's desk. Whenever a bid is made, the proxy bid will outbid it, until it wins or until the proxy bid has been exceeded.

Now imagine a proxy bid in a setting where there are three

identical cases of fine wine. You make a proxy bid of £200 for a single case: you only want one. The auctioneer will raise the bidding until there are only three bidders left. All of them pay the same price, of course. And if that price is £200 or less, you'll be a winner. But it's possible to get more clever than that: imagine that you might want *two* cases of wine, but only if there's a bargain to be had. So now you submit two proxy bids: one at £200 and an additional bid at £150. If all but one of your rivals drop out at £120, you win two cases and pay £120 per case. But if the bidding rises to £180, one of your proxy bids is discarded but you still win a single case for £180.

Here's the curious thing: if the auctioneer is known to be honest, she won't actually need to run this auction in real time. She could simply gather up envelopes from every bidder, each containing bids for one, two and three cases. She would then pick the three highest bids – which may all belong to the same bidder, or not – and would charge all three the *fourth* highest bid, which is the point at which the fourth bidder would have dropped out and the auction would have ended. The dynamic, open-outcry auction would have been replaced by an almost instant sealed-bid process. Very little of practical importance would have changed – except that the auction would have become much faster.

Let's add another twist. Now there are two vintages of wine on offer – some cases of a normal vintage and some cases of a fine vintage. Now when you submit your bids you need to consider how much you'd like to win of either vintage, or both, and what price might tempt you. But that's manageable. Previously, you'd submitted a bid at £200 and a second bid at £150. Now you submit a pair of either-or bids: a first bid offering £300 for the good vintage *or* £200 for the ordinary stuff; and a second bargain-hunting bid offering £200 for the good vintage *or* £150 for the ordinary stuff. If the other bidders drop out early enough you might win two cases of wine, but not more, because your bids were 'either-or'. Whether you win the good vintage or the more everyday wine will depend on how fierce the bidding is for each type of wine.

You might worry that the auctioneer would begin to struggle with the proxy bids on her desk once bidders start submitting multiple, mutually exclusive sets of bids. You'd be right, but that doesn't matter. Because the entire auction has been transformed by proxy bids from a traditional open-outcry auction into a sealed-bid process, the auctioneer can simply feed all the bids into a computer and the computer can figure out which bidders get which bottles of wine and at what prices.

This, then, was the 'product-mix' auction that Klemperer designed for the Bank of England – instead of selling wine, the Bank extended credit, backed by strong or weak collateral. Klemperer made two small refinements. One was to use the lowest winning bid, rather than the highest losing bid, to set interest rates. Recall the embarrassment of the Vickrey auction deployed in New Zealand and you'll understand one of the reasons why. This tweak made little difference, in practice, to the outcome of the auction: bidders would be slightly more conservative, so the lowest winning bid under the Klemperer system would have been much the same as the highest losing bid under the Vickrey system. But the auction retained the attractive Vickrey-ish property that bidders had very little incentive to lie when submitting their proxy bids.

The second refinement was important: the Bank of England pre-committed to varying the total scale of the credit injection depending on how strong the bidding was, and how strong the preference for poor-quality collateral. (The equivalent would be for the auctioneer to decide in advance how much of each type of wine to sell for any given demand.) In effect the Bank was able to decide in advance – without knowing much about the state of the banks who came to the auction – that if the banking sector was in good shape, the Bank would lend modest amounts of cash and insist on strong collateral, while if the banks were fragile, the Bank would lend plenty of cash in exchange for weak collateral, thus keeping interest rates down.

The Bank of England embraced the model – one executive director called it 'a world first in central banking' and 'a major step forward in practical policies to support financial stability' – and now routinely uses the auctions to interact with the UK's banks.

But the multi-unit auction could be used much more widely: for instance when, in 2008, the US government was contemplating buying up 'toxic assets' from troubled banks, the multi-unit auction could have been used to set prices, with the government buying assets – potentially hundreds or thousands of different types of assets – from whoever was willing to sell them for the lowest price. Klemperer and several other auction theorists made this suggestion, before the US government changed direction and decided not to buy troubled assets after all. The auction design could be used to run electricity networks, with big industrial buyers bidding to be supplied more reliable gas, oil and nuclear power, or less reliable renewable energy, depending on their circumstances.

The Bank of England auctions were far less spectacular than the 3G auctions, with their multi-billion-pound price tags and seven-week media circus. In the long run, they may be just as important.

8

Why Poor Countries Are Poor

They call Douala 'the Armpit of Africa'. The description is perfect. Lodged neatly beneath the bulging shoulder of West Africa, the malaria infested city of Douala is humid, unattractive and it stinks. But if you live in Cameroon, Douala is where the action is. Cameroon is a very poor country indeed; the average Cameroonian is eight times poorer than the average citizen of the world, and almost fifty times poorer than the typical American. In late 2001 I went to Douala to find out why.

I'm not sure who first applied the 'armpit' label but I wouldn't be surprised if it was Cameroon's Ministry of Tourism. We all know that in most countries the Ministry of Defence is in charge of attacking other people and that the Ministry of Employment presides over the dole queues. Cameroon's Ministry of Tourism is in that noble tradition. Its job is to discourage tourists from getting into the country.

One colleague had warned me that the Cameroonian embassy in London would be so obstructive that I'd have to go to Paris to get my tourist visa. In the end I had less trouble because I had a man on the inside: a friend in Cameroon paid the equivalent of a half-day's wages to get me an official stamp of invitation. Armed with this official stamp, I paid another five days' Cameroonian wages to get my visa, in a process that required only three journeys to the embassy and some mild grovelling. Funnily enough, my companion and I did not meet many tourists in our three weeks in Cameroon.

But I don't want to give too much credit to the Ministry of Tourism. Discouraging tourists is a real team effort. According to Transparency International, Cameroon is one of the most corrupt countries in the world. In 1999 it was the most corrupt country surveyed. When I visited in 2001 it was the fifth most corrupt, an improvement much celebrated by the government.* A moment's reflection should tell you that earning the title of 'Most Corrupt Country in the World' takes some effort. Because Transparency International ranks countries according to international perceptions of corruption, a winning strategy is to concentrate on screwing bribes out of foreign businessmen – for instance, at the airport. But the Cameroon authorities have spread themselves too thin, because Cameroon is massively corrupt at every level and does not just target foreigners. Perhaps it's this lack of focus that has allowed it to slip from the top spot.

That's not to say that Douala international airport was a well-oiled machine. Far from it: it was a humid, chaotic shambles where we had to fight our way through packed crowds despite the fact that the place only dealt with three or four flights a day. Thankfully, on a torrid evening, we were guided out by my friend Andrew and his driver, Sam, who would have whisked us

*In 2001 Cameroon was jointly 84th–87th most corrupt out of 91 countries, according to Transparency International. In 2010 it was 146th–153rd out of an expanded sample of 178. Perhaps this counts as a further improvement.

immediately to the cooler hillside town of Buea, if Douala were at all conducive to being whisked anywhere. It isn't. Douala, a city of two million people, has no real roads.

A typical Douala street is fifty yards wide, from shack to shack. This is not because the space is required for tree-lined boulevards. It's packed with street vendors, slouched beside a tray of peanuts or an impromptu plantain barbeque, and with little clusters of people, standing around a motorbike, or drinking beer or palm wine or cooking on a small fire. Piles of rubble and vast holes mark unfinished construction or demolition work. Along the middle is a strip of potholes which twenty years ago had been a road. Down that strip drive four streams of traffic, mostly taxis. The stream on the outside is usually made up of stationary – or nearly stationary – taxis picking up fares, while the cabs on the inside weave in and out of the potholes and other cars with all the unpredictability of balls in a lottery machine. There are no hard and fast rules. Sometimes a taxi on the verge, overloaded with passengers, will lurch off and overtake the stuttering traffic on the inside: often the road is more potholed than the verge is. The noise is incredible, because not only does every man, woman and child in Douala seem to carry a ghetto blaster with the volume stuck on full, but the car horn has become a form of universal communication. I worked out some of the most common phrases:

BEEEP – 'You don't see me, but I have spare seats in my cab.'
BEEEP – 'I see you, but I do not have spare seats in my cab.'
BEEEP – 'I cannot take your fare because I'm going in a different direction.'
BEEEP – 'I can take your fare ... get in.'
BEEEP – 'In a moment I will swerve around a pothole, and knock you over. Move!'

Douala used to have buses, but the buses can no longer cope with the decaying roads. So the taxis are all that is left. The cabs are beaten-up old Toyotas, carrying four in the back and three in the front, sprayed New York yellow, each with a unique slogan: for instance, 'God is great', 'In God We Trust', 'Powered by God', or 'Toss Man'.

Nobody who sees a Douala street scene can conclude that Cameroon is poor because of a lack of entrepreneurial spirit. But poor it is, and showing little signs of progress: there has been some growth in recent years, but Cameroon was richer in 1989 than it was in 2005. Is there anything to be done to reverse the decline and help Cameroon grow richer instead? That's no small question. As Nobel laureate Robert Lucas put it:

> The consequences for human welfare involved in questions like these are simply staggering: Once one starts to think about them, it is hard to think about anything else.

The missing jigsaw piece

Economists used to think that economic wealth came from a combination of *man-made resources* (roads, factories, machines, telephone systems), *human resources* (hard work and education) and *technological resources* (technical know-how – or simply high-tech machinery). Obviously, then, poor countries grew into rich countries by investing money in physical resources and by improving human and technological resources with education and technology transfer programmes.

What's wrong with this picture? Nothing, as far as it goes. Education, factories, infrastructure and technical know-how are indeed in abundance in rich countries and severely lacking in poor ones. But the picture is incomplete: a puzzle with the most important piece missing.

The first clue that something is amiss with the traditional story is its implication that poor countries should have been catching up with rich ones for the past century or so, and the further behind they are, the faster the catch-up should be. The poorer countries should catch up quickly because in a country which has very little in the way of infrastructure or education, new investments have the biggest rewards. Rich countries don't gain much from further investment: this is called 'diminishing returns'. For instance, a few roads in a poor country can open up whole new areas for trade; in a rich country, a few more roads just relieve a little congestion. The first few telephones in a poor country are of huge importance; in a rich country, phones are used by school kids to send text messages in class. A little more education in a poor country can make all the difference; in a rich country, people with degrees often can't find jobs. And of course, it should be much easier to copy technology than for a rich country to invent it: the citizens of Douala can enjoy taxis without waiting for a Cameroonian to re-invent the internal combustion engine.

When you look at places like Taiwan, South Korea or China, which have been doubling their incomes every decade or quicker, the theory of catch-up seems reasonable. But many poor countries are not growing faster than rich ones; in fact, they are growing more slowly or, like Cameroon, getting poorer. In order to patch up the traditional story, economists combined their 'diminishing returns' model with one that also takes into account 'increasing returns'. The new theory says that sometimes the more you have, the faster you grow: phones are useful if other people have phones; roads are useful if everyone has a car; technology is easier to invent if you've done a lot of inventing before.

That story would explain why rich countries stay rich and poor countries fall further behind, but it doesn't help explain how countries like China, Taiwan and South Korea – not to mention Botswana, Chile, India, Mauritius and Singapore – are catching up. These dynamic countries, not Japan, the United States or Switzerland, have become the fastest-growing economies on the planet. Sixty years ago (in China's case, much more recently), they were mired in poverty – lacking man-made, human, technical and sometimes natural resources – and have grown much richer since then. Along the way they have improved education, technology and infrastructure.

And why not? Since technology is so widely available and increasingly inexpensive, that is really what economists should expect of every country. In a world of diminishing returns, the poorest countries gain most from new technology, infrastructure and education. South Korea, for example, acquired technology by encouraging foreign companies to invest or by paying licence fees. It wasn't free: in addition to the fees, the investing companies sent profits back home. But the gains to Korean workers and investors, in the form of economic growth, were fifty times greater than the fees and profits that left the country.

As for education and infrastructure, since the returns seem to be so high, there should be no shortage of investors willing to fund infrastructure projects or lend money to students or indeed to governments who provide free education. Banks, domestic and foreign, should be queuing up to lend people the money to get through school or to build a new road or a new power plant. In turn, poor people, or poor countries, should be very happy to take out such loans, confident that investment returns are so high that the repayments will not be difficult. Even if, for some reason, that didn't happen, the World Bank, established after the Second World War with the express aim of providing loans to countries for reconstruction and development, lends billions of dollars a year to developing countries. Investment money is clearly not the issue – either the investments are not being made, or they are not delivering the returns the traditional models predict.

Even the 'increasing returns' model suggests that it should be possible for poor countries to grow richer as long as they can make a number of complementary investments all at once, such as factories, roads, electricity and ports, to allow goods to be manufactured and exported. This 'big push' theory of investment was advanced by the economist Paul Rosenstein-Rodan, who spent some time at the World Bank in its early years. Whether through a big push or otherwise, many poor countries have managed to grow quickly over the past few decades, so why have so many others been left behind?

A theory of government banditry

As our car slowly bumped and lurched through the crowds, I tried to make sense of it all by asking Sam, the driver, about the country.

'Sam, how long was it since the roads were last fixed?'

'The roads, they have not been fixed for nineteen years.' (President Paul Biya came to power in November 1982 and had been in office for nineteen years by the time I visited Cameroon. At the end of 2010, he was still in power, and in late 2009 the European Union declared that the upcoming 2011 presidential election in Cameroon 'has already lost its credibility'. Biya once described his opponents as 'political amateurs' – they are certainly out of practice.)

'Don't people complain about the roads?'

'They complain, but nothing is done. The government tells us there is no money. But there is plenty of money coming from the

World Bank and from France and Britain and America – but they put it in their pockets. They do not spend it on the roads.'

'Are there elections in Cameroon?'

'Yes! There are elections. President Biya is always re-elected with a 90-per-cent majority.'

'Do 90 per cent of people vote for President Biya?'

'No, they do not. He is very unpopular. But still there is a 90-per-cent majority.'

You do not have to spend a long time in Cameroon to realise how much people resent the government. To the residents I spoke to, much of government activity appears to be designed expressly to steal money from the people of Cameroon. I was warned so starkly about government corruption, and the likelihood that officials at the airport would attempt to relieve me of my wad of francs, that I was more nervous about that than any risk of malaria or a gunpoint mugging in the back streets of Douala.

Many people have an optimistic view of politicians and civil servants – that they are all serving the people and doing their best to look after the interests of the country. Other people are more cynical, suggesting that politicians are often incompetent and often trade off the public interest against their own chances of re-election.

An economist called Mancur Olson suggested a working assumption that government motivations are darker still, and produced a remarkable and simple theory of why stable dictatorships should be worse for economic growth than democracies, but better than anarchies. Olson supposed that governments are simply bandits, people with the biggest guns who will turn up and take everything. That's the starting point of his analysis – a starting point that you will have no trouble accepting if you spend five minutes looking around you in Cameroon. As Sam said, 'There is plenty of money ... but they put it in their pockets.'

So imagine a dictator with a tenure of one week: effectively, a bandit with a roving army who sweeps in, takes whatever he wishes and leaves again. Assuming he's neither malevolent nor kind-hearted, but purely self-interested, what incentive does he have to leave anything? The answer is none ... unless he plans on coming back next year.

But imagine that the roaming bandit likes the climate of a certain spot and decides to settle down, building a palace and encouraging his army to avail themselves of the locals. Desperately unfair though it is, the locals are probably better now that the dictator has decided to stay. A purely self-interested dictator will realise that he cannot destroy the economy and starve the people if he plans on sticking around, because then he would exhaust all the resources and have nothing to steal the following year. And so a dictator who lays claim to a land is a preferable leader than one who moves around constantly in search of new victims to plunder.

Although it may seem totally unrelated, biology offers a helpful archetype for the political economist here: viruses and bacteria tend to become much less virulent over time, because the most extreme strains die out rapidly. When syphilis was first recorded in Europe in the late fifteenth century, it was described as being a tremendously aggressive disease which quickly killed the victim. This is not a terribly successful strategy – it's much better to be a disease that allows its victims to live, at least for a little while, to spread the infection. So mutant strains of syphilis that killed people less quickly turned out to be much more successful and longer-lasting than the more virulent strains.

The evolution of diseases certainly stuck in my mind when I thought of Olson's description of a self-interested dictator. Such a dictator, as long as he feels secure in his tenure, will not wish to kill the golden goose. Like the disease whose very existence relies on the bodies it afflicts, the dictator has to keep the economy functioning in order to keep stealing from it. This suggests that a leader who confidently expects to be in power for twenty years will do more to cultivate his economy than one who expects to flee the country after twenty weeks. Twenty years of an 'elected dictator' is probably better than twenty years of one coup after another. Long live the dictator?

This is not to say that Mancur Olson's theory predicts that stable dictatorships should do good things for their countries, simply that they should be better than unstable ones. But dictators – or leaders who never lose 'elections' – are still bad news for the people and economies of their countries. A dictator with absolute power over the distribution of his country's income might decide to steal, say, half of it every year in the form of 'tax', which goes into his personal bank account. That would be bad news for his victims, of course, but it is also bad news for the country's long-term growth. Think of a small businessman considering an investment of £1000 in a new power generator for his workshop. The investment is expected to generate income of £100 a year. That's 10 per cent, a pretty good return. But since his dear ruler plans to take half of it, the return falls to a much less attractive 5 per cent. The businessman decides not to make the investment after all, so he misses out, and so does the dictator. That's an extreme example of the phenomenon we discovered in Chapter 3: taxes cause inefficiency. The dictator's taxes are more arbitrary and larger, but the fundamental effect on the economy is similar in nature.

Of course, the dictator might make his own investments: for instance, providing roads or bridges to encourage commerce. While they would be expensive in the short-term, they would help the economy to prosper, leaving the dictator with opportunities to steal later. But the flip side of the same problem applies: the dictator would be stealing only half of the benefits, not nearly enough to encourage him to provide the infrastructure that the country needs.

I have little doubt in my mind that Olson's self-interested dictator is the star of a fable that goes a long way towards explaining the struggles of undemocratic countries. Those with chaotic leadership, such as the Democratic Republic of Congo, are disastrously poor and war-torn. Those with more stable governments tend to do a little better. And according to Olson's theory, a leader who needs to secure broader support for his policies will need to spend more government revenues on wealth-creating goods and services like roads and courts, and less on himself and his cronies. The greater the democratic pressures, the more healthy the economy is likely to become.

In Cameroon, democratic pressures exist, but they are weak. Biya is certainly no absolute dictator, but he is hardly a democrat. In the 1997 presidential election, the opposition boycotted the election and Biya scooped 93 per cent of the vote. Subsequent elections have been fairer but many reputable observers have cast doubt on the honesty of the polling.

This may explain the situation in Cameroon: widespread poverty, economic growth running in reverse, and crumbling infrastructure. Corruption is widespread and many citizens believe it goes right to the top. Yet Olson's model of the self-interested dictator does not fully represent the situation in Cameroon. No leader is in absolute control of what goes on in his country, and President Biya is no exception.

Bandits, bandits everywhere

If you want to drive from the town of Buea to Bamenda, further north, the most popular way to make the trip is by bus; minibuses ply all long-distance routes in Cameroon. Designed to seat ten people in comfort, they will depart as soon as thirteen paying passengers have boarded. The relatively capacious seat beside the driver is worth fighting for. The vehicles are old boneshakers, but the system works pretty well.

It would work a lot better if not for the malign influence of government. Sometimes the problem is simply neglect. For example the quickest, though certainly not the most direct, route from Buea to Bamenda is through the French-speaking part of Cameroon, which has better roads. Simply drive east for two hours, north for two hours and then west for two hours. This is much faster than driving directly north on the appalling roads of the English-speaking region of Cameroon. Biya's government seems to ignore the interests of the politically impotent English-speaking regions. The English-speaking minority complains that when donors funded Cameroon's ring road, the government just sent them receipts but didn't bother to build the English section.

The second obstacle, literally, is the multitude of police roadblocks. Bullying gendarmes, often drunk, stop every minibus and try their best to extract bribes from the passengers. They usually fail but from time to time they become determined. My friend Andrew was once hauled off a bus and harassed for several hours. The eventual pretext for the bribe was his lack of a yellow-fever certificate, which you need when you enter the country but not when riding a bus. The gendarme explained patiently that Cameroon had to be protected from disease. The price of two beers convinced him that an epidemic had been prevented, and Andrew caught the next bus, three hours later.

This is less efficient even than Mancur Olson's model predicts. Olson himself would have admitted that his theory in its starkest form underestimates the damage that bad governments inflict on their people. President Biya needs to keep hundreds of thousands of armed police and army officers happy, as well as many civil servants and other supporters. If Biya was a 'perfect dictator' interested in maximising his bank balance, he would simply impose the least-damaging taxes possible in whatever quantity was necessary, and distribute the proceeds to his supporters. This approach to government turns out to be impracticable because it requires far more information about and control over the economy than a poor government can possibly muster. The substitute is government-tolerated corruption on a massive scale.

The corruption is not only unfair, it is also hugely wasteful. Gendarmes spend their time harassing travellers in return for rather modest returns. The costs are enormous. An entire police force is too busy extracting bribes to catch criminals. A four-hour trip takes five hours. Travellers will have to take costly steps to protect themselves: carrying less money, travelling less often or at busier times of day, bringing extra paperwork to help fend off attempts to extract bribes.

The blockades and crooked police officers comprise a particularly visible form of corruption, but there are metaphorical roadblocks throughout the Cameroonian economy. The World Bank has thrown light on them with its 'Doing Business' project, which collects data about simple business regulations. The Bank discovered that in order to set up a small business, an entrepreneur in Cameroon must spend on official fees more than the average Cameroonian makes in six months. (Remarkably, this reflected a substantial improvement between 2009 and 2010. My expenditure on a tourist visa pales into insignificance in comparison.) To buy or sell property costs nearly a fifth of the property's value. To get the courts to enforce an unpaid invoice takes more than two years, costs almost half

of the invoice's value and requires forty-three separate procedures. These ridiculous regulations are good news for the
bureaucrats who enforce them. Every procedure is an opportunity to extract a bribe. The slower the standard processes, the
greater is the temptation to pay 'speed money'. As a result,
President Biya enjoys the support of enough officials to keep
him firmly in power.

Yet that is not the only result. Inflexible labour regulations help
make sure that only experienced professional men are given
formal contracts; women and young people have to fend for
themselves in the grey market. Red tape discourages new businesses. Slow courts mean that entrepreneurs are forced to turn
down attractive opportunities with new customers because they
know they cannot protect themselves if they are cheated. Poor
countries have the worst examples of such regulations, and that is
one of the major reasons they are poor. Governments in rich
countries usually perform these basic tasks quickly and cheaply,
whereas governments in poor countries draw out the processes in
the hope of pocketing some extra cash themselves.

Institutions matter

Government banditry, widespread waste and oppressive regulations designed to make it easier to extract bribes: all elements of
that missing piece of the growth and development puzzle. Over
the past fifteen years or so, economists working on development
issues have converged on the mantra that 'institutions matter'. Of
course, it is hard to describe what an 'institution' really is; it is
even harder to change a bad institution into a good one.

But progress is being made. Mancur Olson's theory of government banditry helps us to understand, in a simplified form,

how different kinds of government might affect the incentives of everyone in the country, although it gives us little guidance as to how to make things better.

The World Bank's measurement of red tape gives us an excellent sense of one kind of institution: simple business regulations. That project also shows how simple publicity can improve some of those institutions. For example, after the World Bank advertised the fact that entrepreneurs in Ethiopia couldn't legally start a business without paying four years' salary to publish an official notice in government newspapers, the Ethiopian government relented and decided to scrap the regulation. New business registrations jumped by almost 50 per cent immediately.

Unfortunately, it is not always so easy. Although it is becoming clearer and clearer that dysfunctional institutions are a key explanation of poverty in developing countries, most institutions cannot be described with an elegant model like Mancur Olson's, nor even with careful data-gathering from the World Bank. Most unhappy institutions are unhappy in their own way.

The world's worst library

Just such a uniquely backfiring institutional set-up was responsible for the world's worst library. A few days after I arrived in Cameroon, I visited one of the country's most prestigious private schools, Cameroon's equivalent of Eton. The school grounds were a mix of the familiar and the odd: low, cheaply built classrooms surrounding playing fields reminded me very much of my old school in England, but a tree-lined avenue of crazy paving (Tim Burton meets *Born Free*), along which all the teachers live, did not.

We were being shown round the school by the librarian, a

volunteer for the British-based voluntary organisation VSO, which aims to place skilled volunteers where they are most needed in poor countries. The school boasted two separate library buildings, but the librarian was most unhappy – and I soon understood why.

At first glance the library was very impressive. With the exception of the principal's palatial house, it was the only two-storey structure on campus. Its design was also adventurous: a poor man's Sydney Opera house. The sloped roof, rather than running down from a ridge, soared up in a V from a central valley like the pages of an open book on a stand.

Despite its creative design, I am sure that my memories of the spectacular new library will last far longer than the building does. Standing in the blazing sunlight of the Cameroonian dry season, it's hard to see at first what the problem is with a roof that looks like a giant open book. But that would be to forget, as the architect seemingly did, that Cameroon also has a rainy season. When it rains in Cameroon, it rains for five solid months and so hard that even the most massive storm ditches quickly overflow. When that kind of rain meets not so much a guttered roof, as a roof that is, essentially, a gutter that drains onto the flat-roofed entrance hall, then you know it's time to laminate the book collection.

The only reason the school's books still existed was because they'd never been near the new building: the librarian had refused repeated requests from the principal to transfer them from the old library. I was tempted to conclude that the principal was in an advanced stage of denial when I stepped inside the new library to see the devastation. It was in ruins. The floor contained the stains of countless puddles. The air had the kind of musty smell I associate with a damp cave in Europe, not a modern building on the equator. The plaster was peeling off the walls like a thousand-year-old Byzantine fresco. Yet the library is only four years old.

This is a shocking waste. Instead of building the library, the school could have bought forty thousand good books, or computers with internet connections, or funded scholarships for poor children. Any of these alternatives would have been incomparably better than an unusable new library. This leaves aside the fact that the school never needed a new library in the first place – the old library works perfectly well, could easily hold three times as many books as the school owns, and is waterproof.

The fact that the library was unnecessary goes some way to explaining its poor design. After all, nobody pays too much attention to the functionality of a building whose functions are redundant. But if the library was such a pointless endeavour, why was it built at all?

Napoleon is often credited with the statement, 'Never ascribe to conspiracy that which is adequately explained by incompetence.' That's the natural response: incompetence is an easy scapegoat. It's all too tempting for the visitor to Cameroon to shrug his shoulders and explain Cameroon's poverty by presuming that Cameroonians are idiots. The library looks like good evidence, but Cameroonians are no smarter or more foolish than the rest of us. Seemingly stupid mistakes are so ubiquitous in Cameroon that incompetence cannot be the adequate explanation we're looking for. There is something more systematic at work. Once again, we need to consider the incentives of the decision makers.

First, the principal of this prestigious private school wanted to convert it into a university, and so needed to build a library building of university size and quality. It was hardly the point that the current library was sufficient for the basic purpose of storing the school's books, and that the money could have been better spent in other ways or by other schools.

Second, nobody was effectively monitoring the principal or her spending. In common with many principals in north west

Cameroon, the principal has powerful friends. Members of staff in the education system are not paid or promoted on merit but absolutely on the decisions of the principal. This is a prestigious school with good conditions for teachers, so staff would be particularly eager to keep their jobs, which meant keeping in good favour with the principal. In fact, the only person with the ability to defy the principal was the librarian, who was accountable only to the VSO head office in London. She turned up after the library was built but was at least in time to prevent the book collection from being transferred and destroyed. The principal was either so stupid that she did not realise that water ruins books, or she did not care very much about the books and simply wanted to demonstrate that the library had some books in it. The second explanation seems more likely.

With nobody to object to the wastefulness of building a second library, the principal had full control over the project. She appointed a former pupil of the school to design the library, probably to demonstrate the quality of education provided by the school; she did prove a point, although perhaps not the one she intended. But no matter how incompetent the design, its flaws would have been spotted if anybody concerned had a strong interest in making sure that the library functioned as a library. But that was never the prime concern of anybody with any authority. The people in power simply cared about putting up *something* that could qualify the school as a university.

Consider the situation: money that was provided because of social networks rather than need; a project designed for prestige rather than to be used; a lack of monitoring and accountability; and an architect appointed for show by somebody with little interest in the quality of the work. The outcome is hardly surprising: a project that should never have been built was built, and built badly.

The lesson of the story might appear to be that self-interested or ambitious people in power are often the cause of wastefulness in developing countries. The truth is a little sadder than that. Self-interested and ambitious people are in positions of power, great and small, all over the world. In many places, they are restrained by the law, the press and democratic opposition. Cameroon's tragedy is that there is nothing to hold the consequences of ambition or self-interest in check.

The plot thickens – incentives and development in Nepal

The Cameroonian education system gives administrators such perverse incentives that educating children is the last thing anyone profits from doing, and hence, the last thing education officials focus on.

Other development projects involve more subtle webs of unusual incentives. One example was uncovered by the economist Elinor Ostrom, who looked in detail at the intricate irrigation designs in Nepal.* In addition to older traditional systems of dams and canals, Nepal also has some modern concrete dams and canals, designed by expert engineers and funded by big international donor organisations. Which works best, and why?

When I heard about this study I thought I could guess the punchline. The obvious conclusion is that the best of modern design, materials and engineering, with massive funding, should

*When I first described Ostrom's work, she was something of a cult figure – hugely admired in development circles but not widely known, even to other parts of the economics profession. That has now changed: in 2009 she was awarded the Nobel memorial prize in economics.

produce a better irrigation system than a bunch of farmers using mud and sticks, right? Wrong.

We know better now. We know that large dam projects have often been poorly suited to local conditions, and that in fact 'small is beautiful' – local methods and traditional knowledge handed down over long years from generation to generation turn out to work far better. Right? Wrong again.

It turns out that the real story in Nepal is much more interesting than either of these oversimplified assumptions. Elinor Ostrom identified an apparent paradox. The first part of the paradox is that modern dams, which are professionally designed and built, seem to reduce the effectiveness of irrigation systems. But the second part of the paradox is that when donors pay to have irrigation channels built, or reinforced with modern materials, they strengthen the irrigation system, reliably delivering more water to more people.

Why can donors provide effective irrigation channels, but not effective dams? Clearly there is something more subtle going on than the tired debate between modern technical expertise and traditional wisdom. The truth is clearer to someone who tries to work out the motivations of all concerned.

Start with the obvious insight that any project is most likely to be successful if the people who benefit from its success are the same people who make it possible. That immediately explains why the existing methods of irrigation have an advantage – not because they are full of traditional wisdom (they may be, of course) but because they're designed, built and maintained by the farmers who use them. The modern dams and canals, by contrast, are designed by engineers who will not starve if the dams fail, commissioned by civil servants whose jobs do not rest on success and paid for by donor agency officials who are more likely to be judged by procedure than results. Immediately we start to see why better materials and vastly superior funding do not necessarily lead to success.

Looking deeper still, irrigation systems have to be maintained to be of any use. But who will maintain them? Neither donor agencies nor civil servants have as much interest in maintenance as they should. Nepalese civil servants are promoted mostly by seniority and partly by being associated with 'prestige' construction projects. Maintenance is a dead-end job, regardless of whether it pays dividends for the farmers. What civil servant would want to oversee an unending menial task, far from Kathmandu where his wife shops and his children go to school? On top of that, bribes are always a potential source of income for civil servants, and a large construction contract offers much greater chances of backhanders than does maintenance work.

Like the civil service, donor agencies work under constraints that tend to favour large construction projects. All donor agencies need expensive projects because if they fail to spend cash, they are unlikely to raise more. In addition many bilateral aid organisations, like USAID, are tied to country-specific types of aid: USAID typically has to use equipment purchased in the United States, which tends to be heavy, high-tech machinery. Since bulldozers are of more use in building a dam than maintaining it, the outcome is yet again in favour of big construction projects. Even if the donor agency has no bias towards large projects, they still have to rely on the information they receive from local staff and consultants – who will often have the same incentives as the civil service.

All of this starts to explain why those who commission construction projects do not have as much interest in building good cost-effective systems as do the farmers. But it does not explain Olson's finding that donor-funded dams actually make things worse, and neither does it explain why donor-funded irrigation canals seem to work well despite the fact that the people who commission them don't much care whether they do or not. To understand why, we need to think about the farmers themselves.

Nobody except the farmers is likely to be very interested in maintaining an irrigation system once it is built. This may not be a problem. Before any major modern irrigation systems were built, the farmers had to maintain the traditional systems. If they could maintain the traditional systems, can't they maintain the modern ones, too?

Maintenance requires two big jobs: keeping the dam in one piece, and clearing the canals of obstructions. This is a lot of work. Farmers won't bother unless they see the benefits, and this potentially leads to a problem. The problem is that while all farmers need the dam to be kept in one piece, farmers near the dam don't much care what happens to the drainage canals further down the hill. So why should they bother to help with the drainage canals? Fortunately, most farming communities in Nepal have worked out a system of cooperation; while the details differ the general principle is that the farmers downstream help maintain the dam in exchange for assistance on the canals. So far, so good.

If a big donor pays for new, concrete canals to be installed, then things will improve – the new canals are better, carry more water and require less maintenance. But if a big donor pays for a new dam, everything falls apart. This is not because the dam itself does: quite the reverse. Because the concrete dam needs much *less* maintenance than the traditional one, the cooperative agreement which maintained the entire irrigation system no longer works. The traditional bargain breaks down. Upstream farmers no longer help clear the canals in exchange for help on the dam from downstream farmers. The upstream farmers don't need help, so the downstream farmers no longer have anything to offer on their side of the deal.

Many irrigation systems in Nepal end in failure because although the technical properties of the system may have been understood and improved, the human properties of the system have not been addressed at all.

This Nepalese example is yet another demonstration that if a society cannot provide the right kind of incentives to behave productively, no amount of technical infrastructure can save it from poverty. Development projects are often commissioned by people with no great interest in success but a great interest in bribes and career advancement. If the effectiveness of the project is a minor consideration, then it can hardly be a surprise if the project does not deliver on the publicly announced aims, even if it has delivered on the real aims of enriching bureaucrats. And even if the project was one that would still have been commissioned if genuine development really was the goal, bribes and other distortions are likely to spoil things.

Is there a chance for development?

Development specialists often focus on helping poor countries become richer by improving primary education and infrastructure like roads and telephones, and that's surely sensible. Unfortunately, it's only a small part of the problem. Economists who have pulled apart the statistics, or studied unusual data such as the earnings of Cameroonians in Cameroon and the earnings of Cameroonians who emigrate to the United States, have found that education, infrastructure and factories don't begin to explain the gap between rich and poor. Because of its lousy education system, Cameroon is perhaps twice as poor as it could be. Because of its terrible infrastructure, it's roughly twice as poor again. So we would expect Cameroon to be four times poorer than the United States, but it is fifty times poorer. More importantly, why can't the Cameroonian people seem to do anything about it? Couldn't Cameroonian communities improve their schools? Wouldn't the benefits easily outweigh the costs? Couldn't Cameroonian businessmen build factories, license technology, seek foreign partners . . . and make a fortune?

Evidently not. Mancur Olson showed that kleptocracy at the top stunts the growth of poor countries. If a poor country has a thief for a ruler, that doesn't necessarily spell doom, because the ruler might prefer to boost the economy and then take a slice of a bigger pie. But in general, looting will be widespread either because the dictator is not confident of his tenure, or because he needs to allow others to steal in order to keep their support.

Then further down the pyramid of wealth, development is thwarted because the rules and laws of the society do not encourage projects or businesses, which would be to the common good. Entrepreneurs don't establish official businesses (too difficult) and so don't pay taxes; officials demand ridiculous projects for their prestige or personal enrichment; schoolchildren don't bother to acquire irrelevant qualifications.

It is not news to hear that corruption and perverse incentives matter. But perhaps it is news to find out that the problem of twisted rules and institutions explains not just a little bit of the gap between Cameroon and rich countries but almost all of the gap. Countries like Cameroon fall far below their potential even considering their poor infrastructure, low investment and minimal education. But worse than that, the web of corruption foils every effort to improve the infrastructure, attract investment and improve educational standards.

Cameroon's education system would be better if people had an incentive to get a good education; if a meritocracy were in place, and good grades and real skills – rather than connections – earned jobs. Cameroon would have better technology and more working factories if the investment climate was right, either for foreign or domestic investors, and if the profits weren't eaten up in bribes and red tape. There is so little investment in machinery and computers that extra investment should be very profitable – if the profits weren't eaten up in bribes and red tape.

The small amount of education and technology and infrastructure that Cameroon does have could be much better used if the society was organised to reward good, productive ideas. But it is not.

We still don't have a good word to describe what is missing in Cameroon, indeed in poor countries across the world. But we are starting to understand what it is. Some people call it 'social capital', or maybe 'trust'. Others call it 'the rule of law', or 'institutions'. But these are just labels. The problem is that Cameroon, like other poor countries, is a topsy-turvy world in which it's in most people's interest to take action that directly or indirectly damages everyone else. The incentives to create wealth in any way at all are turned on their heads just as surely at the roof of the school library.

The rot starts with government but it afflicts the entire society. There's no point investing in a business because the government will not protect you against thieves. (So, you might as well become a thief.) There's no point in paying your phone bill because nobody can successfully take you to court (so there's no point being a phone company). There's no point getting an education because jobs are not handed out on merit (and in any case, you can't borrow money for school fees because the bank cannot collect on the loan, and the government doesn't provide good schools). There's no point setting up an import business because the customs officers will be the ones to benefit (and so there is little trade, and so the customs office is under-funded and looks even harder for bribes).

Now we are starting to understand just how important this is, we can begin to put it right. But it's in the nature of the problem to resist solutions, so this is a slow and difficult process. We don't usually find it acceptable to set up democracies by force, and they usually don't last when we do. We don't like development aid to be lost in red tape, but making sure the money is well spent is very time consuming.

These problems cannot be fixed overnight. But there are some simple reforms which – with a modicum of political will – would move poor countries like Cameroon in the right direction. One simple reform is to cut red tape, allowing small businesses to be legally established, which makes it easier for their entrepreneurs to expand and borrow money. The legal reforms necessary are often trivial; and while they still rely on sensible and benevolent government, all it takes is a single minister with his head and his heart in the right place, rather than hoping for an entire civil service to permanently reform.

Another option, and a vital one, is to enlist the world economy for help. Most poor countries are also very small economies; the entire economy of sub-Saharan Africa is about the size of Belgium's. A small African state like Chad has an economy smaller than that of a town like Shrewsbury. Tiny countries like Chad and Cameroon cannot possibly be self-sufficient: they need access to cheap fuel, raw materials, loans from international banks and manufacturing equipment. But Cameroonians are trapped behind high barriers to trade – among the highest tariffs in the world, 12.7 per cent against a world average of just 2.8 per cent. Such barriers generate revenue for the government and allow it to protect the businesses of cronies or hand out profitable import licences. A small country cannot survive without the world economy. With it, small countries can thrive. In the next chapter we shall visit one, and find out how.

9

Beer, Chips and Globalisation

Once upon a time there was a prosperous trading city called Bruges, nestling on the Zwin estuary in what is now Belgium. Bruges grew up around a castle built in the late ninth century by the founder of the Duchy of Flanders. A century later Bruges was Flanders's capital, and it began to grow wealthy as trade expanded across northern Europe. Bruges was a centre for the manufacturing of cloth, and ships sailed up the Zwin estuary to buy the fabric, bringing with them English cheese, wool and minerals, Spanish wine, Russian furs, Danish pork and silks and spices from the East, traded through the mighty Italian cities of Venice and Genoa. The queen of France herself visited Bruges in 1301 and is reported to have commented, 'I thought I alone was queen, but I see that I have six hundred rivals here.'

Bruges's wealth continued to flow in for 250 years, despite conquest by the French and the Dukes of Burgundy. Regardless of who was in charge, Bruges continued to prosper: it was the centre of gravity for the Hanseatic League of trading cities, its arts scene was flourishing, it was developing new industries such as cutting diamonds from India and its population was twice that of London. Fine goods from across the world were traded in the tavern owned by the merchant family Van der Beurs – some would have you believe that this is why, to this day, stock exchanges are called 'bourses'. Tall masts and broad sails adorned the Zwin estuary.

But in the fifteenth century something strange began to happen. The Zwin began to silt up. The great ships could no longer reach the docks of Bruges. The Hanseatic League moved up the coast to Antwerp. Bruges quickly and literally became a backwater. So lifeless did it become that it was nicknamed 'Bruges-La-Morte'. Today it is a quaint museum piece. Perfectly preserved, it hums busily only because of the tourists eager to visit a time capsule: a beautiful and prosperous trading city of the fifteenth century whose wealth and development dried up with the river.

Meanwhile, Antwerp, still connected to the world via the Scheldt River, took over from Bruges as the greatest economic power in western Europe. The wealth of that time is clearly visible today: Antwerp's great cathedral dominates the skyline, and more striking still to the first-time visitor are the great guild houses of the Grote Markt, which soar five, six, seven storeys above the cobblestones, and appear even higher yet because of their spindly architecture of spires and pencil-thin windows. Although the appearance of air, rail and motorised road transport have diminished its geographical advantages, Antwerp remains an economic powerhouse. It is still the diamond capital of the world, and the mighty port on the Scheldt operates round the clock.

The contrasting stories of Bruges and Antwerp suggest a simple message: if you would like to be rich, then it is a good idea to forge close links with the rest of the world. If you prefer nothing to change, then it is best to have a harbour that silts up. If you would like to be rich *and* have nothing change, then you will be disappointed.

There arc few pleasures I enjoy more than sitting in Antwerp, wolfing down hot chips smothered in mayonnaise and cooling my mouth with a heady, fizzy beer. Of course, being an economist, I am inclined to contemplate the world trading system as I do. Chips from Frituur No. 1 simply cannot be matched anywhere in the world. But the glass of Duvel beer to wash them down is obtained without difficulty in London. It may cost twice as much but it tastes every bit as good and is certainly just as potent. So when I am in Antwerp, sitting just off the Grote Markt and enjoying a Duvel, I cannot help but feel a little sad that this thrill has been cheapened by its ready availability in my home city. Of course, when in London – and sober – I can only praise the noble and enterprising merchants who have brought exotic beers such as Duvel, Chimay and Maredsous 10 to my doorstep, and look forward to when Westmalle Trippel is widely available too.

The most visible manifestation of the world's increasing economic interdependence is the availability of foreign products in familiar settings. It is both a blessing and a curse: a blessing because it becomes possible to enjoy a wider variety of treats without straying far from the place you were born. It is a curse because when you do travel you may find that foreign places look a little too familiar. From McDonald's in Moscow to Starbucks in Shanghai, are we not all becoming the same? The whole world seems to have become one seething mass of internationalisation. The commerce with foreign lands that was once the preserve of Florence, Venice and Bruges now appears ubiquitous.

If you spend too much time in airports, hotel chains and capital cities it is easy to feel this way; but we live in a big and varied world. You may be able to visit Starbucks in Shanghai, but

Starbucks is not the whole of Shanghai and Shanghai is not the whole of China. The world has a long way to go before it truly is 'globalised', if by that odd word we mean 'the same everywhere'. No doubt we are on the way. Reading biologist Edward O. Wilson, I discover that in a few dozen generations all human beings will be 'the same', in the sense that whether in London or Shanghai or Moscow or Lagos, the same racial mix would be found. Viewed differently, the variety of human beings would be unprecedented: as this process of racial mixing accelerates, 'many more combinations of skin colour, facial features, talents, and other traits influenced by genes are now arising than ever existed before'.

Personally I find both predictions encouraging, although others might find them alarming.

The same is true for cultures, technology, economic systems and the range of products available. On the one hand they will increasingly resemble each other across the world; on the other, in any one place they will display tremendous diversity and exciting new mixes, as anyone who enjoys Bangladeshi curries in London, Ethiopian stir-fry Tibbs in Washington DC or Japanese sashimi in Antwerp will attest. Like racial intermixing, economic and cultural integration will take a long time. Furthermore, new ideas and new technologies are always arriving. Globalisation will never homogenise what we have, not while new ideas are always appearing and adding fresh ingredients to the slowly turning blender of economic integration. Those who fear a terrible global sameness must remember that new ideas, welcome or unwelcome, will always arise faster than they can be mixed in.

But perhaps by commenting on culture and race I am stepping well outside the boundaries of my expertise. I shall therefore return to economics, where my 'comparative advantage' lies.

*

Comparative advantage is the foundation of the way economists think about trade. Let's picture it this way: who is the better economics writer, me or E. O. Wilson? Professor Wilson is 'one of the twentieth century's greatest thinkers' and 'considered to be one of the world's greatest living scientists' according to the jacket of his book *Consilience*. His chapter on social science was written after interviewing some of the world's greatest economists; the result was an insightful explanation which introduced me to plenty of things I didn't know about economics. The truth is that E. O. Wilson is probably a better economist than I am.

So I know when I'm beaten. Why write a book about economics when Professor Wilson could write a better one? The answer is comparative advantage. Because of comparative advantage, Professor Wilson hasn't written a book about economics, and I'm fairly confident he never will.

We owe the idea of comparative advantage to the star of Chapter 1, David Ricardo. If Wilson and I shared David Ricardo as an agent, he might advise us as follows: 'Tim, if you write biology books you are unlikely to get more than one sale per year of writing – the one your wife buys. But your economics is passable, and we predict sales of twenty-five thousand books for every year you spend writing. Professor Wilson, your economics books will probably sell five hundred thousand copies for every year you spend writing: but why not stick to the biology books and sell ten million?'

E. O. Wilson is twenty times as good an economics writer as I am, but, advised by David Ricardo, he sticks to writing biology, a subject at which he is ten million times more accomplished than I. On a personal level, Ricardo's advice is plain common sense: E. O. Wilson should choose his vocation not with reference to what he does better than I do, but with reference to what he does best. Meanwhile, I would be well advised to make a

living as an economics writer, not because I am the best economics writer in the world but because economics writing is
what *I* do best.

Ricardo's advice becomes more controversial when it comes to
trading with the Chinese. 'Chinese wages are so much lower than
ours,' cry the protectionists. 'They can make televisions and toys
and clothes and all kinds of things much more cheaply than we
can. We should protect our domestic producers with a tax on
Chinese products – or perhaps an outright ban.' And so we do.
Imports of large, high definition television screens to Europe are
subject to a tariff of 14 per cent for no obvious reason, while textiles are subject to horrendously complex trade legislation across
the world. Agriculture is even more highly protected. And other
products – for instance steel, of which China now produces much
more than the United States and Japan combined – are subject to
occasional (and often illegal) trade restrictions.

Isn't this necessary to stem what would otherwise be a flood of
cheap foreign products under which our domestic industry would
drown? It is not. The United States ought to produce goods and
services not by asking what it does more cheaply than China but
by focusing on what the United States does best.

Ricardo's insight is that trade barriers – whether they are subsidies to our farmers, regulations on textiles or taxes on
televisions – make both us and the Chinese worse off. It does
not matter if the Chinese really are better than we are at making
everything: they should stick to producing whatever their economy is most efficient at turning out. Meanwhile, we, despite
(apparently) being worse at everything, should stick to producing what we are least bad at producing. The argument is the
same as one the spirit of David Ricardo gave to me and E. O.
Wilson: I may be worse at everything, but I should still produce

the economics books while E. O. Wilson sticks to biology. Yet barriers to trade are also barriers to this common-sense arrangement.

An example may help to persuade the unconvinced. Let's say a British worker could produce a machine drill in half an hour, or a flat-screen TV in an hour. A Chinese worker could produce a machine drill in twenty minutes or a flat-screen TV in ten. The Chinese worker is evidently the E. O. Wilson of manufacturing. (Incidentally, the productivity numbers in this example are not only fictional but fantastical. Sadly for the Chinese, workers in developing countries are far less productive than workers in developed countries. They are able to compete only because they are paid much less; in fact, the relationship between lower wages and lower productivity is an extremely close one.)

If China and Britain do not trade, it takes ninety minutes' work to produce a flat-screen TV and a drill to mount it on the wall in the UK. In China the TV and drill can be made in half an hour. If the protectionists get their way, then that is how things will stay.

If there are no trade barriers, we can trade with each other and both be better off. The Chinese worker makes two televisions, which take her twenty minutes, and the Briton makes two drills, which take him an hour. Trade one drill for one television and both are better off than when they started, having saved a third of their time. Of course, being more efficient the Chinese worker can quit work earlier, or earn more; but that does not mean the British worker has lost because of trade. Quite the reverse.

It's true that if the Chinese worker put in a bit of overtime, she could do her own job and also do the same work as the Briton would have achieved all week. But why would she be so extraordinarily generous? The Chinese do not export televisions to Britain out of the goodness of their hearts; they do so because we send something in exchange – even if, as with our hypothetical machine drills, the Chinese are better at making them, too.

Contrary to popular belief, it is simply not possible for trade to destroy all of our jobs and for us to import everything from abroad and export nothing. If we did, we would have nothing to buy the imports with. For there to be trade at all, somebody in Britain must be making something to sell to the outside world.

This should be obvious, but somehow it isn't. Think of British workers in, say, Birmingham, producing those machine drills. The workers are paid in pounds sterling. The factory is rented in pounds. The heat and light and telephone bills all come asking for payment in pounds. But the drills are exported to China and sold locally or used to make goods in the Chinese currency, the renminbi. The costs of production are in pounds sterling, the revenues are in renminbi. Somewhere renminbi have to be 'turned into' pounds to pay the Birmingham workers' salaries, but of course there is no process of magically turning pounds into renminbi. The only thing that will work is for an importer in Britain to provide pounds in exchange for renminbi, which he will use to buy imports. Exports pay for imports.

Economics, surprisingly to some, is about the interconnectedness of things: goods and money do not just appear and disappear. Nobody outside Britain would accept pounds in payment if Britain was not exporting things that pounds could be used to buy.

In a more complex world the pounds and renminbi, drills and televisions, will not be directly exchanged for each other. We sell drills to the Saudis, the Saudis sell oil to the Japanese, the Japanese sell robots to the Chinese and the Chinese sell televisions to us.

We can borrow money temporarily* – the UK is currently doing this – or we can produce assets like machine drill factories and sell the factories rather than the machine drills. But the circular flow of currencies will balance out completely in the end. The UK can afford imports only if we eventually produce exports to pay for them, and the same is true for every country.

A more extreme example may clarify things further. Think of a country whose government is very keen on self-sufficiency. 'We need to encourage our local economy,' says the Minister for Trade and Industry. So the government bans all imports and patrols the coast to prevent smuggling. One effect will be that a lot of effort will be devoted to producing locally what was once imported: this certainly is encouragement to the local economy. But another effect is that all of the export industries will quickly shrivel and die. Why? Because who would want to spend time and money exporting goods in exchange for foreign currency, if nobody is allowed to spend the foreign currency on imports? While one part of the local economy is encouraged, another is crippled. The 'no imports' policy is also a 'no exports' policy. And indeed, one of the most important theorems of trade theory, the Lerner theorem, named after the economist Abba Lerner, proved in 1936 that a tax on imports is exactly equivalent to a tax on exports.

Lerner's theorem tells us that restricting imports of Chinese televisions to protect British jobs in television manufacturing makes as much sense as restricting exports of British machine drills to protect British jobs in television manufacturing. In fact,

---

*Let's be careful here. By 'we can borrow money temporarily', I'm not referring to a government deficit, which is the amount a government is borrowing (usually per year) from domestic and foreign creditors. I'm talking about the amount that the UK as a whole, both public and private sectors, is borrowing from overseas investors.

the British television manufacturing industry is not really competing against the Chinese television manufacturing industry at all; it is competing against the British machine drill industry. If the machine drill industry is more efficient, the television manufacturing industry will not survive, just as surely as E. O. Wilson's promising career as an economic journalist never got off the ground in the face of his superior skills as a scientist.

This certainly makes us look at trade barriers in a new light. But it doesn't prove that trade barriers cause any harm: after all, mightn't the benefit of trade barriers to the British television manufacturing industry outweigh the harm to the British machine drill industry? David Ricardo's theory of comparative advantage tells us that the answer is no. As we know, under free trade, both Chinese and British workers can quit work earlier than they could under restricted trade, having produced the same amount as before.

The common-sense answer based on practical experience is also no: compare North Korea with South Korea, or Austria with Hungary. To take a very rough guide to how much better it is to have an open, liberal economy than a closed one, simply note that in 1990, just after the fall of the Berlin wall, the average Austrian was between two and six times richer than the average Hungarian (depending on how you measure it). The average South Korean is wealthy while the average North Korean is starving. North Korea is so isolated that it's hard to get any measurement of quite how poor the country is.

Trade barriers will always cause more harm than good, not just to the country against which the barrier is erected but also the country that erects the barriers. No matter if other countries choose to inflict trade restrictions on themselves, we're better off without. The great economist Joan Robinson once quipped that just because others throw rocks into their harbour, that is no reason to throw rocks into our own. As the Zwin silted up, the citizens of Bruges were no doubt realising the same truth centuries before.

None of this is to say that free trade is good for everybody. Competition from cheaper or better foreign products cannot put all of our domestic industries out of business, because otherwise we couldn't afford to buy the foreign products. But it can alter the balance of our economy. To go back to the example of machine drills and televisions, although in our example the Chinese are better at producing both machine drills and televisions, we still produce machine drills when trading with the Chinese. In fact, we produce twice as many machine drills as we did before, but our television manufacturing industry has been wiped out. Good for the machine drill industry, bad for the television manufacturing industry. People will lose their jobs. They will have to try to learn new skills and get re-employed in the machine drill sector, which may be easier said than done. Overall, the UK is better off, but some people will lose out, and the losers will curse free trade and demand restrictions on imported televisions, although we know now that they could equally demand restrictions on exported machine drills.

Even the most casual historian will be reminded of the Luddite rebellion in Britain. Luddism began in 1811 in the Midlands, a desperate response by skilled textile workers to competition from the latest technology: stocking and shearing frames. The Luddites were well-organised, destroying mills and machines ('frame-breaking') and protesting against the new economic system. Contrary to the modern stereotype of an unimaginative thug, the Luddites were responding to a real threat to their livelihoods.

So did technological change hurt some people? Without a doubt. Did it impoverish Britain as a whole? A ridiculous notion. Without minimising the genuine suffering to those who lost their livelihoods along the way, it's obvious that technological progress made us far better off.

Trade can be thought of as another form of technology. Economist David Friedman observes, for instance, that there are two ways for the United States to produce cars: they can build them in Detroit, or they can grow them in Iowa. Growing them in Iowa makes use of a special technology that turns wheat into Toyotas: simply put the wheat onto ships and send them out into the Pacific ocean. The ships come back a short while later with Toyotas on them. The technology used to turn wheat into Toyotas out in the Pacific is called 'Japan', but it could just as easily be a futuristic biofactory floating off the coast of Hawaii. Either way, car workers in Detroit are in direct competition with farmers in Iowa. Import restrictions on Japanese cars will help the car workers and hurt the farmers: they are the modern-day equivalent of 'frame-breaking'.

The solution, in a civilised but progressive society, is not to ban new technology or to restrict trade. Neither is it to ignore the plight of those people put out of work by technology, trade or indeed anything else. It is to allow progress to continue while helping support and retrain those who have been hurt as a result.

Perhaps that sounds callous. After all, even one person who wants a job and cannot find one is suffering a personal tragedy. Yet the interest groups who oppose free trade for their own profit have vastly overblown the effects of trade. Between 1999 and 2009, 338.9 million private-sector jobs were lost in the United States. Over the same period, more than 337.5 million private-sector jobs were created.* In other words, more than one job was

---

*The net result is 1.4 million fewer jobs over the decade, although if I had picked a decade beginning in a recession and ending in a boom the net picture would look cheerier.

destroyed for every man, woman and child in the United States over the course of the decade, and roughly the same number was created: the churn of jobs in the economy is colossal. Each of the 338.9 million times somebody lost a job, that person was entitled to sympathy and to help, whether or not foreign competition had anything to do with it. Trade or no trade, a healthy economy loses jobs all the time, and creates them as well.

But is globalisation a good thing?

It is one thing to say that trade makes countries like the United States richer. It is quite another to say that globalisation is a good thing. To do justice to all the arguments about globalisation would take an entire book. In a short chapter there is time to address two common complaints about globalisation. The first is that globalisation is bad for the planet; the second is that globalisation is bad for the world's poor.

We first need to be somewhat clearer about what globalisation means, without becoming too technical. Even leaving aside non-economic phenomena such as the spread of American television, Indian cooking and Japanese martial arts, there is plenty to international economic integration besides trade. I would list at least five distinct issues: trade of goods and services; migration of people; the exchange of technical knowledge; 'foreign direct investment', or building or buying factories and companies abroad; and cross-border investments in financial assets like shares and bonds.

Many discussions of globalisation confuse all these. At the risk of oversimplification, let me set three to one side: migration, exchange of technology and cross-border investments in financial assets. This is not because they are unimportant, but because they are not what people tend to think of when they talk about globalisation. Migration is controversial for other reasons; generally, xenophobia and selfishness. On the other hand, few object to the spread of peaceful scientific and technical know-how. Cross-border investments in financial assets are the subject of considerable technical debate among economists; they are a great opportunity for both rich and poor but an opportunity that brings dangers.* For the sake of space, we shall say no more about these three trends.

For most purposes, when people argue about globalisation they are talking about the two trends that remain: more trade, and more direct investment by companies from rich countries, such as building factories in poor countries. A substantial proportion of foreign investment in poor countries is designed to produce goods for shipment back to rich countries; while this remains true, trade and foreign investment will be closely linked together. Foreign investment is widely recognised to be good for economic growth in poor countries: it is an excellent way for them to create jobs, learn cutting-edge techniques and do so without having to invest their own scarce money. Unlike investments in shares, currency or bonds, foreign direct investment cannot quickly be reversed in a panic. As economics journalist Martin Wolf puts it, 'factories do not walk'.

Although trade with and investment in poor countries has risen rapidly in recent years, we should be clear that both trade and foreign investment overwhelmingly take place between the richest countries, not between rich and poor. People look at their Nike shoes and assume, perhaps, that everything is made in Indonesia and China. However, far more money is spent importing wine

---

*I wrote this sentence in 2002. In the wake of the financial crisis, forgive my understatement.

from Australia, pork from Denmark, beer from Belgium, insurance from Switzerland, computer games from Britain, cars from Japan and computers from Taiwan, all carried on ships from South Korea. These rich countries are mostly trading with each other. Mighty China, with 20 per cent of the world's population, produced less than 10 per cent of the world's exports in 2009; the impressive thing about Chinese exports is not so much their absolute size but the fact that they have grown so quickly. Mexico, a country of over 100 million people, in a free trade agreement with the world's largest economy, the United States, exported less than gallant little Belgium in 2009. Meanwhile India, despite well over a billion citizens, gained a 1 per cent share of world exports for the first time in the modern world only in 2006. These figures are for physical merchandise: if you look at trade in commercial services, fuss over 'offshoring' notwithstanding, many developing countries participate even less. India is an exception, but was still responsible for less than 2.7 per cent of world services exports in 2008.

What about the very poor countries? Sadly for them, rich countries trade very little with them – and as trade expands elsewhere in the world, the poorest countries are largely limited to trading commodities. The wealthy OECD (Organisation for Economic Co-operation and Development) sourced only 0.8 per cent of its imports from the least developed countries in 2008. (The figure was 0.6 per cent in 1988 and 0.5 per cent in 1998, which suggests that the number is rising and falling with the price of oil.) For the really poor countries, their problem certainly isn't excessive participation in the world trading system. A similar story holds true for foreign investment.

The theory of comparative advantage, common sense and experience all tell us that trade is good for economic growth; foreign direct investment is closely related to trade, and it, too, is good for growth. The poorest countries miss out on those benefits. This is a simplification but a fair one. In both cases, though, questions remain: what is the effect of trade and foreign investment on the environment? And what is the effect of foreign investment in poor countries on those who have to accept so-called sweatshop jobs, poorly paid jobs in awful conditions?

Globalisation is green

Take the environment first. We saw in Chapter 4 that the economist's concept of externalities gives us a powerful tool to appreciate the risks of environmental damage, and externality charges give us a solution. Many – perhaps most – economists understand the risks of environmental damage and want action to preserve the environment.

But the link between trade and environmental damage just doesn't stand up to close scrutiny. There are three reasons for concern. The first concern is of a 'race to the bottom': companies rush overseas to produce goods under cheaper, more lenient environmental laws, while hapless governments oblige them by creating those lenient laws. The second is that physically moving goods around inevitably consumes resources and causes pollution. The third worry is that if trade promotes economic growth, it must also harm the planet. While each has some initial plausibility, the idea that trade is bad for the environment is based on weak thinking and little evidence.

The first worry, that free trade causes environmental problems because goods produced overseas are subject to more lenient environmental standards, or no standards at all, should first be qualified by reminding ourselves that the overwhelming majority of trade is between rich countries, who have similar environmental standards. But what about investment in poor countries?

The environmentalist Vandana Shiva speaks for many when she declares that 'pollution moves from the rich to the poor. The result is a global environmental apartheid.' Strong words – but are they true?

In theory, they might be true. Companies that can produce goods more cheaply will be at a competitive advantage. They can also move around more easily in a world of free trade. So the 'race to the bottom' is a possibility. After the first edition of this book went to press, a research paper in the *Journal of International Development* was published with a statistical analysis of pollution and foreign direct investment. The authors concluded that there was some evidence that foreign direct investment into middle-income countries causes a rise in pollution.

Yet the idea that globalisation is a major cause of increased pollution is implausible. Environmental regulations are not a major cost; labour is. If American environmental standards are really so strict, why do the most pollution-intensive American firms spend only 2 per cent of their revenues on dealing with pollution? Most spend much less: perhaps 0.5 or 0.6 per cent of revenues on average. When companies move abroad they are seeking cheap labour, not a pollution haven. And companies do not pollute for fun; the latest manufacturing techniques are often cheaper and less polluting at the same time. Energy efficiency, for instance, saves money and reduces pollution. This is why many companies regard environmental performance as part of general quality control and good efficient manufacturing. Even if it was possible to save some costs by cutting environmental corners, many firms build factories everywhere in the world using the same latest, cleanest technology from the developed world, simply because that kind of standardisation itself saves costs. As an analogy: if ten-year-old computer chips were still produced in bulk, they would be simpler and cheaper to make than modern chips, but nobody

Does globalisation cause pollution?
Air quality and net foreign direct investment in China

Source: UN Environment Program http://geodata.grid.unep.ch/ and
http://databank.worldbank.org/2010.

Protected agriculture is intensive
Agricultural protection and use of fertilisers in agriculture

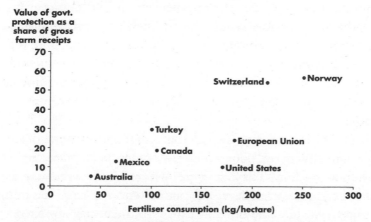

Iceland (58%, 3467 kg and New Zealand (0.67%, 1147 kg) are not shown due to scale

Source: OECD Agriculture and Fisheries database; http://databank.worldbank.org

bothers any more. It's now hard to buy an old computer even if you want to. And these arguments leave aside the possibility that firms want to offer high environmental standards to please their workers and their customers.

So ... a 'race to the bottom' is possible in theory; but there are also good grounds for doubting its significance in practice. Foreign investment in rich countries is far more likely to go into polluting industries than foreign investment in poor countries. Foreign investment in polluting industries is also the fastest-growing segment of foreign investment coming into the United States. In contrast, foreign investment in clean industries is the fastest-growing segment of American investments abroad. In other words, foreigners are bringing dirty industries to the United States, but American companies are bringing clean industries to the world.

You may have blinked a little when you read that last paragraph. To those brought up on a diet of environmentalist guilt, those statistics seem insane. They are not so insane when you consider that poor countries produce goods like clothes, children's toys and coffee, while the seriously polluting industries like bulk chemical production require high levels of skill, reliable infrastructure and – since a lot of capital investment is involved – political stability. Why jeopardise that by moving the plant to Ethiopia to save a few dollars on environmental costs?

Another indicator of the environmental performance of foreign investment in poor countries comes from measures of pollution in China. The first figure on page 249 shows how, as the Chinese economy has developed, air pollution in China has been reduced. At the same time, foreign investment has exploded as foreign firms build factories in China, either to cater for the Chinese market or to take advantage of cheaper labour and export to the rest of the world. Brazil and Mexico have shown very similar patterns.

This is not to give foreign investment all the credit. As China has grown richer, the government has imposed tighter environmental restrictions at the same time that foreign investment has arrived.

While there is no room for complacency, the overall picture does not match the scare stories of a 'race to the bottom'. Even if there was some increase in pollution in globalising middle-income countries, that needs to be set against the benefits of gender equality, better schooling, and longer life expectancy that are strongly correlated with higher income. Overall, the protectionist hype about the 'race to the bottom' is much stronger than the evidence for it, meaning protection for established industries at the expense of customers and the developing world alike.

The truth is that protectionism itself can have tremendous environmental costs. The most obvious case: the splendidly 'multifunctional' Common Agricultural Policy in the European Union, a package of trade barriers and subsidies designed to protect European farmers. To its defenders, multifunctionality is supposed to convey self-sufficiency, security, environmental performance and a fair deal for poor farmers. But instead, the policy subsidises farmers in the European Union to the tune of almost half the Union budget, with the largest quarter of the farms getting over two-thirds of this, for example, the third richest man in the UK, the Duke of Westminster, received over 6.5 million euros in farming subsidies between 1999 and 2009. The Queen has received even more, and almost 800,000 euros in 2009 alone.

Generally the Common Agricultural Policy encourages intensive farming with the obvious results of poor food quality and high use of pesticides and fertilisers, and all the while dumps food on the developing world and depresses the prices received by farmers in poor countries. Into the bargain it is helping to derail the current round of world trade liberalisation – although there are many other parties to blame for that. As Martin Wolf commented in the *Financial Times*: 'This is a multifunctional policy indeed: regressive, wasteful, damaging to food quality and the environment and an obstacle to trade liberalisation everywhere.'

Other rich nations, especially Japan and South Korea, privilege their farmers the same way as the European Union: almost a quarter of the typical OECD farm's revenue comes from government support, and as the second figure on page 249 shows, the more agriculture is subsidised, the more fertilisers it consumes. If the Common Agricultural Policy and other examples of agricultural protectionism were abolished, there is little doubt that the world's environment would be substantially improved as the intensity of farming could be reduced. At the same time, both European consumers and third-world farmers would get a much better deal.

The United States provides less subsidy for its farmers, but it can still lay on trade protection and cause environmental damage when it has to. In 1998, domestic sugar producers enjoyed a $1-billion subsidy, half of which went to just seventeen farms. Because of the distortions caused by protection, this cost consumers nearly $2 billion, half of which was pure waste. (Fortunately the situation has improved since then: the subsidy was $470 million in 2009, down by two thirds since a peak in 1999.) The protection has damaged sugar producers in Colombia, who have turned to producing cocaine instead. Of course, the environmental lobby might still approve if the environment was benefiting, but it is not: chemical run-off from the intensive farms in southern Florida is damaging the Everglades.

Intensive farming is an unusually clear-cut case. Not all environmental problems will be automatically solved by free trade.

One example is the tendency to monoculture: growing only rice, only coffee or only wheat. This lack of biodiversity renders crops more vulnerable to pests and to fluctuations in the weather.

That might seem like an argument against free trade, since increased trade encourages countries to specialise in single crops for which they have a competitive advantage. But trade barriers are a terrible way to deal with the problem of intensive farming. First, local biodiversity and global biodiversity are both important, but national biodiversity is irrelevant: environmental problems do not notice political boundaries. To the extent that lack of biodiversity is a problem, the solution is direct environmental regulation: the keyhole economics of Chapter 5. Hoping that a trade barrier will fix the problem is ludicrous.

This is a special case of another important piece of trade theory. There will always (in theory) and usually (in practice) be an alternative policy, which will fix the environmental problem more directly and efficiently than any trade barrier. Jagdish Bhagwati, an eminent trade theorist, comments in this context that 'You cannot kill two birds with one stone.' Trade barriers are a clumsy and damaging way to pursue worthwhile objectives, like a healthy environment.

Transport costs are another instance of Bhagwati's principle. Again, it seems superficially attractive to restrict international trade to cut down on the pollution caused by container ships and freight airplanes. Yet, again, direct regulation in the form of an externality charge is the solution. Trade barriers attack the transport of goods across borders: but there is nothing especially environmentally damaging about crossing a border. The transport costs of moving a CD player from Osaka harbour to the port of Los Angeles are less than the transport costs of moving it from the port of Los Angeles across to Arizona, or even into a branch of Best Buy in Los Angeles itself. The transport costs of somebody then driving to Best Buy and back home with the CD player are often higher still, when the true environmental costs of congestion and pollution are figured in. Just because goods are moved within countries, or even quite locally, doesn't mean that the environmental costs of transporting them are small. Again, the Undercover Economist has to recommend policies that attack the problem directly: an externality charge would encourage the use of cleaner methods of transport, whether within or between countries.

The final concern, then, is that trade is not bad in its own right but because it leads to environmentally damaging economic growth: that is, trade makes people richer, and this will damage the environment. This claim is worth some attention.

The most deadly and certain environmental problems of today – and possibly the most serious of the future, even given the threat of climate change – are also those that afflict the very poorest people in the world. One example is domestic pollution from wood-burning stoves, which causes blindness and fatal respiratory conditions. Another example is unsafe drinking water, which kills millions. The cure for these environmental problems is economic growth, and trade can help.

Other pollutants, such as airborne particulates emitted from cars, do get worse as people get richer – for a while. Typically, this pollution becomes less serious after people earn around $5000 a head (as in Mexico), because at this point they are rich enough to afford improved environmental standards, and they will demand them. Trade helps both indirectly, by boosting growth, and directly, because free trade in poorer countries has been associated with the end of subsidies to heavily polluting prestige industries such as petrochemicals and steel as well as the import of new, cleaner technologies.

It is true that energy consumption, and with it carbon dioxide emissions and the threat of climate change, do increase long after people reach $5000 a head. It seems likely, although we do not know for sure, that the richest countries in the world are just reaching the point where even energy consumption per head is about to stop rising. After all, our cars and domestic appliances get more efficient every year, and when we all have two cars and a large air-conditioned house, it's hard to see where extra energy demand will come from.

If we are honest, then, the argument that trade leads to economic growth, which leads to climate change, leads us to a stark conclusion: we should cut our trade links to make sure that the Chinese, Indians and Africans stay poor. The question is whether any environmental catastrophe, even severe climate change, could possibly inflict the same terrible human cost as keeping three or four billion people in poverty. To ask that question is to answer it.

Does this mean that we are doomed to choose between mass starvation and environmental Armageddon? Not at all. There is plenty we can do to aid the environment without using the counterproductive method of restricting trade. Externality taxes have already cut sulphur emissions in the United States (and more direct regulations have done so in China, too). They could also be used to cut carbon dioxide emissions and fight climate change; if we demanded the commitment from our leaders, this could be done. It might not even be that expensive. We could make a start by stopping outright subsidies of fossil fuels; Germany, a country fond of its green credentials and a firm supporter of international efforts to fight climate change, spends tens of thousands of euros per coal miner protecting its coal industry from international competition. (It has recently passed a law to phase out such subsidies by 2018. Fingers crossed.)

What, really, are we to make of the environmentalist attack on free trade? We've seen that the race to the bottom is modest if it is happening at all; that polluting industries are still based in rich countries, rather than poor countries; that environmental standards are rising in China, Brazil and Mexico, the major destinations for foreign investment into poor countries; that protectionist measures such as those on farming, steel and coal, which sometimes claim environmental justifications in fact are tremendously harmful to the environment; that taxes on transport fuels are consistent with free trade and much better for the environment than trade restrictions; and that the worst environmental problems, at least of today, are caused by poverty not wealth. The environmentalist movement should be manning the barricades to demand global free trade immediately. One day, perhaps they will.

Sweatshops, or, is trade good for the poor?

Nice running shoes! But don't they make you feel a little, well, guilty?

A number of multinational companies have been accused of subjecting workers in developing countries to poor working conditions. For example, Nike has been a frequent target of campaigners. To consider just one particularly splendid example, an enterprising student at MIT named Jonah Peretti took advantage of Nike's offer to create customised shoes. In his own words:

> Confronted with Nike's celebration of freedom and their statement that if you want it done right, build it yourself, I could not help but think of the people in crowded factories in Asia and South America who actually build Nike shoes. As a challenge to Nike, I ordered a pair of shoes customized with the word 'sweatshop.'

Even economists think this is pretty funny. Nike did not; Jonah Peretti did not get his customised shoes.

Jonah Peretti and his sympathisers have rightly drawn attention to the fact that in developing countries workers endure terrible working conditions. Hours are long. Wages are pitiful. But sweatshops are the symptom, not the cause, of shocking global poverty. Workers go there voluntarily, which means hard as it is to believe – that whatever their alternatives are, they are worse. They stay there, too; turnover rates of multinational-owned factories are low, because conditions and pay, while bad, are better than those in factories run by local firms. And even a local company is likely to pay better than trying to earn money without a job: running an illegal street stall, working as a prostitute or combing reeking landfills in cities like Manila to find recyclable goods. Manila's most famous landfill, Smokey Mountain, was closed down in the 1990s because it had become such an embarrassing symbol of poverty. But other rubbish dumps continue to support scavengers who can earn up to £3 a day. Over 130 people were killed in a landslide at Payatas, another dump in Manila, in July 2000. Even those ways of eking out an urban living are attractive compared with scraping an existence in rural areas. In Latin America, for instance, while extreme poverty is relatively rare in cities, it is commonplace in the countryside. Anybody with a scrap of concern for other human beings should be disgusted at the situation, but they should also recognise that multinational companies are not its cause.

The solution to this poverty is not going to come by boycotting shoes and clothes made in developing countries. On the contrary, as countries like South Korea have opened up to multinational companies, slowly but surely they have become richer. As more multinational companies have set up factories, they have competed with each other for workers with the best skills. Wages have risen, not because the companies are generous but because they have no choice if they want to attract good workers. Local firms learn the latest production techniques and become big employers, too. It becomes more and more attractive for people to work in a factory and to acquire the necessary skills: education improves. People move away from the countryside, raising rural earnings for those who remain to a more tolerable level. Formal employment is easier to tax, so government revenues rise and infrastructure, health clinics and schools improve. Poverty falls, and wages inexorably rise. After adjusting for inflation, the typical South Korean worker earns five times more than his father did thirty-five years ago. South Korea is now a world technology leader and rich enough to subsidise the hell out of its agriculture like the rest of the rich countries in the world. The sweatshops have moved elsewhere.

It is difficult to be unmoved by conditions in sweatshops. The question is how to get rid of them. Most economists believe that sweatshops are good news in two ways: they are a step up from the immediate alternatives, and they are also a rung on the ladder to something better.

But plenty of people think otherwise. William Greider, a left-of-centre political commentator, praised New York's city council for passing a resolution in 2001 requiring that the city refuse to buy uniforms for police and firefighters unless they were produced under 'decent wages and factory conditions'. Such a resolution can only harm sweatshop labourers: they'll be out of a job and – literally, for those in Manila – back on the rubbish heap. Of course, it will be good news for textile workers in rich countries, who'll get the business instead. I doubt it is a coincidence that the city council resolution was drafted by UNITE, the Union of Needletrades, Industrial, and Textile Employees, exactly the people who would benefit if imports of textile goods decreased.

The power of special-interest groups

Harry Truman is credited with the request for a one-handed economist, who would be unable to give advice and then say, 'on the other hand'; Ronald Reagan, who always had better speech-writers, once said that there should be a version of trivial pursuit for economists 'with one hundred questions and three thousand answers'.

True enough, economists don't always agree. But it is a rare economist who will not be enthusiastic about the merits of free trade. The near universal opinion among economists is that global free trade would be a great advance, and that even if other countries refuse to lower trade barriers we would be idiots not to lower our own.

Economists estimate that the benefits of free trade are enormous. For example, when Japan was forced by the United States to open its ports to trade in the 1850s, following decades of isolation, it began to export silk and tea to an eager world market, in exchange for cotton and woollen clothes, which were cheap internationally but expensive in Japan. As a result its national income increased by two-thirds.

The Uruguay round of trade negotiations, which reduced trade barriers across the world from 1994, is estimated to have increased world income by roughly $100 billion. If tariffs on agricultural and industrial goods, and services, were reduced by a third, there would be a further gain of $600 billion – about 2 per cent of world income. Removal of all trade barriers would deliver over 6 per cent of world income. These numbers, collected by the economist Douglas Irwin, are likely to be underestimates of the benefits, because they include only the most straightforward gains of bringing cheaper goods from world markets into protected markets: that is, the straightforward application of David Ricardo's theory of comparative advantage. Other advantages are likely, since, contrary to popular belief that trade is the friend of the multinational, free trade also destroys the scarcity power of big firms by subjecting them to international competition. It encourages the use of new ways of working and better technology. Some people even think it promotes peace by giving trading nations powerful reasons not to go to war with each other.

If free trade really has so many benefits, why does the world still have so many trade barriers? Why don't politicians grab easy votes by lowering trade barriers? Why did the Japanese have to be *forced* to implement a policy that almost doubled the country's income? Unfortunately, in most countries, rich and poor, special-interest groups with disproportionate influence have reasons to oppose free trade.

Tariffs tend to impose a small and disguised cost on most of the country, in the form of higher prices, and a further cost on foreigners, who do not have a vote. The benefits of the tariffs are substantial for a narrowly concentrated group of people, often sectors with organised unions and large businesses. If voters are well informed and fully understand economic theory, then in a democracy the protectionists will be voted down. But if people are not well informed about the costs of tariffs imposed on them, then given the small effect on any particular voter of any particular tariff, the tariff may not even enter their thoughts – especially if the campaign for trade restrictions is disguised as a campaign about sweatshops. Reform efforts may also be stymied by inertia and nervousness on the part of these poorly informed voters, while the special-interest groups are well aware that they stand to gain from protection and find it worthwhile to devote substantial funds and lobbying effort to defend their narrow interests.

In a healthy democracy special interests should have less power than in a fragile democracy or an undemocratic country, like Cameroon. If special-interest groups are part of the explanation behind trade barriers, we might expect countries with better established democracies to have lower trade barriers.

The numbers tell us exactly that. In 2008, the United States had average tariffs of 1.49 per cent. In the European Union, average tariffs were 1.15 per cent. High-income countries in general averaged 1.76 per cent. In the giant economies of China and India, 3.9 per cent and 6.1 per cent respectively. We have already heard that the poverty and corruption of sad little Cameroon is not being relieved by tariffs averaging over 12.7 per cent.

It seems that even if we are able to pressure our politicians to do the right thing for everyone by reducing tariffs, an equal responsibility lies with the governments of these poor countries. Why do they maintain tariffs, which harm their citizens? Perhaps because international isolation is good for political stability. The world's longest-serving political leaders have been men such as Kim Jong Il, Robert Mugabe and Fidel Castro, none of whom have suffered political weakness as a result of their economic isolation. Saddam Hussein's rule seemed stronger than ever after a decade of sanctions: it was external force, not internal change, that removed him. Myanmar and North Korea are international pariahs with frustratingly stable governments.

This explains why the Japanese had to be forced to liberalise and vastly increase the country's income. The policy of isolation was not designed for the good of the Japanese people but for the good of their rulers, the Tokugawa clan. Historian Janet Hunter concludes:

Mechanisms of political control were backed up by a harsh system of regulation, which attempted to minimize all social, political and economic change among the population at large ... Potentially damaging foreign influences were minimized after 1640 by cutting off the country from virtually all contact with the outside world.

While these careful measures succeeded in preserving Tokugawa rule for some two and a half centuries, they could never hope to prevent all social, economic and political change ... The reopening of foreign contacts with the United States and the imperialist powers of Europe rapidly brought matters to crisis point ... From 1853 [during] the crisis over US demands for formal relations ... Tokugawa authority went rapidly downhill.

Special-interest groups have tried to define the trade policy of the United States, with varying success. Tariff barriers have to be approved by Congress, and congressional representatives defend the interests of their own constituents, demanding protection of farming in Iowa, steel in Pennsylvania, sugar in Florida or car manufacturing in Michigan. By trading votes with each other they could get tariff after tariff passed, and if the president came back from some trade negotiation with a treaty in his hand reducing trade barriers, they would refuse to ratify it.

Presidents tend to be more enthusiastic supporters of free trade because they need votes from the whole nation, and so would be relatively less likely to favour locally concentrated protectionism. Sure enough, after 1934, when President Roosevelt persuaded Congress to grant him and future presidents rolling pre-approval for trade treaties, tariff rates in the United States fell from about 45 per cent to about 10 per cent in two decades. Now that the president has responsibility for trade policy, they have been falling ever since.

Of course, presidents are not totally immune from special-interest politics: the importance of Florida's vote in recent presidential elections guarantees protection of sugar producers at the expense of the nation. No political system is perfect, but democracies tend to favour trade more than others, because lowering trade barriers is good for the ordinary person.

How can we make things better for the poor?

You will have gathered by now that I am a big fan of both coffee and beer. My favourite coffee comes from Timor. My favourite beer comes from Belgium. My life is much happier because of the Timorese coffee pickers and the Belgian brewers. I hope that I have done enough to persuade you that their lives are happier because of me. A fundamental characteristic of the kinds of social interactions that economists usually study is that … everybody wins.

Unfortunately, some win much more than others. I am doing well, and so are the Belgians. The Timorese are not. They would be doing worse if it were not for trade, but that is not enough for us to relax and forget about them.

Coffee growers are poor because they have no scarcity power. There are many places where coffee can be grown. Growing mass-market coffee requires hard work but little skill. No individual coffee grower has any power to affect the market price. Even if countries can act in unison, they have no scarcity power: when the top coffee producers attempted to set up a cartel controlling two-thirds of world coffee production, the Association of Coffee Producing Countries, it failed and shut down. Whenever the cartel succeeded in raising prices, new farmers in new countries quickly found it attractive to start growing coffee. Vietnam is a great example. In the 1980s, coffee was hardly grown in the country at all, but now it is the world's second-largest producer of coffee. A cartel designed to exploit scarcity power can work only if new producers cannot easily enter the market.

We should not forget that one of the reasons it is so easy for poor farmers to produce coffee is that coffee does not grow in France or Florida, and so rich farmers are not interested in agitating for high tariffs. Unprocessed coffee is relatively free of trade barriers, so one further effect of trade barriers on beef and rice and grain is that farmers in poor countries are forced into niches like coffee, which cannot sustain all of them.

Because coffee is such an easy business to get into, I am willing to make a prediction: coffee farmers will never be rich until most people are rich. If coffee farmers became rich but other farmers or workers in sweatshops were poor, the others would switch to farming coffee. High coffee prices will always collapse, until workers in sweatshops become well-paid blue-collar workers in skilled manufacturing jobs, who don't find the idea of being even a prosperous coffee farmer attractive.

We need to understand that narrowly focused initiatives on 'fair trade coffee' or 'sweatshop-free clothes' will never make a substantial improvement to the lives of millions. Some, like the campaign to prevent New York City from buying uniforms from poor countries, will actively cause damage. Others, like the numerous brands of fair trade coffee, are likely to improve the income of a few coffee producers without causing a great deal of harm. But they cannot fix the basic problem: too much coffee is being produced. At the slightest hint that coffee farming will become an attractive profession, it will always be swamped with desperate people who have no alternative. The truth of the matter is that only broad-based development of poor countries will ever lift the living standards of the very poor, increase coffee prices and improve wages and labour standards in shoe factories.

Can such broad-based development happen? Undoubtedly. Billions of people in the developing world are much richer than their parents were. Life expectancy and education are improving, even in countries that are not getting richer. This is only partly because of free trade; there is far more to the story. For a developing economy to grow strongly, many different reforms have to be put in place. There is one country in the world that has done this for more people, more quickly and from a worse starting point than any in history. It is where we shall finish our journey.

10

How China Grew Rich

'My God,' I said.

It was 2003. I was standing with my wife in Renmin Gongyuan, the People's Park, in the middle of Shanghai. Renmin Gongyuan is the Central Park of the twenty-first century. It gave me the same dizzying rush as my first visit to Manhattan. Walking out into the space of the park allowed us to feel the full visual impact of Shanghai's skyscrapers. One was a modern-day Chrysler building, with a striking crown of four mirrored tines meeting at a perfect point; the entire tower was rotated forty-five degrees around its axis so that the top forty floors sat at a diagonal to the bottom forty. Another building boasted a vast glass atrium hanging suspended sixty floors above the city. Not every design was in the best of taste: one had a domed penthouse that looked like it had been stolen from the set of a 1950s flying-saucer movie. There must have been thirty skyscrapers, half a dozen of which were on an incredible scale. All of them were brand new.

'My God,' said Fran.

'When were you last in Shanghai?'

'Ten years ago.'

'How many of these buildings were up ten years ago?'

She thought for a moment. 'You see that one?'

'The boxy forty-storey office building over there?'

'No. That one just beneath it.' She was pointing to a twelve-storey red-brick building, dwarfed on every side by more modern constructions.

'I see. Yes.'

'That was the tallest one standing ten years ago.'

'My God,' I said.

The ambition of it all was simply exhilarating. In just a decade, the builders of Shanghai had put up a fair imitation of Manhattan. What New Yorkers would have made of it, I don't know. It made us Londoners feel like country bumpkins.

Yet it could all have been so different. For most of the twentieth century, China was poorer than Cameroon. In 1949, when the People's Republic of China came into being, the world's largest country was torn by civil war and ruled by a communist dictatorship. In the late 1950s, millions of people died in a famine induced by the failed policies of the government. In the 1960s, the university system was destroyed by the Cultural Revolution, when millions of educated citizens were forcibly relocated to work in the countryside. After all this, how did China become the greatest economic success story in history?

Two farming revolutions

A visit to Shanghai is enough to provoke the question. Clues to the answer can be found all over China. I picked up several of them on a train to the inland Chinese city of Zhengzhou.

The train itself was the first clue: it was more comfortable, faster and more punctual than those back in England. China's road and rail network appeared to be in superb condition. Second, the Chinese seemed to have an excellent education system – I was soundly but politely thrashed at chess by a PhD in economics, a young man who had never been outside China but who spoke mildly and thoughtfully in good English. Third, although the train was packed, there were few children and no large families. China's 'one child family' policy has created a society where women have time to work and where the bulk of people are neither old nor young but in middle age, saving for the future. Those vast savings have provided the investment money for the roads, the trains and more. At the minimum China clearly had the human resources, infrastructure and financial capital required by traditional models of economic growth. Yet it did not always seem as though these resources would be well used; we already know that without the right incentives they will be wasted.

Under Mao, that waste was legendary. China's initial development efforts were two-pronged: massive investment in heavy industry such as steel, plus application of special agricultural techniques to make sure that China's vast population was fed. The policy focus was understandable. China's northern provinces are rich in high-quality coal, which logically could provide the basis of an economic revolution. Coal, steel and heavy manufacturing had been the basis of the industrial revolution in the leading economies: the United Kingdom, the United States and

Germany. Meanwhile, agriculture had to be a priority for any Chinese government because there was barely enough fertile land to feed the country's hundreds of millions of people. From the window of the train to Zhengzhou I was looking out over Henan, China's most densely populated province. It is a freezing desert.

This two-pronged push was called the 'Great Leap Forward'. It seemed to make sense, but it was the greatest economic failure the world has ever seen. Mao conducted economic policy on the hidden premise that if people tried hard, the impossible would happen. Zeal alone was sufficient. Villagers were ordered to build steel furnaces in their backyards but had no iron ore to put into them. Some villagers melted down good iron and steel – tools, even doorknobs – in order to meet the quotas demanded by the state. Even Mao's personal doctor worried about the wisdom of a policy to 'destroy knives to produce knives'. The steel that emerged from the furnaces was unusable.

If industrial policy was a farce, agricultural policy was a tragedy. The Great Leap Forward had already pulled many workers off the land to labour at the furnaces or in public works like dams and roads. Mao ordered the people to kill grain-eating birds, and the population of insect pests exploded as a result. Mao personally redesigned China's agricultural techniques, specifying closer planting and deeper sowing to increase yields. Rice planted so closely together could not grow, but party officials, anxious to please Mao, staged shows of agricultural and industrial success. When Mao travelled by train to admire the fruits of his policy, local officials built furnaces in strips along the railroad and brought rice from miles away to replant, at the officially specified density, in adjacent fields. Even this charade could not be maintained without the use of electric fans, which were used to circulate air and prevent the rice from rotting.

Crop yields fell, of course, but even this would not have been disastrous without the state's insistence that the policy was working. When the defence minister raised the issue of the famine in a ministerial meeting, he was punished and ordered to write a 'self-criticism'. Less powerful figures who denied that there was a surplus were tortured. While crops were failing, China doubled its exports of grain from 1958 to 1961 as a symbol of its success. In Henan province, across which we were travelling in comfort just forty-five years later, state grain stores contained enough food to provide for the people but remained shut because the official government position was that there was a grain surplus. Meanwhile, people starved to death outside in the snow. Some were left unburied, others were eaten by desperate family members; neither fate was uncommon.

Estimates of the death toll from the famine range from 10 million to 60 million people, roughly the entire population of England, or of California and Texas combined. Even Chinese government figures later acknowledged that 30 million people had died, although they blamed bad weather.

In the 'world of truth' described in Chapter 3, such disasters cannot happen. Mistakes, certainly, will be made – perhaps more frequently than under central planning. But the mistakes stay small; in market economies we call them 'experiments'. If venture capitalists back them, they do not expect many to succeed. When they succeed, they make some people rich and bring innovation to the whole economy. When they fail – which is more often than not – some people will go bankrupt, but nobody will die. Only command economies can promote experimentation on such a fatally extravagant scale and suppress informed criticism. (Mao was not alone. The Soviet president, Nikita Khrushchev, made a similar mistake following a visit to the United States, when he ordered Soviet fields to be replanted with the corn he had seen growing in Iowa. The failure was a catastrophe.) It is worth remembering that market failures, while sometimes serious, are never as tragic as the worst failures of governments like Mao's.

In 1976, after many more crimes against his own people, Mao died. After a short interregnum, he and his followers were replaced by Deng Xiaoping and his allies in December 1978. Just five years later, the change in China's economy was incredible. Agricultural output, always the headache of the Chinese planners, had grown by 40 per cent. Why? Because those planners had brought the 'world of truth' into China. As we discovered in Cameroon, incentives matter. Before 1978, China had some of the most perverse incentives in the world.

Before Deng took power, Chinese agriculture had been locally organised into collectives of twenty or thirty families. People were rewarded with 'work points', which were awarded according to the output of the collective as a whole. There was little opportunity for personal improvement either through extra effort or ingenuity. As a result there was little of either.

The government also purchased and redistributed food from regions that produced a surplus, but did so at a severely depressed price, discouraging more fertile regions from making the most of their agricultural land. Many rural workers were underemployed. The very system that was designed to boost China's agricultural output and make the nation self-sufficient was undermining it. China's output of grain, per person, was as low in 1978 as it had been in the mid-1950s, just before the Great Leap Forward.

Deng had little time for such folly and immediately embarked on a programme of reform, announcing that 'socialism does not mean poverty'. To improve agriculture, he had to get the incentives right. He started by raising the price paid by the state for crops by nearly a quarter. The price paid for surplus crops rose by more than 40 per cent, substantially increasing the incentive for fertile areas to produce more crops.

At the same time, a few collectives experimented with subcontracting land to individual households. Instead of clamping down, the government allowed the innovation to see whether it would work, just as a market economy allows small-scale experiments. Households who were renting land from collectives had every incentive to work hard and think of smarter ways of doing things because they were rewarded directly for their successes. Crop yields immediately increased. The experiment spread: just 1 per cent of collectives had used the 'household responsibility system' in 1979; by 1983 98 per cent had switched to the system.

These reforms were linked with a number of other pieces of liberalisation: the retail price of grain was allowed to rise, further increasing the incentive to produce what was needed. Restrictions on trade between regions were eased, so that each region could enjoy its comparative advantage. Production quotas were soon abandoned altogether.

The results were dramatic: agricultural output expanded by 10 per cent a year in the first half of the 1980s. More impressively still, more than half of the increase was attributable not to working harder or using more machinery but to more efficient farming and harvesting methods. Much of that productivity increase was directly attributable to the abandonment of the collective system. In the five years following the reforms, the average real income of farmers doubled. It was not Mao but Deng, by using the power of markets and prices, who had achieved the great leap forward.

All these statistics are best understood by thinking back to Chapter 3 and the world of truth. Partly by accident, partly by benign neglect and partly by design, Deng introduced the world of truth to Chinese agriculture. Those who had good ideas, good luck and who worked hard prospered. Bad ideas were quickly abandoned. Good ones spread rapidly. Farmers grew more cash crops and devoted less effort to crops that were difficult to grow;

all of this was the unsurprising result of introducing a price system. China had begun to travel along the so-called capitalist road.

Such a journey cannot be completed on rice alone. The success of the agricultural reforms created the momentum and popular support for Deng to continue. Attention needed to be turned to the rest of the economy – and to cities like Zhengzhou.

Investing for the future

Zhengzhou is not a stunning city like Shanghai. It is ugly and crowded and, despite being a major rail intersection, somewhat insular: we spent nearly a week in the Zhengzhou area without seeing a single foreign face. In its own way, though, Zhengzhou is as impressive as Shanghai. A city the size of London far from the Western world, affectionately described by our guidebook as 'a sprawling paradigm of ill-conceived town planning', Zhengzhou at least demonstrates that China's economic revolution has spread beyond the coastal provinces. Forty-storey high-rises loom solidly over the enormous train station; there are plenty of modern banks, huge department stores and hotels and brutal concrete overpasses. Advertising is everywhere.

To construct such buildings, railways and roads requires an enormous investment. Economists have a label for the roads and factories, homes and office buildings which result from investment: they call such constructions 'capital', and all sustained development needs capital. Capital can come from private investors, both domestic and foreign, who hope to recoup profits, or it can come from the government, either by taxing people and investing the proceeds, or by a programme of compulsory saving.

Common sense suggests that if you want to be richer tomorrow than you are today, you should invest money rather than spending it on goods and services to be enjoyed immediately. You could invest it in an education, in a house or in a bank account. Either way, if you consume less today and invest the money, you will be richer tomorrow – if the investments are good ones. (Building blast furnaces in the back garden will not do. Neither will building a library with a leaky roof.)

An unmysterious chunk of the development of countries is based on the same simple principle that saving and investing today makes you richer tomorrow. Savings rates have been very high in the fast-growing economies of the Pacific Rim. However, that is not the whole story, as we learned in Chapter 8. A market economy cannot simply decide to save and invest more. Most people don't bother saving in Cameroon: they have few ways to recoup investments in basic infrastructure like roads, and little confidence that they will be allowed to do so if they build factories or shops. The few exceptions, such as the mobile-phone sector, which can be funded by pay-as-you-go cards, have been the stunning successes you might expect. Many poor economies seek foreign investment but cannot even retain the confidence of their own citizens, who are eager to invest money overseas. Small wonder that savings rates are low, and the percentage of those savings invested inside Cameroon lower still. Without offering a secure environment for investment, the Cameroonian government can do little to encourage it.

China's socialist government had no problem with access to capital. While a market economy cannot simply decide to save and invest more, a socialist economy can and usually does. Capital came from government programmes; almost all saving was done either by the government or by state-owned corporations. In both cases money was being taken out of the pockets of individuals and invested on their behalf. There was plenty of capital available, too: about a third of national income was saved rather than consumed, roughly twice as much as in Cameroon.

Initially, China was able to get fairly good returns out of this capital. In the early 1950s, when the main task was to rebuild essential infrastructure and industry, every 100 yuan invested added 40 yuan to China's annual output, an impressive return. This should not be surprising. The tasks facing the Chinese government were clear enough: in particular, what had been broken during the war and the revolution needed to be fixed. All that was needed was for the government to give the orders.

The trouble came later. Even setting aside the chaos of the Great Leap Forward and the Cultural Revolution, the Chinese state found itself increasingly unable to get value out of its investments. By the time Mao died in 1976, every 100 yuan invested was adding only 18 yuan to China's annual output. This was less than half as efficient as two decades before. Given that the government and state enterprises were, between them, investing such a large chunk of the nation's income, this reduction in the efficiency of investment was a crippling waste.

A sympathetic observer might conclude that it was inevitable that after the obvious investments had been made, returns would fall. This might be true for a cutting-edge economy like Japan or the United States, but in 1976 China was still desperately poor. Few people had cars, telephones, electricity or running water. In such a poor country, the right investments can achieve very high returns by providing such basics of modern life. There was plenty of effective investment to be made, but the state didn't know how to make it.

As long as it was obvious what to order people to make or to build or to grow, this didn't matter much. But as the population grew, technology advanced and long-demanded investments were made, the communist economies slipped further and further away from the memory of the price system. Real market economies change quickly. In South Korea, 80 to 90 per cent of workers, land and capital were working or being used for different purposes in the 1970s than they had been in 1960 – in 1960, agricultural output was 45 per cent of the economy and manufacturing output less than 10 per cent. By the early 1970s, the manufacturing sector was larger than the agricultural sector. More importantly, within those sectors, workers were training and retraining, firms were starting up and closing down. South Korea's export industries used to make toys and underwear, but now they make memory chips and cars. If, in 1975, a planner for the South Korean government had tried to run the economy on outdated information from 1960, the result would have been a catastrophe. Fortunately, nobody did. Such folly was left to the North Koreans. Command economies from North Korea to the Soviet Union to China simply lacked the information necessary to keep making the right choices.

Unlike Cameroon, where individuals and companies have little incentive to invest, Maoist China had no problem with incentives – after all, the leaders had the power of life and death over their followers. But incentives alone are not enough. Chapter 3 showed that the world of truth created by markets produces good outcomes not just because it provides incentives, but because it generates information about the costs and benefits of all kinds of goods and services through the price system. The socialist systems of the Soviet Union and China provided the strongest incentives imaginable, but not the information necessary to use them correctly. Rather than responding to demand from world markets, like the South Koreans did, the Chinese responded to demands from Mao: plant crops more closely, kill birds, melt down your tools to make new tools.

To get any value out of the vast sums of investment capital available, the Chinese government began a gradual shift to a market system. Where successful agricultural reforms had paved the way, more complex and far-reaching reforms of the whole economy were to follow. Fifteen years after Deng came to power, returns on investment had quadrupled: for every 100 yuan invested, China's annual output grew by 72 yuan: each investment paid for itself after just 500 days. Nor was this because the government had scaled back its investment and was cherry-picking only the very best projects. Quite the reverse: investment levels were even higher than in the 1970s. It's small wonder the economy grew spectacularly. But how were the high returns to investment achieved?

Growing out of the plan

Like the Soviet bloc economies, China's industrial sector was controlled by planners. The plan specified, for instance, that a particular steel mill would produce a defined quantity of steel, that that steel would then be used for certain specified purposes and that a standard quantity of coal (0.8 tons of coal were said to be required for each ton of steel) would be delivered to the steel mill in order to make production possible, and so on. The calculations required were tremendously complex, even presuming that junior bureaucrats were supplying honest information about costs and quality. (Everybody had an incentive to claim that the machinery and materials they had to manage were insufficient and of poor quality, and to claim that nevertheless their output was vast and excellent. Without a world of truth, the real story was impossible to uncover.) But, leaving aside Mao's fatal utopian whims, such a system could work tolerably well for a time because each year the planners had the previous year's plan to guide them.

As the economy grew and changed, the process of adjusting output requirements and making wise capital investments became increasingly difficult: this is why the returns to capital in China were so much lower in 1976 than in the 1950s. A market system would have done much better, but it was no simple matter to create one. Markets do not work well without market-supporting institutions: in a market economy, people need banks for commercial loans, contract law to resolve disputes and confidence that their profits will not be confiscated. Such institutions cannot be set up overnight. Meanwhile, many workers in a socialist economy are engaged in unproductive activities and might simply starve unless the adjustment process was phased in or they received some kind of compensation. The problems were most acute for the industrial sector of the economy because it was most closely tied into the plan system, was the vehicle the government used to generate savings and was the source of most government investment.

Had Deng decided simply to abandon the plan and switch to a market system overnight, the likely outcome would have been a scramble to establish property rights, the collapse of the financial sector (because many government-run banks had made loans that could never be repaid) and widespread unemployment, even starvation. It is conceivable that things might have worked out for the best quite quickly, but it is likely that they would not. (In the former Soviet Union in the 1990s, such 'shock therapy' resulted in economic collapse.)

What is more, such extreme reforms would have offended so many vested interests – including huge numbers of ordinary people – that they might have been politically impossible. Deng, who had been purged twice under Mao's chairmanship yet returned to lead the country, well understood the value of political credibility.

So Deng and like-minded reformers adopted a more tentative strategy. In 1985 the size of the 'plan' was frozen: the production levels specified by the government did not grow as the economy grew. Instead, state-owned firms were allowed to do as they wished with any extra production. Efficient coal manufacturers would find that efficient steel manufacturers wanted to buy extra coal to make extra steel, which would be sold on to efficient construction firms. Inefficient firms that tried to expand got nowhere.

This strategy turned out to work very well for several reasons. First, it was easy to understand, and the commitment to freeze the size of the plan was a credible one. Such a credible commitment was important: if the planners had constantly tried to expand and update the plan in the light of the information emerging from the fringe market, that market would quickly have ceased producing useful information. Plant managers, realising that any successful changes they made would quickly be absorbed into next year's plan, would have stuck to safe choices.

Second, because the plan was kept fixed, a certain stability was guaranteed. Workers who had jobs could keep them. Things were guaranteed not to get worse – but if growth resulted, there was the possibility that they could get better. Many people grabbed that possibility, preferring long hours and poor conditions in a textile factory, even if they had to travel thousands of miles from their families, to their previous occupation of scraping a living – or failing to do so – on the most marginal, arid farmland.

Third, the market operated exactly where it needed to: at the margin. Remember that marginal costs and marginal benefits are what really matter for the efficiency of an economy. Imagine the decision of a factory manager trying to decide whether to produce one extra ton of steel, from which he can keep the profits. If he knows the marginal cost (the cost of producing one extra ton) and the price he is offered is a market price (which reflects the benefits to someone else of one extra ton), then he will make the right decision: produce if the price is higher than the marginal cost. The output of the factory will be efficient.

Decisions about what happens to the rest of the steel are not important for whether the quantity of output is efficient. Nine tons out of ten could be produced and allocated in accordance with the plan, but it is the decision about the tenth ton that matters for efficiency.

What this meant was that efficient firms expanded to meet extra demand: an eleventh ton and a twelfth followed the tenth. That demand was coming from expanding sections of the economy, which really needed supply, rather than from the planners. Managers got to keep profits and reinvest them – and had an incentive to make sure that the investments were profitable.

Inefficient firms, by contrast, did not grow. As long as the government kept subsidising them through the plan (it gradually stopped doing so in the 1990s), they could still keep producing for ever; but since the Chinese economy was well over four times as big in 2003 as it had been when the plan was frozen in 1985, the relative importance of those firms shrank very quickly. The economy, quite literally, grew out of the plan.

Entry and scarcity power

We know that a market system limits the scarcity power of firms; most firms face competition, and sectors of the economy that are not very competitive tend to attract new competition over time. The competition and free entry of new firms, by limiting scarcity power, pushes powerfully towards efficient production, new ideas and consumer choice.

The Chinese reformers needed to encourage entry and limit scarcity without resorting to a dangerously unpredictable strategy of rapid liberalisation. They hoped to improve the performance of the state sector, introduce new public sector companies as competitors, gradually foster a private sector and slowly open up to international competition. If one source of competition didn't work out, there was always another. The most important competitors at first were local-government-owned 'township and village enterprises'. Despite the name they were often huge industrial monsters. Later, privately owned and foreign companies were allowed to set up and grow, too.

As late as 1992, only 14 per cent of industrial output was being produced by privately owned or foreign firms, while the state sector was responsible for nearly half of output. The output of local-government township and village enterprises made up most of the remainder. The Chinese economic miracle was not really about privatisation. What mattered was not who owned the companies, but that the companies were forced to compete in a relatively free market, driving down scarcity power and bringing in the information and incentives of the world of truth.

The effects are even measurable. Remember, way back in Chapter 1, we discovered that high profits were often a signal of scarcity power. If new entry and stronger competition were removing the scarcity power of state-owned firms, we would expect their profit rates to fall.

That is indeed what happened. Chinese firms in the 1980s had very high rates of profit: many sectors had profit rates of over 50 per cent (for a fairly competitive economy, you would expect not more than 20 per cent and often much less). Profits also varied a lot from sector to sector depending on the arbitrary pricing of the plan: the oil refining sector had a profit rate of almost 100 per cent, the iron mining sector just 7 per cent. In all cases, the government confiscated the profit and reinvested it.

As the economic reforms began to bite, profits started to fall; they also started to converge, as the most profitable sectors faced the fiercest competition from local government, private firms and foreign firms. During the 1990s, average profit rates fell by over a third; in the juiciest sectors they fell by at least a half. The effect of all this was to reduce waste, give Chinese customers better return for their money and make China a potential player on world markets. Scarcity power disappeared.

China and the world

There have been times in China's history when it has been an insular place. This is not one of them. Far from the coast in the inland cities of Xi'an and Zhengzhou we had no difficulty finding Coke, McDonald's, pool rooms and internet cafés. In Shanghai it was almost impossible to escape from familiar brand names.

Anyone who visited China in the early 1990s could tell you that this is all very new. But it's more than an anecdotal impression: the statistics tell the same story. As recently as 1990, China was a minnow on the global trading scene. The United States and Germany exported almost ten times as much. But in 2009, China became the largest exporter in the world; it is also the second-largest importer. This is no accident. The dramatic entry of China on to the world's economic stage has been one of the last acts of China's economic reform.

Why did China need the world? A country of over a billion people seems better placed than most to be self-sufficient. But China's economy was still tiny in 1978 – smaller than Belgium's –

and the reformers realised that engaging with the world could help. There were three advantages. First, China could tap into world markets for labour-intensive goods: toys, shoes and clothes. Second, the foreign currency these exports earned could be spent on raw materials and on new technology to develop the economy.

Finally, by inviting foreign investors in, the Chinese could learn modern production and business techniques from them – hugely important for a country that had been communist for decades. In 2009, China and Hong Kong managed to attract almost 40 per cent of all the foreign direct investment into the world's developing countries. (India, the other Asian giant, is finally starting to catch up, but is still well behind at 11 per cent.) As we discussed in Chapter 9, one advantage of such investment is that it supplies capital to an economy that cannot be instantly withdrawn if investors get nervous. This happened to China's neighbours in the Asian currency crisis of 1997, where purely financial investments like loans were rapidly withdrawn in a mass panic. The capital investment expands the future capacity of the economy, but as we have already seen, China did not need foreigners to supply capital. It was the expertise that really counted: expertise, for example, in quality control or in logistics.

American and Japanese firms made investments in transport and electronics, turning China into a high-technology manufacturer. You can see the effect of these investments in the statistics: China is now the largest producer of the majority of important consumer electronics; more than half the world's DVD players and digital cameras are now made in China. You can also see the effect while wandering around the country. Sitting on the buses around Zhengzhou, I was surrounded by people talking on high-tech gizmos that I'd never seen before, and which didn't arrive back home for months. The foreign investors who made the technology possible hope for a good return on their investments, but it is obvious to anyone that plenty of the money is staying with Chinese consumers.

Foreign investment has been a major factor in keeping China's reforms on track. Not only did foreign firms bring capital, and not only did they bring expertise and connections to the world economy, they also continued the competitive process of the earlier reforms by competing with China's domestic firms, driving them to continue improving their efficiency.

If foreign investment is such a boon for the economy, how did China do it? Luck plays a role. In contrast to Cameroon, the Chinese had a substantial and rapidly growing domestic market, always attractive to foreign investors. No Cameroonian leader, no matter how gifted, could copy this: fate dealt Cameroon a different hand. There was nothing lucky, however, about the Chinese commitment to education – one happy legacy of the communist years – which meant that by 1978 there was a huge reservoir of skilled and potentially productive workers, waiting to flood the economy with talent when the dam of the command economy burst. Cameroon's government was unable to do likewise, although it was scarcely poorer in the 1970s than it is today. But India also has a large and growing domestic market and a well-educated workforce, even though that education is less broadly available than in China; the statistics show, popular hysteria about outsourcing notwithstanding, that India has only recently begun to attract foreign investors at a scale its potential would seem to justify.

China had other natural advantages that India did not. The often-painful process of international economic engagement was made smoother and more effective because of mainland China's links with Hong Kong and Taiwan. Both were successful internationally integrated economies back in the days when China was very isolated from world markets, and despite the different economic systems there were close ties of family and friendship between businessmen in the three economies. These social ties helped compensate for problems in China's legal system in the early years of reform. China was (and still is) striving to improve the commercial framework of property rights and contract law, which all successful economies need. Without such a framework it is hard to do business with confidence. How can you trust that your business partners will not rip you off? How can you feel safe if local government officials can confiscate your profits or your property?

For entrepreneurs from Hong Kong and Taiwan, personal connections meant that they were often able to rely on promises with no legal basis. A formal contract would have been better, but a businessman's word could be good enough if the opportunity for profit was attractive.

In this case, it certainly was. There was a perfect fit between China and Hong Kong. Chinese firms, producing cheap goods but unused to international deals, tapped into the expertise of Hong Kong traders. Chinese exports to Hong Kong grew dramatically in the 1980s, and Hong Kong re-exported them to the world. Taiwan joined in during the 1990s. As the economist Dwight Perkins observed at the time, 'the formidable marketing talents of Hong Kong and Taiwan are being grafted onto the manufacturing capacity of the mainland'.

India lacked Hong Kong and Taiwan, but for many years also lacked any interest in welcoming foreigners. The noted Indian economist Jagdish Bhagwati described his own government's policies from the 1960s to the 1980s as 'three decades of illiberal and autarkic policies' – in other words, the government sat hard on the market and did its best to prevent trade and investment.

China, on the other hand, worked hard to attract foreign

investors and to make the most of the links with Hong Kong and its other neighbours. The plan was to create 'special economic zones', such as Shenzhen, where the normal rules of the command economy would not apply to foreign investors. At the same time, the infrastructure of the special economic zones could be improved quickly. That method perfectly complemented China's connections with Hong Kong, Macao and Taiwan: the zones were exclusively in Guandong Province, next to Hong Kong and Macao, and Fujian, next to Taiwan. Over half of all investment into China in 1990 came from the tiny country of Hong Kong, while Japan and the United States together supplied only a quarter. Further, almost half of all investment arrived in Guandong; Fujian was the second-largest recipient. The city of Shenzhen, across the border from Hong Kong, was a fishing village in 1980 when it became a special economic zone. Twenty years later property developers were pulling down skyscrapers mid-construction to start building bigger skyscrapers. The Chinese say, 'You'll think you're rich until you set foot in Shenzhen.'

Unfair and arbitrary as they were, the special economic zones worked well at attracting investors without turning the entire Chinese mainland upside down. They also provided a toehold for reforms to spread. Whenever the rules for foreign firms seemed to be working well, administrators started applying them to domestic firms within the zones. Then they started applying them to domestic firms outside the zones. Other coastal provinces looked at the booming economies of Fujian and Guandong and started to demand similar privileges. Unfair or quirky rules were straightened out as foreign investors protested at any special favours for domestic firms, while domestic firms circumvented special favours for foreign firms by laundering their money through Hong Kong and bringing it back as 'foreign investment'.

As so often with the rest of China's reform programme, good policies were copied and foolish ones died out quickly.

Epilogue: does the economy matter?

This chapter is called 'How China Grew Rich'. That's an exaggeration. China is not rich – yet. But it is growing richer faster than any country in history. There is no guarantee that the growth will continue – many observers are concerned about the balance sheets of China's banks, and the possibility of a bubble in the Chinese property market – but at least we can say that as far as economic growth is concerned, so far, so good.

But also . . . so what? With this economic growth comes tremendous upheaval. Chinese people are confused; many are unemployed or dislocated from the modern China. A group of workers in Sichuan came to believe that Mao was running a factory in the afterlife – according to socialist principles, naturally. One account claims that some of them killed themselves with the aim of joining him.

Contemporary Chinese films also tell a story of bemusement and at times agonised searching. Many films, such as *Shower* and *Happy Times Hotel*, feature families split up after someone seeks his fortune in Shenzen. The movies show the heartache but not the riches. The message is that the new opportunities are destroying the old way of life. Another common theme is of total confusion: the hapless bike messenger of *Beijing Bicycle* discovers that property is indeed theft, and his attempt to engage with the capitalist system ends in misery and violence. In the touching farce *Happy Times Hotel*, well-meaning friends, unemployed after their factory unit has closed down, are so busy trying to look after a blind girl by faking the existence of a business that they fail to appreciate it would be easier simply to run a real business. It is only the girl, who grew up in the 1990s, who comes to see clearly that she has the ability to make a living for herself.

It is not easy to be part of a revolution. Young men and women growing up in rural China in the 1970s worked as part of a farming community, collecting 'work points', doing as they were told, moving where they were told and having basic needs provided for by the community and the state. Their sons and daughters grew up in a different China in the 1980s and 1990s. Life was still hard, but there was more money around and much more choice. Land was valuable; as farming methods improved, there was still less need for spare workers on the farm. Some people did what their fathers had been forbidden to do: sold their land and moved to the cities to look for work. Migration tore families apart. While new opportunities opened up, the old safety nets were becoming tattered as some state enterprises became obsolete.

Meanwhile, conditions in factories were terrible. Badly paid employees worked long shifts under conditions of dubious safety. A BBC reporter picked up the stories of Li Chun Mei, who died in late 2001 at the end of a sixteen-hour shift; she was found by her co-workers lying on the toilet floor, blood oozing from her nose and mouth. Then there is Zhou Shien Pin, whose feet melted after he touched a high-voltage wire in a paint factory. Is this the price of economic growth? Is it worth paying?

Economists like Paul Krugman, Martin Wolf and Jagdish Bhagwati have repeatedly tried to argue that Chinese sweatshops beat the alternatives. This is not a popular view. After Martin Wolf's book *Why Globalisation Works* was reviewed in the *Guardian Weekly*, the paper published an outraged letter from a reader who fantasised with glee about Wolf himself being forced to work in a sweatshop.

This response is about as vicious as wishing that anyone who wears a 'Mao' T-shirt be condemned to starvation – but less logical. Martin Wolf is correct to suggest that the sweatshops are better than the horrors that came before them, and a step on the road to something better. Mao's 'Great Leap Forward' was a leap into hell.

Nor is it unfair or irrelevant to compare modern China with Mao's utopia. Countries that are rich or rapidly growing have embraced the basic lessons of economics we have learned in this book: fight scarcity power and corruption; correct externalities; try to maximise information; get the incentives right; engage with other countries; and most of all, embrace markets, which do most of these jobs at the same time. Cameroon's poverty costs lives – because poverty kills – and it also robs people of their autonomy and ability to make meaningful choices about their own lives. Meanwhile communist China and the Soviet Union killed tens of millions, often through pure economic failure. Economics matters. The contrast between Cameroon, Soviet Russia or Mao's China and America, Britain or Belgium could not be greater.

In the end, economics is about people – something that economists have done a very bad job at explaining. And economic growth is about a better life for individuals – more choice, less fear, less toil and hardship. Like other economists, I believe that sweatshops are better than the alternatives and without a doubt better than starvation under the Great Leap Forward or in 'modern' North Korea. But if I did not also believe that they were a step to something better, I would not be such an enthusiastic supporter of China's reforms.

That is why I was cheered when I discovered that wealth – while very unevenly spread – has been slowly seeping inland from the 'Gold Coast' of Shanghai and Shenzhen. Between 1978 and 1995, two-thirds of China's provinces grew faster than any country elsewhere in the world. Most importantly, the people of China are feeling the difference. After years of paying low wages – because the supply of migrant labour from China seemed unlimited – factories on the Gold Coast are starting to run out of willing workers. (Foreign-owned factories pay a bit more and enjoy easier recruitment and lower turnover.) Between 2002 and 2006, average wages rose by 9 per cent per year (and by 11 per cent in the cities) – these numbers measured in dollars rather than local currency. Strikes are now commonplace, and after a change in the law in January 2008, workers now have more rights built into their contracts. All this is feeding through into higher pay and better conditions.

But these steps forward don't just come through strikes and changes in the law. They are also forced on employers by the fact that as China develops, workers have more and better alternatives to working in abusive settings.

In 2003, Yang Li did what many Chinese workers have done: she left home to work in a sweatshop in the Pearl River delta. A month later, after working thirteen-hour shifts, she decided to go home and start her own business – a hair salon. 'Every day at the factory was just work, work,' she said. 'My life here is comfortable.' Yang Li's parents had to survive the Cultural Revolution; her grandparents, the Great Leap Forward. Yang Li has real choices, and she lives in a country where those choices mean something for her quality of life. She tried factory work and decided it wasn't for her. Now she says that 'I can close the salon whenever I want.'

Economics is about Yang Li's choice.

Notes

Introduction

The quotation is from Paul Seabright's book *The Company of Strangers* (Princeton: Princeton University Press, 2004), 15. The story of the cappuccino was inspired by what I thought was a folk story economists told each other. I have since discovered the original version, an essay by Leonard Read called *I, Pencil*. It's available here: http://www.econlib.org /library/Essays/rdPncl1.html

Chapter 1

David Ricardo's account of economic rents is in *On the Principles of Political Economy and Taxation* (London: John Murray, 1817). The book is available online at: http://www.econlib.org/library/Ricardo/ricP.html. His example of settlers farming different grades of agricultural land is in Chapter 2, sections 2.3–2.5.

John Kay's application of Ricardo's theory to companies is in *Foundations of Corporate Success* (Oxford: Oxford Paperbacks, 1995).

To find out about the economics of criminal enterprise, see Steven D. Levitt and Sudhir Alladi Venkatesh, 'An economic analysis of a drug-selling gang's finances', *NBER Working Paper Series 6592* (June 1998), and Thomas Schelling's *Choice and Consequence* (Cambridge, MA: Harvard University Press, 1984), Chapters 7 and 8.

The underlying cost of a cup of coffee is artfully calculated by Brian McManus, 'Nonlinear pricing in an oligopoly market – the case of speciality coffee' (working paper, Olin School of Business, Washington University, St Louis, MO, 2004), http://www.olin.wustl.edu/faculty/mcmanus/coffee12-04.pdf. The effects of high rents on coffee company profits is explained by Astrid Wentlandt, 'Avoiding a coffee has-been', *Financial Times*, 7 August 2002, 19.

A discussion of, and statistics about, immigration and wages come from Martin Wolf, 'A Matter of More Than Economics', *Financial Times*, 14 April 2004; and George Borjas, 'Economics of Migration' (working paper, Kennedy School of Government, Harvard University, Cambridge, MA, 2000). My discussion simplifies the issue: a full consideration of the impact of immigration would also consider investment in capital, and much else. The 'Measuring Worth' database at MeasuringWorth.com shows that there was 452 per cent consumer price inflation between 1970 and 2009, and a very similar 468 per cent in the nominal unskilled wage. By contrast, nominal GDP per head rose 816 per cent.

Other sources for statistics:
The number of people passing through Waterloo station from Network Rail, http://www.networkrailstations.co.uk/index.cfm?fuseaction=retail.statistics.

Office rents from Insignia, reported in *The Economist*, 20 April 2002, 116.

Milk prices from Dairyco.org.uk and the *Farmers Guardian*.

Chapter 2

I worked out the premium on Fair Trade coffee using the Cafédirect website, http://www.cafedirect.co.uk/fairtrade/gold_prices.php. The exact premium depends on the type of beans and on the world price. (Cafédirect guarantees a minimum price, so when the world price is particularly low the premium rises.) For more discussion of the fair trade coffee market, see Tim Harford, 'Fair Trade Coffee has a Commercial Blend', *Financial Times*, 12 September 2003, 15.

For more on Amazon.com's 'money on' vouchers see 'Keeping the customer satisfied', *The Economist*, 14 July 2001.

Hal Varian is always insightful on the subject of price-targeting. The model of price-targeting through periodic sales is detailed in Hal R. Varian, 'A Model of Sales', *American Economic Review* 70, no. 4 (September 1980): 651–59. Varian's textbook *Intermediate Microeconomics*, 4th ed. (New York: W. W. Norton, 1997) covers the subject extensively, including the quotation about French railways, which comes from Emile Dupuit, an eighteenth-century French economist, translated by R B. Ekelund, 'Price Discrimination and Product Differentiation in Economic Theory: An Early Analysis', *Quarterly Journal of Economics* 84 (1970): 268–78. The amazing stories of price discrimination in high-tech goods are from Hal Varian and Carl Shapiro, *Information Rules* (Cambridge, MA: Harvard Business School Press, 1999), 59. Another excellent source is Preston McAfee's article, 'Price Discrimination' in *Issues in Competition Law and Policy 465* http://www.mcafee.cc/Papers/PDF/ABAPriceDiscrimination.pdf

I learned why popcorn costs so much at the cinema by reading Steven Landsburg's *Armchair Economist* (New York: Free Press, 1993), and why wine costs so much at restaurants in discussion with my former colleague Bill Sjostrom.

Chapter 3

Figures for the cost of the London Olympics: *Daily Telegraph*, 20 April 2010, http://www.telegraph.co.uk/sport/othersports/olympics/london 2012/7650638/London-2012-Lord-Coe-allays-fears-over-mooted-public-spending-cuts.html It is striking that when I first gathered this data, in 2005, the public subsidy was budgeted at only £2.5 billion.

The Wilt Chamberlain example is from Robert Nozick's *Anarchy, State and Utopia* (Oxford: Basil Blackwell, 1974). Tiger Woods' sponsorship earnings were reported in the *Daily Telegraph*, 21 July 2010, http://www.telegraph.co.uk/sport/golf/tigerwoods/7903222/Tiger-Woods-still-the-worlds-highest-earning-athlete.html

Other sources for statistics:
Rockefeller being the only man to pay the top rate of tax, from Cato Policy Analysis no. 192, http://www.cato.org/pubs/pas/pa-192.html.

The number of deaths of the elderly due to cold, from *Age Concern*, press release, 7 March 2003.

Information about environmental taxes paid by motorists in the UK: see *Tax by Design* from the Institute for Fiscal Studies, Table 10.1, http://www.ifs.org.uk/mirrleesreview/design/ch10.pdf. US figures from the Department of Transportation 'Highway Statistics 2008'. $72 billion is collected by states and $32 billion by the federal government.

Chapter 4

Many of the statistics on the costs of congestion and pollution, especially in the United Kingdom, are in David Maddison, David Pearce et al., *Blueprint 5: The True Costs of Road Transport* (London: Earthscan Publications, 1996).

The impact of environmental taxes on different groups in Britain, such as the poor or rural residents, is discussed in *Blueprint 5* with figures from Johnson et al.; 'The Distributional Consequences of Environmental Taxes', *Institute for Fiscal Studies Commentary* 23 (1990): 55; and S. Smith, 'The Distributional Consequences of Taxes on Energy and the Carbon Content of Fuels', *European Economy Special Edition* (1992). A separate, more recent, study focused on London is Ian Crawford's *The Distributional Effects of the Proposed London Congestion Charging Scheme* (briefing note, no 11, Institute for Fiscal Studies, Oct. 2000), http://www.ifs.org.uk/consume/gla.pdf. Distributional consequences in the United States are explored by Howard Chernick and Andrew Reschovsky, 'Who Pays the Gasoline Tax', in the *National Tax Journal* 50, no. 2 (June 1997): 233–59. More recent data, telling a similar story, available for some states – for example, Texas, at http://www.window.state.tx.us/taxinfo/incidence/table33_66.html.

For a fairly technical review of estimates of the value people place on their own lives, see Kip Viscusi and Joseph Aldy, *The Value of Statistical Life: A Critical Review of Market Estimates Throughout the World* (AEI-Brookings Joint Center for Regulatory Studies, Related Publication 03-02, Jan. 2003), http:// www.aei.brookings.org/publications/abstract.php?pid=305.

I learned about the Camelback houses from David Friedman, *Hidden*

Order (New York: HarperBusiness, 1997), 91; and the window tax from David Smith, *Free Lunch* (London: Profile Books, 2003), 148.

On tradeable permits in the United States, see Paul L. Joskow, Richard Schmalensee and Elizabeth Bailey, 'The Market for Sulfur Dioxide Emissions', *American Economic Review* 8, no. 4 (Sept. 1998): 669–85. The Chinese programme is explained in 'A Great Leap Forward', *The Economist*, 9 May 2002. For a design intended to work on a global level see Peter Cramton and Suzi Kerr, 'Tradeable Carbon Permit Auctions' (working paper, University of Maryland, 1998), http:// www.market-design.com/files/98wp-tradeable-carbon-permit-auctions.pdf. Paul Klemperer, the auction designer who features in Chapter 7, helped to design an auction for the United Kingdom government to kick-start its programme of tradable emission permits.

Anyone doubting my statement that 'economists have long been in the forefront of analysing environmental problems' will be surprised to hear that one of the first environmentalists was also one of the first and most famous economists, Thomas Malthus, whose study of overpopulation was published in 1798. ('An Essay on the Principle of Population' (London: Murray). Only slightly less famous is the inspiration for this entire chapter: Arthur Pigou, professor of economics at Cambridge University, whose seminal book *The Economics of Welfare* (London: Macmillan, 1920) developed the theory of externalities and the solution of externality pricing. Some readers may also doubt my claim that economists don't care much about GDP. Consider then, this quotation from Steven Landsburg's *The Armchair Economist* (New York: Free Press, 1995, 135–36), which is a characteristically elegant explanation of what most economists believe:

The gross national product is the most frequently reported measure of general economic well-being. As such, it has some obvious deficiencies. It counts the value of all goods and services produced in the economy, but not the value of time spent relaxing on the beach . . . Another deficiency is that increased output of goods and services can be either a good or a bad thing. A construction boom that creates thousands of desirable new houses is a good thing; a construction boom that replaces thousands of old houses destroyed by a hurricane consists of running as fast as possible just to stay in one place. The GNP counts them equally.

Other sources for statistics:
Deaths in the United States caused by particulate matter, from EPA brochure, *Diesel   Exhaust   in   the   United   States,* http://www.epa.gov/otaq/retrofit/documents/ 420f03022.pdf.

The tax bill paid by British drivers from D. Newbery, 'Fair and Efficient Pricing and the Finance of Roads', *Proceedings of the Chartered Institute of Transport* 7, no. 3, 1998, cited in G. Roth, 'Road Pricing in a Free Society', *Economic Affairs,* December 1998. The tax bill paid by American drivers from the US Department of Transportation, http://www.fhwa.dot.gov/ohim/2000hfbt.pdf.

Transport for London publishes regular updates on the impact of the congestion charge. See for example: http://www.tfl.gov.uk/assets/downloads/sixth-annual-impacts-monitoring-report-2008-07.pdf

For more detail about the Chinese efforts to introduce sulphur dioxide trading, see Julia Tao and Daphone Ngar-yin Mah, 'Between Market and State: Dilemmas of Environmental Governance in China's Sulphur Dioxide Trading System', *Environment and Planning C: Government and Policy 2009,* Vol. 27, *pp. 175–88,* and Zhang Bing, Yu QinQin and Bi Jun 'Policy Design and Performance of Emissions Trading Markets: An Adaptive Agent-based Analysis', *Environmental Science and Technology 2010,* Vol. 44, *pp. 5693–9.*

Chapter 5

The classic article on lemons and asymmetric information is George Akerlof, 'The Market for "Lemons": Quality Uncertainty and the Market Mechanism', *Quarterly Journal of Economics* (August 1970). Akerlof's book *An Economic Theorist's Book of Tales* (Cambridge: Cambridge University Press, 1984) contains many of his most interesting papers up to that date – not only the lemons paper but, for instance, economic theories of the caste system.

In conversation, John Kay has made me realise that the explanation of bad restaurants in tourist traps is more subtle than it appears. Tourists can, of course, tell the difference between an upmarket and a downmarket restaurant, just as in the market for cars, buyers can tell a Ferrari from a Ford. But in both cases, the ignorant buyers cannot tell good from bad within the obvious categories: there are good burger joints and bad ones, and even Ferraris, when second-hand, are likely to be lemons.

Data on health-care spending in different countries is from David M. Cutler, 'A Guide to Health Care Reform', *Journal of Economic Perspectives* 8, no. 3 (1994): 13–29; Cutler also reports on the survey of satisfaction with health-care systems carried out by Karen Donelan, Robert Blendon, Cathy Schoen, Karen David and Katherine Binns: 'The Cost of Health System Change: Public Discontent in Five Nations', *Health Affairs* 18, no. 3: 206–16. The responses are: 'On the whole, the health system works pretty well, and only minor changes are necessary to make it work better' (these are the respondents I described as 'content'); 'There are some good things in our health-care system, but fundamental changes are needed to make it work better'; 'Our health-care system has so much wrong with it that we need to completely rebuild it.'

The World Health Organisation website provides a rich resource on European health systems, http://www.euro.who.int/observatory/hits/20020525_1, while the WTO's *World Health Report 2000* provides detailed statistics on the cost of public and private health care across the world.

The cost of the American health-care system to taxpayers is analysed by S. Woolhandler and D. Himmelstein, 'Paying for national health insurance – and not getting it', *Health Affairs* 21 (August 2002): 88–98, and administrative costs are from Harvard Medical School press release, '*New England Journal of Medicine* Study Shows U.S. Health Care Paperwork Cost $294.3 Billion in 1999 Far More Than in Canada', August 20, 2003, http://www.hms.harvard.edu/news/releases/0820wool-himmel.html. The US Census Bureau (2003) measures coverage of the American health system: http://www.census.gov/Press-Release/www/2003/cb03-154.html.

The study of hospital management standards in marginal political constituencies is Nick Bloom, Carol Propper, Stephan Seiler and John Van Reenen (2010), 'The Impact of Competition on Management Quality: Evidence from Public Hospitals', CEP Discussion Paper, No. 983. Centre for Economic Performance, London School of Economics and Political Science, http://eprints.lse.ac.uk/28731/ and it is described in more detail by me here: http://timharford.com/2010/07/a-healthy-dose-of-competition-will-help-the-nhs-pull-through/

A review of age-related macular degeneration therapies is: Miriam Karmen, 'AMD Therapies: Comparing Costs and Quality of Life', *EyeNet* magazine, October 2006. It is available online at: http://www.aao.org/publications/eyenet/200610/feature.cfm

The Leksell Gamma Knife is discussed in *Honolulu Star Bulletin*, 25 May 2001, http://starbulletin.com/2001/05/25/news/index.html; Steve Goetsch, San Diego Gamma Knife Center, http://www.medphysics.wisc.edu/medphys_docs/seminars/goetsch.html.htm; *Hawaii Business*, http://www.hawaiibusiness.cc/hb72001/default.cfm?articleid=26; and BBC Online News, 8 September 1998, http://news.bbc.co.uk/1/hi/health/166993.stm. The Gamma Knife is manufactured by Elekta (www.elekta.com).

The Singaporean health system is described by T. A. Massaro and Y. Wong, *Medical Savings Accounts: The Singapore Experience*, National Centre for Policy Analysis report, no. 203 (April 1996), http://www.ncpa.org/studies/s203/s203.html; and R. Taylor and S. Blair, 'Financing Health Care: Singapore's Innovative Approach', http://rru.worldbank.org/PublicPolicyJournal/Summary.aspx?id=261.

Chapter 6

There are now too many good books about the crisis to list, but for an accessible introduction I wholeheartedly recommend John Lanchester, *Whoops!* , Michael Lewis, *The Big Short*, Andrew Ross Sorkin, *Too Big to Fail* and Gillian Tett, *Fool's Gold*. Lewis's article in the March 2011 edition of *Vanity Fair*, 'When Irish Eyes Are Crying', is a must-read, including Theo Phanos 'worst bank' quote. As is Tett's prescient 'The Dream Machine' in the *FT Magazine*, 24 March 2006. My favourite more technical source is the *Squam Lake Report*, which consists of a series of brief notes that are available online. Readers may also be interested in my book, *Adapt: Why Success Always Starts with Failure*, which includes a chapter drawing some unexpected lessons from nuclear meltdowns and industrial accidents such as the Deepwater Horizon oil spill, and applying them to the financial system.

Fiona Exon's Eggs: The *Daily Telegraph* was among several newspapers to report 'Woman's Amazing Trillion to One Find' – by Andrew Hough,

Daily Telegraph, 2 February 2010, http://www.telegraph.co.uk/news/
newstopics/howaboutthat/7127206/Womans-amazing-a-trillion-to-one-
find-all-eggs-in-box-had-double-yolks.html. My little calculation about
how often double-yolk cartons eggs would turn up assumes (simplistically)
that the world population stays fixed at its current level. I am indebted to
Alex Tabarrok for putting together a quick spreadsheet to perform similar calculations, which I modified for my own eggy purposes. The key
formula in Microsoft Excel is [1-BINOMDIST(x,6,y,TRUE)] where x is
the egg's position out of six in a carton (usually 2 in my examples) and y
is the probability that the egg is rotten. It's 0.05 initially and then the formula can be applied recursively to calculate the probability of default in
the RMBS, CDO, CDO-squared and so on. Tabarrok's original spreadsheet can be downloaded from: http://www.marginalrevolution.com/
marginalrevolution/2010/05/the-dark-magic-of-structured-finance.html

David Viniar's bad luck: Viniar was quoted by Peter Thal Larsen in
the *Financial Times*, 13 August 2007, http://www.ft.com/cms/s/0/
d2121cb6-49cb-11dc-9ffe-0000779fd2 ac.html. The short academic
paper that calculated just how unfortunate Mr Viniar was is: K. Dowd,
J. Cotter, C. G. Humphrey and M. Woods, 'How Unlucky is 25-Sigma?'
Journal of Portfolio Management, Volume 34 (Number 4), 2008, pp.76–80.
http://www.nottingham.ac.uk/ business/cris/papers/2008-3.pdf

The costs of the crisis: I interviewed Andrew Haldane on Monday 20
December 2010 on behalf of BBC Radio 4's *More or Less*. The Hank
Paulson bailout is discussed in Tim Harford, 'Why US Banks and
Taxpayers Owe Big Thanks to Hank', *Financial Times*, 23 January 2010,
http://timharford.com/2010/01/why-us-banks-and-taxpayers-owe-big-
thanks-to-hank/ and Veronesi, Pietro and Zingales, Luigi, 'Paulson's
Gift' (1 December 2009). Chicago Booth Research Paper No. 09-42.
Available at SSRN: http://ssrn.com/abstract=1498548. The UK government budgets contain estimates of the direct cost of the various
interventions to support the banking system. In June 2010 they were estimated at £2bn, a figure that has shrunk dramatically over time. In January
2011, I interviewed Edwin Latter of LINK and Paul Smee of the UK
Payments Council about the robustness of the UK payments system.

Alan Greenspan's confession is reported by Mark Felsenthal,
'Greenspan "shocked" at credit system breakdown', *Reuters*, 23 October
2008. http://www.reuters.com/article/idUSTRE49M58W20081024

Chapter 7

See *Prisoner's Dilemma* by William Poundstone (New York: Doubleday, 1992) to find out more about Von Neumann and the use of game theory in the cold war. For an analysis of poker models by Emile Borel, Von Neumann, John Nash and Lloyd Shapley, see Chapter 12 of Ken Binmore's textbook *Fun and Games* (Lexington: D. C. Heath, 1992). This is the same Ken Binmore who later went on to lead the auction design team for the UK 3G auction.

The United States spectrum auctions are expertly discussed in John McMillan's 'Selling Spectrum Rights', *Journal of Economic Perspectives* 8, no. 3 (Summer 1994): 145–62; also McAfee and McMillan's 'Analysing the Airwaves Auction', *Journal of Economic Perspectives* 10, no. 1 (Winter 1996): 159–75. McMillan also draws lessons from failures in Australia and New Zealand. The collusion theory is explained in *The Economist*, 'Economics Brief', 17 May 1997. Not all economists believe that this was the result of collusion – it may also have been a dramatic reevaluation of the licences.

The design team for the UK auction was assembled by the ESCRC Centre for Economic Learning and Social Equilibrium (ELSE). See www.paulklemperer.org and http://else.econ.ucl.ac.uk/research/spectrum.shtml for papers and contemporary press. Paul Klemperer's *Auctions: Theory and Practice* (Princeton: Princeton University Press, 2004), especially Chapter 6, contains a wealth of material on the spectrum auctions. The book describes (187) analysts' forecasts of the auction revenues (£2–5 billion); the auction raised five to ten times this amount. It also contains Klemperer's defence of the auctions (207), originally published as 'The Wrong Culprit for Telecom Trouble', *Financial Times*, 26 November 2002. A subsequent study has found no evidence that spectrum auctions harm consumers: M. Park, S-W. Lee, Y-J. Choi, 'Does Spectrum Auctioning Harm Consumers? Lessons from 3G Licensing', *Information Economics and Policy* (2010), doi: 10.1016/j.infoecopol.2010.10.002

William Vickrey's classic paper on auctions is 'Counterspeculation, Auctions and Competitive Sealed Tenders', *Journal of Finance* 16 (March 1961): 8–37.

Bulow and Klemperer's paper on the merits of auctions relative to other forms of negotiations is 'Auctions vs. Negotiations', *American Economic Review* (March 1996): 180–94. Also available at www.paul-klemperer.org.

The UK auction history is still available at http://www.ofcom.org.uk/static/archive/spectrumauctions/3gindex.htm.

The section on the crisis auction is based on discussions with Paul Klemperer, Anthea Milnes, 'Creating Confidence in Cash', *Blueprint* (October 2010), and Paul Klemperer, 'The Product-Mix Auction: A New Auction Design for Differentiated Goods,' *Journal of the European Economic Association* (2010), Paul Klemperer.

Chapter 8

Cameroon's level of corruption is rated by Transparency International at www.transparency.org.

Robert Lucas's memorable statement on the importance of economic growth is from 'On the Mechanics of Economic Development', *Journal of Monetary Economics* (1988).

The legitimacy of Cameroon's electoral process is a matter for debate. At the time of talking to Sam, Biya's most recent mandate had been to win 93 per cent of the votes in the 1997 presidential election, which was boycotted by the opposition. In October 2004, after I had visited Cameroon, Biya won another election with around 75 per cent of the vote. Many external observers regarded the election as reasonably fair (see http://news.bbc.co.uk/1/hi/world/africa/3746686.stm). BBC reporters were sceptical; they concluded that many people were unaware of the election or did not vote because they felt their vote would not count. The BBC reported short queues at the polls despite official reports of a high turnout. The number of registered voters is only four million, with a voting-age population of eight million. http://news.bbc.co.uk/1/hi/world/africa/3732512.stm. My own pessimistic view of Cameroon's democracy was formed by talking to Cameroonian citizens who, like Sam, believe it to be a sham.

Mancur Olson's theories are expounded in his *Power and Prosperity* (New York: Basic Books, 2000). The World Bank measures red tape every year in the 'Doing Business' reports, http://rru.worldbank.org/

DoingBusiness/. Data on Cameroon's income per capita is available from the World Bank: http://data.worldbank.org/indicator/NY.GNP. PCAP.CD/countries/1W-CM?display=graph. Using the 'Atlas' method it was $950 in 1989 and $910 in 2005. It was $1170 in 2009, an encouraging but – thus far – brief growth spurt.

All you ever wanted to know about Nepalese dams is in Elinor Ostrom, 'Incentives, Rules of the Game, and Development' (Annual Bank Conference of Development Economics, World Bank, May 1995); Nepal is now in a state of civil war and there are other reasons for civil servants not to leave Kathmandu. At the time of Ostrom's study, though, it was tedium rather than danger that discouraged them.

Other sources for statistics:
South Korea's gains from foreign investment from Bohn-Young Koo, 'New Forms of Foreign Direct Investment in Korea' (working paper no. 82-02, Korean Development Institute, June 1982).

In the first edition of *The Undercover Economist* I reported that Cameroon's trade barriers were even higher. They have fallen slightly, but I am also using what I think is a superior measure of trade barriers, the World Bank's 'Tariff rate, applied, weighted mean, all products' series. Cameroon is still in the quarter of countries with the highest tariff rates. The data source is: http://data.worldbank.org/indicator

Chapter 9

Globalisation and trade has been the subject of some excellent books in recent years, and ideas and statistics in this chapter are drawn liberally from Martin Wolf's *Why Globalisation Works* (New Haven: Yale University Press, 2004), Philippe Legrain's *Open World* (London: Abacus, 2002), Douglas Irwin's *Free Trade Under Fire* (Princeton: Princeton University Press, 2002) and Jagdish Bhagwati's *Free Trade Today* (Princeton: Princeton University Press, 2002). David Friedman's book *Hidden Order* (New York: Harpercollins, 1996, 65–77) contains an excellent chapter on trade theory.

E. O. Wilson's discussion of homogenisation is from his splendid display of his comparative advantage. See Wilson's *Consilience – The Unity of Knowledge* (London: Abacus, 2003), 304.

The original paper proving that a tax on imports is a tax on exports is Abba P. Lerner's 'The Symmetry Between Import and Export Taxes', *Economica* 3 (August 1936): 306–13.

I leave to one side discussion of migration, capital flows and technological transfers. You can find out more in Martin Wolf's *Why Globalisation Works* or in a speech by Stanley Fischer, 'Globalization and its challenges' http://www.iic.com/fischer/pdf/fischer011903.pdf (delivered to the American Economics Association, 3 January 2003).

Vandana Shiva's view on environmental apartheid is from 'On the edge: living with Global Capitalism', Will Hutton and Anthony Giddens, eds., cited in Philippe Legrain's *Open World* (London: Abacus, 2002).

Statistics on the cleanliness of US investment overseas from the American Census Bureau and from R. Repetto and J. Albrecht, both cited in Legrain, *Open World*. Data on pollution in Mexico and China are from D. Wheeler, 'Racing to the Bottom: Foreign Investment and Air Pollution in Developing Countries', *Journal of Environment and Development* 10, no. 3: 225–45, reported in an overview by Dasgupta et al., 'Confronting the Environmental Kuznets Curve', *Journal of Economic Perspectives* 16, no. 1 (Winter 2001): 147–68. The data in Figure 6 come from the World Bank: http://databank.worldbank.org. The 2005 US census reports that all US industry spent a total of $26.6 billion on pollution abatement, while the total value of shipments that year was over $4700 billion. See http://www.census.gov/prod/2008puba200-05.pdf. The paper suggesting some evidence that foreign investment causes pollution is Robert Hoffman, Chew-Ging Lee, Bala Ramasamy and Matthew Yeung (2005) 'FDI and Pollution: A Granger Causality Test Using Panel Data', *Journal of International Development*, Vol. 17, pp. 311–17.

On agricultural subsidies see Martin Wolf, 'Weeding Out Subsidies', *Financial Times*, 5 November 2002; and Douglas Irwin, *Free Trade Under Fire*, 61–62. The latest figures on sugar subsidies are from the OECD's Producer and Consumer Support Estimates database.

Jonah Peretti tells his story in 'My Nike Media Adventure', *The Nation*, 22 March 2001, http://www.thenation.com/doc.mhtml?i=

20010409&s=peretti. The Smokey Mountain example is from Paul Krugman, 'In Praise of Cheap Labor', *Slate*, Thursday, 20 March 1997, http://web.mit.edu/krugman/www/smokey.html. News of the landslide came from *The Economist*, 13 July 2000. William Greider explains his support of New York's rules on imported clothes in 'No to Global Sweatshops,' *The Nation*, 19 April 2001, http://www.thenation.com/doc.mhtml?i=20010507&s=greider. Douglas Irwin and Philippe Legrain both have good arguments and data to support the view that multinationals pay more and offer better conditions than local firms.

The political economy of trade restrictions explains the stability of Tokugawa, Japan, described by Janet E. Hunter, *The Emergence of Modern Japan* (London: Longman, 1989), 4–7; it is fully explored by Douglas Irwin in *Free Trade Under Fire*, Chapter 5.

The BBC has covered the fate of the poor coffee farmers in depth: http://news.bbc.co.uk/1/hi/business/1493104.stm ('Coffee Farmers Switch to Drugs', 15 August 2001); http://news.bbc.co.uk/1/hi/business/1333204.stm ('Coffee Farmers Face Destitution', 16 May 2001); http://news.bbc.co.uk/1/hi/business/1488758.stm ('The Cappuccino Trail', 16 August 2001); http://news.bbc.co.uk/1/hi/business/1608356.stm ('Coffee Cartel Shuts Up Shop', 19 October 2001).

Other sources for statistics:
Job creation and destruction in the United States, from Bureau of Labor Statistics, http://bls.gov/news.release/cewbd.htm Table 1. October 2010..

The Duke of Westminster and the Queen have their agricultural handouts analysed at http://farmsubsidy.org/lists/11/duke-of-westminsters-farm-subsidies/ and http://farmsubsidy.org/lists/2/queen-elizabeth-iis-farm-subsidies/.

Various estimates of the benefits from trade are gathered from Douglas Irwin's *Free Trade Under Fire*, 30–48.

Data on trade barriers and export shares from the World Bank: http://data.worldbank.org/indicator and the OECD International Trade by Commodity Statistics database: http://stats.oecd.org/

Other trade statistics from the *World Trade Overview 2000*, World Trade Organisation, 2001.

Chapter 10

The effects of Mao's Great Leap Forward are discussed by J. M. Roberts in *Penguin History of the World* (London: Penguin, 1995), 1013, and especially Jonathan Glover, *Humanity: A Moral History of the 20th Century* (New Haven: Yale University Press, 1999). John Kay tells the story of Khrushchev's great experiment in *The Truth about Markets* (London: Allen Lane, Penguin Press, 2003), 88.

A symposium in the *Journal of Economic Perspectives* 8, no 2 (Spring 1994) is a wonderful analysis of Deng's reforms in the 1980s. Articles include Dwight Perkins, 'Completing China's move to the market'; Shahid Yusuf, 'China's Macroeconomic performance and management during transition'; and Gary Jefferson and Thomas Rawski, 'Enterprise reform in Chinese industry'. Other invaluable resources are Barry Naughton, *Growing Out of the Plan* (Cambridge: Cambridge University Press, 1995); Justin Yifu Lin, 'Rural reforms and agricultural growth in China', *American Economic Review* 82, no 1 (March 1992); and Robert F. Dernberger, 'The People's Republic of China at 50: The Economy', in *The People's Republic of China After 50 Years*, ed. Richard Louis Edmonds (New York: Oxford University Press, 1999). More recent views on China come from Martin Wolf, 'Asia's Awakening', *Financial Times*, 21 September 2003; and from David Hale and Lyric Hughes Hale, 'China takes off', *Foreign Affairs* 86, no 6 (Nov/Dec 2003).

Jagdish Bhagwati's condemnation of Indian economic policy is from 'Review of Sachs-Varshney-Bajpai and Lal', *Times Literary Supplement*, January 2000. Available at: http://www.columbia.edu/~jb38/TLS_SV.pdf.

On the cult of Mao see Richard McGregor, 'Mao and Forever', *Financial Times Magazine*, 14 August 2004. Lucy Ash reports on harsh working conditions in 'Inside China's Sweatshops', BBC Online News, 'From Our Own Correspondent', 20 July 2002, http://news.bbc.co.uk/1/hi/programmes/from_our_own_correspondent/2139401.stm. Yang Li's choice is described in Alexandra Harney, 'Migrant workers shun long hours and low pay', *Financial Times*, 2 November 2004. A more recent update from *The Economist* describes Chinese labour disputes and rising rages: 'The Next China', *The Economist*, 29 Jul 2010, http://www.economist.com/node/16693397

Other sources for statistics:
Statistics on Chinese growth rates and the size of the economy relative to others from the World Bank http://databank.worldbank.org/ and the World Trade Organisation, http://www.wto.org/english/news_e/pres10_e/pr598_e.htm.

The statistics on the transformation of South Korea's economy are from Anne Krueger, 'Institutions of the New Private Sector', in *The Emergence of Market Economies in Eastern Europe*, eds. Christopher Clague and Gordon Rausser (Cambridge, MA: Blackwell, 1992), cited in Mancur Olson, *Power and Prosperity* (New York: Basic Books, 2003).

Index

ADAPT
Why Success Always Starts with Failure

read the first chapter from Tim Harford's
next book, now available in Abacus paperback . . .

1

Adapting

The curious task of economics is to demonstrate to
men how little they really know about what they
imagine they can design.

Friedrich von Hayek

Cross the river by feeling for stones.

Attributed to Deng Xiaoping

1 'You could easily spend your life making a toaster'

The electric toaster seems a humble thing. It was invented in
1893, roughly halfway between the appearance of the light bulb
and that of the aeroplane. This century-old technology is now a
household staple. Reliable, efficient toasters are available for less
than an hour's wage.

Nevertheless, Thomas Thwaites, a postgraduate design student at the Royal College of Art in London, discovered just what
an astonishing achievement the toaster is when he embarked on

what he called the 'Toaster Project'. Quite simply, Thwaites wanted to build a toaster from scratch. He started by taking apart a cheap toaster, to discover that it had over four hundred components and sub-components. Even the most primitive model called for:

> Copper, to make the pins of the electric plug, the cord, and internal wires. Iron to make the steel grilling apparatus, and the spring to pop up the toast. Nickel to make the heating element. Mica (a mineral a bit like slate) around which the heating element is wound, and of course plastic for the plug and cord insulation, and for the all important sleek looking casing.

The scale of the task soon became clear. To get iron ore, Thwaites had to travel to an old mine in Wales that now serves as a museum. He tried to smelt the iron using fifteenth-century technology, and failed dismally. He fared no better when he replaced bellows with hairdryers and a leaf-blower. His next attempt was even more of a cheat: he used a recently patented smelting method and two microwave ovens, one of which perished in the attempt, to produce a coin-sized lump of iron.

- Plastic was no easier. Thwaites tried but failed to persuade BP to fly him out to an offshore rig to collect some crude oil. His attempts to make plastic from potato starch were foiled by mould and hungry snails. Finally, he settled for scavenging some plastic from a local dump, melting it down and moulding it into a toaster's casing. Other short cuts followed. Thwaites used electrolysis to obtain copper from the polluted water of an old mine in Anglesey, and simply melted down some commemorative coins to produce nickel, which he drew into wire using a specialised machine from the RCA's jewellery department.

Such compromises were inevitable. 'I realised that if you started absolutely from scratch, you could easily spend your life making a toaster,' he admitted. Despite his Herculean efforts to duplicate the technology, Thomas Thwaites's toaster looks more like a toaster-shaped birthday cake than a real toaster, its coating dripping and oozing like an icing job gone wrong. 'It warms bread when I plug it into a battery,' he told me, brightly. 'But I'm not sure what will happen if I plug it into the mains.' Eventually, he summoned up the courage to do so. Two seconds later, the toaster was toast.

2 Problem solving in a complicated world

The modern world is mind-bogglingly complicated. Far simpler objects than a toaster involve global supply chains and the coordinated efforts of many individuals, scattered across the world. Many do not even know the final destination of their efforts. As a lumberjack fells a giant of the Canadian forest, he doesn't know whether the tree he topples will make bed frames or pencils. At the vast Chuquicamata mine in Chile, a yellow truck the size of a house growls up an incline blasted into the landscape; the driver does not trouble himself to ask whether the copper ore he carries is destined for the wiring of a toaster or the casing of a bullet.

The range of products, too, is astounding. There are a hundred thousand or so distinct items in an ordinary Wal-Mart. Eric Beinhocker, a complexity researcher at the McKinsey Global Institute, reckons that if you were to add up all the different sizes and shapes of shoes, shirts and socks, the different brands and flavours and sizes of jams and sauces, the millions of different books, DVDs and music downloads on offer, you would find that a major economy such as New York or London offers over ten billion distinct types of product. Many of these products were undreamed of when the toaster was first invented, and millions of new ones appear every month. The complexity of the society we have created for ourselves envelops us so completely that, instead of being dizzied, we take it for granted.

I used to view this sophistication as cause to celebrate. Now I am less sure. Certainly, this complex economy produces vast material wealth. Not everyone gets a share, but far more people today enjoy a high material standard of living than at any time in history; and, notwithstanding the occasional recession, the wealth continues to grow more quickly than it ever used to. The process that produces this wealth is near miraculous, and the job is far harder than we tend to acknowledge. Alternative systems, from feudalism to central planning, have attempted the same task and been consigned to the history books.

Yet the Toaster Project should give us pause for thought. Because it is a symbol of the sophistication of our world, the toaster is also a symbol of the obstacles that lie in wait for those who want to change it. From climate change to terrorism, fixing the banks to ending global poverty, there is no shortage of big policy problems out there. They are always up for debate, yet we never seem to move any closer to a solution. Humbler problems in business and everyday life also tend to conceal the same unexpected complexity as the Toaster Project.

This is partly a book about those problems. But more fundamentally, it's a book that aims to understand how any problem – big or small – really gets solved in a world where even a toaster is beyond one man's comprehension.

The toasting problem isn't difficult: don't burn the toast; don't electrocute the user; don't start a fire. The bread itself is hardly an active protagonist. It doesn't deliberately try to outwit you, as a team of investment bankers might; it doesn't try to murder you, terrorise your country, and discredit everything you stand for, as a terrorist cell or a group of insurgents in Iraq would. The toaster is merely an improved way to solve an old problem – the Romans loved toast – unlike the World Wide Web or the personal computer, which provide solutions to problems we never realised we had. The toasting problem is laughably simple compared to the problem of transforming a poor country such as Bangladesh into the kind of economy where toasters are manufactured with ease and every household can afford one, along with the bread to put into it. It is dwarfed by the problem of climate change – the response to which will require much more than modifying a billion toasters.

Such problems are the stuff of this book: how to fight insurgents who, of course, fight back; how to nurture ideas that matter when so many of those ideas are hard even to imagine; how to restructure an economy to respond to climate change, or to make poor countries rich; how to prevent rogue investment bankers from destroying the banking system again. These are complex, fast-moving problems in a complex, fast-moving world. I will argue that they have far more in common with each other than we realise. Curiously, they also have something in common with the more humble problems we face in our own lives.

Whenever such problems are solved, it is little short of a miracle. This book is about how such miracles happen, why they matter so much, and whether we can make them happen more often.

3 The experts are humbled

We're proud of the change we've brought to Washington in these first hundred days, but we've got a lot of work left to do, as all of you know. So I'd like to talk a little bit about what my administration plans to achieve in the next hundred days. During the second hundred days, we will design, build and open a library dedicated to my first hundred days ... I believe that my next hundred days will be so successful I will be able to complete them in 72 days. And on the 73rd day, I will rest.

This was President Obama addressing the White House Correspondents' Dinner, traditionally a venue for a joke or two, a few months after a tidal wave of hope and high expectations had swept him into power in November 2008. It seems a long time ago now, but Obama's joke cut close to the bone even then: people were expecting too much of one man.

We badly need to believe in the potency of leaders. Our instinctive response, when faced with a complicated challenge, is to look for a leader who will solve it. It wasn't just Obama: every president is elected after promising to change the way politics works; and almost every president then slumps in the polls as reality starts to bite. This isn't because we keep electing the wrong leaders. It is because we have an inflated sense of what leadership can achieve in the modern world.

Perhaps we have this instinct because we evolved to operate in small hunter–gatherer groups, solving small hunter–gatherer problems. The societies in which our modern brains developed weren't modern: they contained a few hundred separate products, rather than ten billion. The challenges such societies faced, however formidable, were simple enough to have been solved by an intelligent, wise, brave leader. They would have been vastly simpler than the challenges facing a newly elected US president.

Whatever the reason, the temptation to look to a leader to fix our problems runs deep. Of course, a leader doesn't have to solve every problem by himself. Good leaders surround themselves with expert advisers, seeking out the smartest specialists with the deepest insights into the problems of the day. But even deep expertise is not enough to solve today's complex problems.

Perhaps the best illustration of this comes from an extraordinary two-decade investigation into the limits of expertise, begun in 1984 by a young psychologist called Philip Tetlock. He was the most junior member of a committee of the National Academy of Sciences charged with working out what the Soviet response might be to the Reagan administration's hawkish stance in the Cold War. Would Reagan call the bluff of a bully or was he about to provoke a deadly reaction? Tetlock canvassed every expert he could find. He was struck by the fact that, again and again, the most influential thinkers on the Cold War flatly contradicted one another. We are so used to talking heads disagreeing that perhaps this doesn't seem surprising. But when we realise that the leading experts cannot agree on the most basic level about the key problem of the age, we begin to understand that this kind of expertise is far less useful than we might hope.

Tetlock didn't leave it at that. He worried away at this question of expert judgement for twenty years. He rounded up nearly three hundred experts – by which he meant people whose job it was to comment or advise on political and economic trends. They were a formidable bunch: political scientists, economists, lawyers and diplomats. There were spooks and think-tankers, journalists and academics. Over half of them had PhDs; almost all had postgraduate degrees. And Tetlock's method for evaluating the quality of their expert judgement was to pin the experts down: he asked them to make specific, quantifiable forecasts – answering 27,450 of his questions between them – and then waited to see whether their forecasts came true. They rarely did. The experts failed, and their failure to forecast the future is a symptom of their failure to understand fully the complexities of the present.

It wasn't that expertise was entirely useless. Tetlock compared his experts' responses to those of a control group of undergraduates, and the experts did better. But by any objective standard, they didn't do well. And the return on expertise was distinctly limited. Once experts have acquired a broad knowledge of the political world, deeper expertise in a specific field doesn't seem to help much. Predictions about Russia from experts on Russia were no more accurate than predictions about Russia from experts on Canada.

Most accounts of Tetlock's research savour the humbling of the professional pundits. And why not? One of Tetlock's more delicious discoveries was that the more famous experts – those who spent a lot of time as talking heads on television – were especially incompetent. Louis Menand, writing in the *New Yorker*, enjoyed the notion of bumbling seers, and concluded, 'the best lesson of Tetlock's book may be the one that he seems most reluctant to draw: Think for yourself'.

Yet there is a reason why Tetlock himself hesitates to draw that conclusion: his results clearly show that experts do outperform non-experts. These intelligent, educated and experienced professionals have insights to contribute – it's just that those insights go only so far. The problem is not the experts; it is the world they inhabit – the world we all inhabit – which is simply too complicated for anyone to analyse with much success.

So, if expertise is of such limited help in the face of our complex, ever-changing human society, what can we do to solve the problems we face? Perhaps we should look for clues in the success story we've already encountered: the amazing material wealth of modern developed countries.

4 The long, tangled history of failure

In 1982, just a couple of years before Philip Tetlock began his painstaking examination of expertise, two management consultants, Tom Peters and Robert Waterman, concluded their own detailed study of excellence in business. *In Search of Excellence* was published to great acclaim and launched Peters's career as one of the world's most recognisable management gurus. The two authors, working with their colleagues at McKinsey, used a mixture of data and subjective judgement to settle on a list of forty-three 'excellent' companies, which they then studied intensively in a bid to unlock their secrets.

Just two years later, Business Week ran a cover story entitled 'Oops! Who's Excellent Now?' Out of the forty-three companies, fourteen, almost a third, were in serious financial trouble. Excellence – if that was what Peters and Waterman really found when they studied the likes of Atari and Wang Laboratories – appears to be a fleeting quality.

It seems strange that so many apparently excellent companies could find themselves in deep trouble so quickly. Perhaps there was something uniquely silly about Peters and Waterman's project. Or perhaps there was something uniquely turbulent about the early 1980s – *In Search of Excellence* was published during a severe recession, after all.

But perhaps not. The 'who's excellent now?' experience is reinforced by a careful study from the economic historian Leslie Hannah, who in the late 1990s decided to trace the fortunes of every one of the largest companies in the world in 1912. These were corporate giants that had survived a merger shakedown over the preceding few years and typically employed at least ten thousand workers.

At the top of the list was US Steel, a gigantic corporation even by today's standards, employing 221,000 workers. This was a company with everything going for it: it was the market leader in the largest and most dynamic economy in the world; and it was in an industry that has been of tremendous importance ever since. Yet US Steel had disappeared from the world's top hundred companies by 1995; at the time of writing, it was not even in the top five hundred.

Next on the list was Jersey Standard, which these days continues to prosper under the name Exxon. General Electric and Shell were also in the top ten both in 1912 and in 1995. But none of the other top-ten titans was in the top ten by 1995. More remarkably, none of them was even in the top hundred. Names such as Pullman and Singer recall a bygone age. Others, such as J&P Coats, Anaconda and International Harvester, are barely recognisable. It is hard to imagine just how large and powerful these companies once were – the closest parallels would be the likes of Microsoft and Wal-Mart today – and how permanent their success must have seemed. And while it could be said that Pullman and Singer suffered from being market leaders in declining industries, their fate was not inevitable. Singer made sewing machines, but Toyota's origins as a manufacturer of looms were no more promising. Other former titans, such Westinghouse Electric, Cudahy Packing and American Brands, were in the same dynamic industries as the rare success stories General Electric and Procter & Gamble. Yet they failed.

Just as Philip Tetlock's experts have proved less capable than we tend to think, in the face of a complex world, these great companies are more transient than we realise. Ten of Hannah's top hundred had vanished within a decade; over half disappeared over the next 83 years. The lesson seems to be that failure is fundamental to the way the market creates sophisticated and wealthy economies. But perhaps what Peters, Waterman and Hannah found merely reflects the fact that if you start at the top, the only way is down. What happens when we look at survival rates in young, dynamic industries?

The answer is that failure rates are even higher. Consider the early printing industry. The printing press was invented by

Johannes Gutenberg, a man who changed the world utterly, and produced the celebrated Gutenberg Bible in 1455. But the Gutenberg Bible was a ruinous project that put him out of business. The centre of the printing industry quickly moved to Venice, where twelve companies were established by 1469. Nine of them were gone in just three years, as the industry fumbled for a profitable business model. (It eventually found one: printing pre-packaged relief from divine punishment in the form of religious indulgences.)

At the dawn of the automobile industry, two thousand firms were operating in the United States. Around 1 per cent of them survived. The dot-com bubble spawned and killed countless new businesses. Today, 10 per cent of American companies disappear every year. What is striking about the market system is not how few failures there are, but how ubiquitous failure is even in the most vibrant growth industries.

Why, then, are there so many failures in a system that seems to be so economically successful overall? It is partly the difficulty of the task. Philip Tetlock showed how hard it was for expert political and economic analysts to generate decent forecasts, and there is no reason to believe that it is any easier for marketers or product developers or strategists to predict the future. In 1912, Singer's managers probably did not forecast the rise of the off-the-peg clothing industry. To make things even more difficult, corporations must compete with each other. To survive and be profitable it is not enough to be good; you must be one of the best. Asking why so many companies go out of business is the same as asking why so few athletes reach Olympic finals. In a market economy, there is usually room for only a few winners in each sector. Not everyone can be one of them.

The difference between market-based economies and centrally planned disasters, such as Mao Tse-tung's Great Leap Forward, is not that markets avoid failure. It's that large-scale failures do not seem to have the same dire consequences for the market as they do for planned economies. (The most obvious exception to this claim is also the most interesting: the financial crisis that began in 2007. We find out why it was such a catastrophic anomaly in Chapter 6 of *Adapt*.) Failure in market economies, while endemic, seems to go hand in hand with rapid progress.

The modern computer industry is a striking example: the most dynamic sector of the economy has also been the one in which failure is everywhere you look. The industry started with failure: when transistors replaced vacuum tubes as the basic elements of the computer, vacuum-tube manufacturers failed to make the switch. The likes of Hughes, Transitron and PhilCo took over, before stumbling in turn as integrated circuits replaced transistors, and the baton passed to Intel and Hitachi.

Meanwhile, Xerox, struggling to survive the expiry of its patents on photocopying, established the Palo Alto Research Center (or Parc), which developed the fax machine, the graphical interface that defines all modern computers, the laser printer, the Ethernet, and the first personal computer, the Alto. Yet Xerox did not become a powerhouse in personal computing. Many of the Alto's successors – including the ZX Spectrum, the BBC Micro and Japan's MSX standard – were dead-ends in the history of computing. It fell to IBM to produce the direct ancestor of today's personal computer – only to then unwittingly hand over control of the most valuable part of the package, the operating system, to Microsoft. IBM eventually bowed out of the personal computer business in 2005, selling its interests to a Chinese company. Apple also lost out to Microsoft in the 1980s, despite perfecting the user-friendly computer (although it was later to bounce back selling music, iPods and phones). Microsoft itself was caught unawares by the internet, lost the search-engine war with Google, and may soon lose its dominant position in software altogether. Who knows? Only the most arrogant forecaster would be able to convince himself that he could predict the next twist or turn in this market. The most successful industry of the last forty years has been built on failure after failure after failure.

The humble toaster which so baffled Thomas Thwaites is itself a product of trial and error. The Eclipse of 1893 was not a success: its iron heating element was prone to rust and tended to melt and start fires. The company that marketed it no longer exists. The first successful toaster did not emerge until 1910. It boasted a superior nickel-chrome alloy for the heating element but was still flawed. Most notably, that heating element was exposed, making it a potential source of household fires, burns and electrocutions. It took several decades for the practical and familiar pop-up toaster design to emerge, by which time many manufacturers had quit the business or gone bankrupt.

The market has solved the problem of generating material wealth, but its secret has little to do with the profit motive or the superior savvy of the boardroom over the cabinet office. Few company bosses would care to admit it, but the market fumbles its way to success, as successful ideas take off and less successful ones die out. When we see the survivors of this process – such as Exxon, General Electric and Procter & Gamble – we shouldn't merely see success. We should also see the long, tangled history of failure, of all of the companies and all of the ideas that didn't make it.

5 A shifting landscape

Biologists have a word for the way in which solutions emerge from failure: evolution. Often summarised as survival of the fittest, evolution is a process driven by the failure of the less fit. Disconcertingly, given our instinctive belief that complex problems require expertly designed solutions, it is also completely unplanned. Astounding complexity emerges in response to a simple process: try out a few variants on what you already have, weed out the failures, copy the successes – and repeat for ever. Variation, and selection, again and again.

We are used to thinking about evolution as something that happens in the natural world – a biological phenomenon. But it doesn't have to be. Anyone can watch evolution taking place in a digital world, thanks to a graphics expert named Karl Sims. If you've ever seen *Titanic*, or the *Lord of the Rings* trilogy, or the *Spider-Man* films, then you've enjoyed the work of Karl Sims, who founded the special-effects company GenArts. But in the early 1990s, before Sims turned his attention to the visual-effects business, he produced moving images that are far cruder and yet, in some ways, more remarkable.

Sims wanted to watch evolution in progress. More than that, he wanted to create a virtual environment in which he could set its direction. Sims programmed simulations of settings such as a tank of water, and into them he dropped crude virtual creatures consisting of simple control systems, some sensors and random assortments of articulated blocks. Most of these jumbled creatures sank to the bottom and thrashed about without any great success. A few, however, were able to swim a little. Sims then applied the evolutionary process, instructing his computer to discard the floundering creatures and to create mutations based on the more successful swimmers: variation and selection. Most of the mutations were failures, of course. But the failures were continuously discarded, the occasional successes were allowed to flourish. From the most mindless and random of processes, remarkable results emerged: virtual creatures that resembled tadpoles, eels and rays, along with a number of apparently successful entities that looked like nothing on earth.

On another evolutionary run, Sims rewarded creatures for successfully taking possession of a green cube, in competition with each other. The trial-and-error process of evolution produced a wide range of workable solutions, some obvious, others less so, from ignoring the cube and lunging at the opponent, to making a quick grab for the cube and then dashing off, to simply toppling forward and covering the cube with a heavy slab of a body. Sims was not the designer, nor even the subjective judge of success after the fact: he simply set up an evolutionary environment and recorded what happened. The process he created was entirely blind and stupid: there was no foresight, planning or conscious design in any of the mutations. Yet the blind evolutionary process produced marvellous things.

Why is trial and error such an effective tool for solving problems? The evolutionary algorithm – of variation and selection, repeated – searches for solutions in a world where the problems keep changing, trying all sorts of variants and doing more of what works. One way to think about this quest for solutions is to imagine a vast, flat landscape, divided into a grid of billions of squares. On each square is a document: a recipe describing a particular strategy. Evolutionary theorists call this a 'fitness landscape'. If the fitness landscape is biological, each strategy is a different genetic recipe: some squares describe fish; some describe birds; some describe human beings; while the majority describe a genetic mush that represents nothing that could ever survive in reality. But the fitness landscape might equally represent recipes for dinner: some produce curries; others produce salads; many produce dishes that are nauseating or even poisonous. Or the fitness landscape might contain business strategies: different ways to run an airline or a fast-food chain.

For any problem, it's possible to imagine a huge range of potential solutions, each one carefully written down and scattered on this vast landscape. Imagine, too, that each recipe is very similar to its neighbours: two adjacent dinner recipes might be identical save for one demanding a little more salt and the other a slightly longer cooking time. Two neighbouring business strategies might advocate doing everything the same, except that one prescribes slightly higher prices and a bit more marketing.

We've been imagining a flat plane stretching in every direction, but now let's change the picture and say that on our fitness landscape: the better the solution, the higher the altitude of the square that contains it. Now the fitness landscape is a jumble of cliffs and chasms, plateaus and jagged summits. Valleys represent bad solutions; mountain tops are good. In an ecosystem, the latter are creatures more likely to survive and reproduce; in the market place, they are the profitable business ideas; and at the dinner party, they are the tastiest dishes. In our dinner-party landscape, a deep, dark pit might contain a recipe for spaghetti with fish fingers and a jar of curry sauce. From there, the only way is up. Trek in one direction and you might eventually ascend to the soaring peak of Bolognese ragù. Head off in the opposite direction and you might eventually climb to the summit of a Bangladeshi fish curry.

Problem-solving on a contoured fitness landscape means trying to find the high peaks. In dinner-party space, that's not so hard. But in a biological ecosystem, or an economy, the peaks keep moving – sometimes slowly, sometimes quickly. Pullman and Singer went out of business because the peaks they were standing on suddenly disappeared. The peak that McDonald's currently occupies has been around for a while, moving slowly as new technologies become available and new tastes develop. The Google peak is very young, and it exists only because of earlier developments, such as the computer and the World Wide Web, just as squirrels exist only because there are trees for them to inhabit. And the Google peak is moving fast, more like a rolling wave than a mountain. At the moment, Google is surfing along, adapting its strategy to stay on or near the crest of the wave. Like surfing itself, this is harder than it looks.

As one peak subsides, others may not be clearly visible. The biological process of evolution through natural selection is entirely blind; finding a corporate strategy may or may not be a more deliberate and far-sighted process, as we shall shortly see. But Tetlock's research on expertise suggests that, even if other peaks in corporate strategy are sometimes visible, executives see them only fleetingly, through heavy cloud.

We can imagine many ways to search for peaks in this changeable and mysterious landscape. Biological evolution usually moves in small steps, but occasionally takes wild leaps – a single mutation might give a creature an extra pair of legs or totally different skin pigmentation. This combination, along with the culling of failed experiments, works well. Some strategies will cling to a familiar summit as it shifts around; others, by darting off, may find a new peak rising up. The process of evolution strikes a balance between discovering the new and exploiting the familiar very well. In fact, Stuart Kauffmann and John Holland, both complexity theorists affiliated with the multidisciplinary Santa Fe Institute, have shown that the evolutionary approach is not just another way of solving complex problems. Given the likely shape of these ever-shifting landscapes, the evolutionary mix of small steps and occasional wild gambles is the best possible way to search for solutions.

Evolution is effective because, rather than engaging in an exhaustive, time-consuming search for the highest peak – a peak that may not even be there tomorrow – it produces ongoing, 'works for now' solutions to a complex and ever-changing set of problems. In biological evolution, solutions include photosyn-thesis, pairs of eyes and mothers' milk. In economic evolution, solutions include double-entry book-keeping, supply-chain man-agement and 'buy one, get one free'. Some of what works seems to be perennial. The rest, such as being a Tyrannosaurus rex or the world's most efficient manufacturer of VHS video cassettes, is rooted in a particular place and time.

We know that the evolutionary process is driven by variation and selection. In biology, variation emerges from mutations and from sexual reproduction, which mixes the genes from two par-ents. Selection happens through heredity: successful creatures reproduce before they die and have offspring that share some or all of their genes. In a market economy, variation and selection are also at work. New ideas are created by scientists and engineers, meticulous middle managers in large corporations or daring entrepreneurs. Failures are culled because bad ideas do not sur-vive long in the market place: to succeed, you have to make a product that customers wish to buy at a price that covers costs and beats obvious competitors. Many ideas fail these tests, and if they are not shut down by management they will eventually be shut down by a bankruptcy court. Good ideas spread because they are copied by competitors, because staff leave to set up their own businesses, or because the company with the good ideas grows. With these elements of variation and selection in place, the stage is set for an evolutionary process; or, to put it more crudely, solv-ing problems through trial and error.

6 We are blinder than we think

This is all rather counter-intuitive, not to say uncomfortable. Many people assume that top corporate executives must be good for something: the shareholders who pay them handsome salaries certainly do; as do the millions of people who buy books purporting to convey the wisdom of successful business chiefs. Tetlock's experts were almost helpless in the face of the complex situations he asked them to analyse. Are chief executives just as impotent, fumbling around for workable strategies in an impenetrable fog?

That would be what the evolutionary analogy implies. In biological evolution, the evolutionary process has no foresight. It is the result of pure trial and error over hundreds of millions of years. Could that also be true in an economy, despite the best efforts of managers, corporate strategists and management consultants?

A compelling clue comes from the economist Paul Ormerod. Ormerod had been reviewing what the fossil record tells us about extinctions over the last 550 million years – including mass extinctions that make the death of the dinosaurs look almost trivial. That record revealed a clear relationship between the scale of an extinction event and how often such events occur: if the extinction event is twice as severe, it is four times as rare; if it is three times as severe, it is nine times as rare. Eras in which very few extinctions take place are the most common of all. The pattern is very clear, and biologists now have mathematical models that show how a blind evolutionary process, when combined with an ever-changing contest for resources and the occasional asteroid strike, produces this distinctive signature.

Ormerod is a blunt, widely read iconoclast from Lancashire in northern England, with a taste for disarming fellow economists with their own favourite weapon – mathematics. He decided to take a look at the data for corporate extinctions as well. He studied Leslie Hannah's statistics on the death of corporate titans and compared them with half a billion years of data from the fossil record. The timescales were different, but the relationship between the size of an extinction event and its frequency proved to be exactly the same. (By far the worst year for the corporate titans was 1968, when six of them 'died'.) Next, Ormerod turned to a much bigger database of smaller corporate extinctions in the United States, state by state, sector by sector, with thousands of data points describing literally millions of small companies. He discovered the same thing. He cast the net even wider, looking at corporate extinctions across eight other rich countries. He found the same thing again.

Biological extinctions and corporate extinctions share that special signature. This does not prove that the economy is an evolutionary environment and that corporate strategies evolve through trial and error rather than successful planning, but it does offer a big hint. And Ormerod went further, again building on work by biologists. He took a stripped-down mathematical model of biological extinction that produced the tell-tale extinction signature and adapted it to represent corporate life and death. But he added a twist: he changed the rules of his model so that some companies were allowed to be successful planners. These planners were able to adjust their strategies to maximise the advantage they gained from interacting with other companies in the economy; some could do this perfectly, while others had just a tiny edge over a company whose strategy was determined entirely at random.

Ormerod discovered something disturbing: it was possible to build a model that mimicked the real extinction signature of firms, and it was possible to build a model that represented firms as modestly successful planners; but it was not possible to build a model that did both. The patterns of corporate life and death are totally different from reality in the 'planning is possible' model, but uncannily close to reality in the 'planning is impossible' model. If companies really could plan successfully – as most of us naturally assume that they can, despite what Tetlock tells us about the limitations of expert judgement – then the extinction signature of companies would look totally different to that of species. In reality, the signatures could hardly be more similar.

We should not leap to conclusions based on an abstract mathematical model, but Ormerod's discovery strongly implies that effective planning is rare in the modern economy. I wouldn't go so far as to suggest that Apple might as well replace Steve Jobs with a dart-throwing chimpanzee – even though it would certainly liven up Apple product launches. But the evidence suggests that in a competitive environment, many corporate decisions are not successful, and corporations constantly have to cull bad ideas and search for something better.

The same conclusion is suggested by Tetlock's studies of expert judgement and by the history of 'excellent' companies that so often lose their way: we are blinder than we think. In a complex, changeable world, the process of trial and error is essential. That is true whether we harness it consciously or simply allow ourselves to be tossed around by the results.

While trial and error is fundamental to the way that markets work, it makes for a challenging approach to life. Who wants to grope her way to a successful solution, with her repeated failures in full view of the world? Who wants to vote for a politician who takes that approach, or promote a middle manager whose strategy seems to be to throw around random ideas and see what works? Remember that President George W. Bush vowed to 'stay the course' while his opponent, John Kerry, lost the Presidential election in part because he had a reputation for changing his mind. Kerry's fans agreed that 'flip-flopper' was an insult, although they felt it was ill-deserved. But if we took trial and error seriously, 'flip-flopper' would be a badge of flexibility, worn with pride. A similar attitude prevails in British politics. Margaret Thatcher famously declared, 'You turn if you want to. The lady's not for turning.' Tony Blair was proud of the fact that he didn't have a reverse gear. Nobody would buy a car that didn't turn or go backwards, so it is unclear why we think of these as desirable qualities in Prime Ministers. But British voters rewarded Thatcher and Blair for their self-professed lack of adaptability with three general election victories apiece.

But whether we like it or not, trial and error is a tremendously powerful process for solving problems in a complex world, while expert leadership is not. Markets harness this process of trial and error, but that does not mean that we should leave everything to the market. It does mean – in the face of seemingly intractable problems, such as civil war, climate change and financial instability – that we must find a way to use the secret of trial and error beyond the familiar context of the market.

We will have to make an uncomfortable number of mistakes, and learn from them, rather than cover them up or deny they happened, even to ourselves. This is not the way we are used to getting things done.

7 A failure to adapt

A railroad foreman named Phineas Gage has the unfortunate distinction of being the world's most famous victim of a brain injury. In 1848, he was preparing an explosive charge when it detonated unexpectedly, driving his tamping iron – a rod over a yard long and an inch thick – through his cheek, behind his left eye, through his left front brain and out of the top of his head. The rod landed eighty feet away. Astonishingly, Gage survived, but his character was changed radically: previously sober and reliable, he became feckless, stubborn, unable to settle on any plan and prone to yelling obscenities. Along with a chunk of his brain, a particular part of his mind had gone. His friends said he was 'no longer Gage'.

The Soviet Union is to economics what Phineas Gage is to neuroscience. Neuroscientists study patients with damage to specific regions of the brain because their plight illuminates how the brain is ordinarily supposed to work. In much the same way, economists study dysfunctional economies when attempting to figure out the secrets of healthy ones. It is of course not a new insight that the Soviet system failed, but the unexpected details of why it failed are often glossed over – and they hold an important lesson for our mission to understand how to harness trial and error to solve problems.

The story starts in Russia's coal-rich Don Basin, north of the Black Sea, in 1901, before the Soviet Union even existed. A twenty-six-year-old engineer named Peter Palchinsky was sent by the Tsar's government to study the area's coal mines. Palchinsky gathered reams of data, paying attention to every local detail, and in particular building up a dossier on working conditions. The miners, he discovered, were housed forty or even sixty to a room, stacked in shared wooden bunks like cheap goods in a warehouse. In order to sleep, they had to crawl into position from the foot of the bed because there was no headroom to clamber over their fellows. Toilets and other facilities were rudimentary.

When Palchinsky sent back his findings, his superiors realised that his research was political dynamite: Palchinsky was sent to Siberia to perform less sensitive assignments. Palchinsky and his stubborn streak were inextricably linked. A few years earlier, winning a place at Russia's top engineering school, he had taken pride that he had based his application on the strength of his exam results, rather than relying on the right connections. In short,

Palchinsky was bright, energetic, confident – and almost absurdly honest.

Palchinsky's early brush with the authorities worked to his advantage. He slipped across the Russian border to work in Western Europe. Palchinsky soaked up knowledge in Paris, Amsterdam, London and Hamburg, making copious notes on the new industries those cities were developing, and paying just as much attention to new ideas in management as in engineering. He wanted to absorb the latest thinking on organising a work-force as well as cutting-edge science and technology. Hungry to understand as much as he could, he became a successful industrial consultant, and was as eager to spread expertise as to gain it.

Incredibly, Palchinsky began writing articles suggesting suit-able reforms for the Russian economy, advising the very Tsarist government that had exiled him to Siberia. But that was Palchinsky through and through: he just couldn't stop telling it the way he saw it. He wrote letters to his wife Nina freely admit-ting that he had had an affair while travelling in Europe. (She received the news stoically.) When he returned to Russia after receiving a pardon in 1913, he became an influential adviser to the Tsar's government, and – after narrowly escaping being bay-oneted during the revolution – later he advised the Soviet government, too. But his stubborn honesty continued: he refused to join any scientific or engineering organisation that was con-trolled by the Communist Party, on the grounds that engineering advice should not be distorted by politics. He frequently criticised foolhardy engineering. He even drafted a letter to the Soviet lead-ership, offering the helpful observation that technology and science were more important than communism; friends begged him not to send it, and he relented.

Yet while Palchinsky's political antennae were missing, his technical judgement and humanitarian instincts were sharp. He warned against prestige projects: why drill oil wells just for the spectacular 'gush' when cheap coal and gas were widely available? He defended small projects that, according to his own painstaking research, were often more efficient than gigantic ones. He defended workers' rights throughout.

It is easy to forget just how successful the Soviet economy was ... for a time. We tend to assume that the planned economy fell apart because it lacked the galvanising force of the profit motive and the creativity of private-sector entrepreneurs. But this does not really make sense: there were many creative people in the Soviet Union, including Palchinsky. It is not immediately obvious why they would lose their creativity merely because they worked for state-owned enterprises. Nor did the Soviet Union lack motivational techniques: in fact, it possessed as great a range of incentives, positive and horrifyingly negative, as any civilisation in history, and deployed them ruthlessly. And the results were initially impressive. So much so that, by the 1950s, many Western experts had concluded that communism – while anti-democratic and cruel – was more effective than capitalism as a way to run an economy.

The Soviet failure revealed itself much more gradually: it was a pathological inability to experiment. The building blocks of an evolutionary process, remember, are repeated variation and selection. The Soviets failed at both: they found it impossible to tolerate a real variety of approaches to any problem; and they found it hard to decide what was working and what was not. The more the Soviet economy developed, the less of a reference point the planners had. The whole system was unable to adapt.

Peter Palchinsky, with his international experience and his painstaking analysis of local conditions, was just the kind of man who could have changed that. He was assigned to advise on two of the most important projects in Stalin's first five-year plan: the

Lenin Dam and Magnitogorsk. The Lenin Dam, on the Dnieper River in modern Ukraine, was the world's largest when it was commissioned in the late 1920s. Palchinsky was unmoved by its scale. Stalin's brainchild it might be, but he warned that the river was too slow and, on a flood plain, the reservoir would be huge and would swamp many thousands of homes and much prime farming land. Nobody knew how much, he pointed out, because no hydrological surveys had been carried out; but the reservoir eventually proved to be so large that simply growing hay on the land it had covered and burning it in a power plant would have generated as much energy as the dam did. There was a dry season, Palchinsky admonished, so coal-fired power stations would have to be built and run for three months a year in any case. He advocated a step-by-step approach as the local economy expanded, combining small coal-fired plants with more modest dams. He pointed out that smaller dams would likely be more effective. In every detail, his concerns were later proved correct. But Stalin was not interested: he simply wanted the world's largest hydroelectric project and gave the order to proceed anyway. The project suffered huge cost overruns and was an economic and engineering disaster, even setting aside the ecological costs, the forced relocation of ten thousand farmers and the appalling labour conditions.

The steel mills of Magnitogorsk, the 'City of Magnet Mountain', were if anything more ambitious. The city was to be built in the remote heart of Russia, far to the east of Moscow, but near apparently plentiful iron-ore deposits. It was designed to exceed the entire steel output of the United Kingdom. Again, Palchinsky counselled caution – he wanted more analysis and a step-by-step approach. His old studies of workers' conditions in the coal mines of the Don Basin led him to worry about the fate of Magnitogorsk's workers. But he also pointed out the key technical objections to the project, which seemed to be cast from the same mould as the Lenin Dam: it was begun without a detailed study of the area's geology and without any interest in the availability of the coal needed to fire the mills.

Palchinsky's warnings were ignored, and again they were horribly accurate. One witness described conditions on the cattle wagons transporting workers to the site: 'For a day and a half, the door was not even opened ... mothers had children die in their arms ... From only the wagon in which we travelled, four little corpses were removed. More were carried out from other wagons.' Over three thousand people died in the first winter of construction work. Promised a garden city, Magnitogorsk's forced labourers were housed downwind of the blast furnaces. The iron ore ran out in the early 1970s, and then both coal and iron has had to be shipped to what were the world's largest steel mills over vast distances. When the US historian Stephen Kotkin spent time living in the city in 1987, he discovered endemic alcoholism, shortages of almost everything, crumbling infrastructure, 'almost unfathomable pollution and a health catastrophe impossible to exaggerate'.

What Palchinsky realised was that most real-world problems are more complex than we think. They have a human dimension, a local dimension, and are likely to change as circumstances change. His method for dealing with this could be summarised as three 'Palchinsky principles': first, seek out new ideas and try new things; second, when trying something new, do it on a scale where failure is survivable; third, seek out feedback and learn from your mistakes as you go along. The first principle could simply be expressed as 'variation'; the third as 'selection'. The importance of the middle principle – survivability – is something which will become clear in Chapter 6 of *Adapt*, which explores the collapse of the banking system.

The monstrous moral flaws of the Soviet system are now obvious. The economic flaw was more subtle: its inability to produce variation and selection, and therefore its inability to adapt. Central planners decided what would be built, lulled into a sense of omniscience by having a map or a table of statistics in front of them. Such plans inevitably missed the messy complexities of the situation on the ground, and also produced far too little variation. Almost every apartment in 1960s Moscow had the same iridescent orange lampshade. In Magnitogorsk, there were two types of apartment, named 'A' and 'B'. They were the city's sole concession to variety.

Above all, feedback is essential for determining which experiments have succeeded and which have failed. And in the Soviet Union, feedback was ruthlessly suppressed.

One icy Leningrad night in April 1928, there was a knock on the door of Peter Palchinsky's apartment. He was arrested by the secret police and was never seen by his wife again. Over a year later, it was announced that he had been executed. There had been no trial, but a secret police dossier on Palchinsky, unearthed and smuggled out of Moscow many decades later by the historian Loren Graham, documented his 'crimes'. He was accused of 'publishing detailed statistics' and sabotaging Soviet industry by trying to set 'minimal goals'. In other words, Peter Palchinsky was murdered for trying to figure out what would work, and for refusing to shut up when he saw a problem.

Palchinsky was not alone. Three thousand of the USSR's ten thousand engineers were arrested in the late 1920s and early 1930s, mostly bound for near-certain death in Siberia. (Palchinsky's wife, Nina, also met that fate.) Anyone who tried to object to looming technological disasters and to suggest alternatives was denounced as a 'wrecker'. Palchinsky's secret execution was unusual – perhaps because, stubborn to the end, he refused to recant. His persecution was not.

The Soviet Bloc began to fall apart in the late 1980s, punctuated with famous events such as the victory of the newly legalised Solidarity movement in the Polish elections of June 1989, and the fall of the Berlin Wall in November of that year. In the heart of the Soviet Union itself, a momentous but less famous revolt was also taking place: the first major strike in Soviet history. In July 1989, a quarter of a million coal miners walked away from their jobs. Part of the protest was about grotesquely dangerous conditions: the death rate for Soviet miners was fifteen to twenty times higher than it was for their American equivalents, with the local pits claiming the lives of over fifty men every month. But the strike was also provoked by simple deprivation: the miners often had no meat or fruit to eat, and few had access to soap or hot water. After risking their lives each day in the suffocating depths, they couldn't even wash themselves or rest in a comfortable bed. President Mikhail Gorbachev was forced to appear on national television, acknowledging the justice of the miners' cause and offering substantial concessions. It was a notable moment in the downfall of the Soviet system.

The miners who had walked out and humiliated Gorbachev worked, of all places, in the Don Basin. Sixty years after Peter Palchinsky's execution, and eighty-eight years after he had initially pointed to the problem of working conditions in the Don coal mines, the Soviet system had still failed to adapt.

8 Beyond Coca-Cola problems

The Soviet Union, like poor Phineas Gage, is a grotesquely extreme example. Only the worst dictatorships have exhibited the same pathological immunity to feedback. Yet, in a gentler way, most organisations and most forms of politics have the same difficulty in carrying out the simple process of variation and selection.

Variation is difficult because of two natural tendencies in organisations. One is grandiosity: politicians and corporate bosses both like large projects – anything from the reorganisation of a country's entire health-care system to a gigantic merger – because they win attention and show that the leader is a person who gets things done. Such flagship projects violate the first Palchinsky Principle, because errors are common and big projects leave little room to adapt. The other tendency emerges because we rarely like the idea of standards that are inconsistent and uneven from place to place. It seems neater and fairer to provide a consistent standard for everything, whether it's education, the road network or the coffee at Starbucks. Such uniformly high standards sound tempting: as Andy Warhol once commented, 'You can be watching TV and see Coca-Cola, and you know that the President drinks Coke, Liz Taylor drinks Coke, and just think, you can drink Coke, too. A Coke is a Coke and no amount of money can get you a better Coke than the one the bum on the corner is drinking. All the Cokes are the same and all the Cokes are good.'

But Warhol found Coke intriguing because it was an exception; and it still is. Producing a sweet, fizzy drink is a static, solved problem. No further experimentation is necessary, and it is perfectly possible to set uniformly high standards in the production of Coca-Cola. (The *delivery* of Coke to remote parts of the world is another matter, and is a minor miracle of local adaptation.) Ensuring uniformly high standards in more complex situations is much harder: it's the chief achievement of Starbucks and McDonald's, and even then the standardisation comes at a price in charm, flexibility and quality.

Running a hospital or a school is another matter altogether. We love the idea that every single one should deliver the same high quality. In the UK, we even have our own catchphrase, the 'postcode lottery', to describe the scandal that standards vary from place to place. It is something of a national obsession. We want all of our public services to be like Coca-Cola: all identical, all good. And they can't be.

If we are to take the 'variation' part of 'variation and selection' seriously, uniformly high standards are not only impossible but undesirable. When a problem is unsolved or continually changing, the best way to tackle it is to experiment with many different approaches. If nobody tries anything different, we will struggle to figure out new and better ways to do anything. But if we are to accept variation, we must also accept that some of these new approaches will not work well. That is not a tempting proposition for a politician or chief executive to try to sell.

It seems to be equally hard for traditional organisations to deliver the selection component of variation and selection. The difficulty is in selecting what is really working on the ground. Peter Palchinsky was all for taking things step by step, but politicians resist pilot schemes with objective measures of success. This is partly because politicians are in a hurry: they expect to hold on to a role for two to four years, not long enough for most experiments to deliver meaningful results.* Even more politically inconvenient is the fact that half of the pilot schemes will fail – many things do in a complex world – so the pilot will simply produce stark evidence of that failure. This is our fault as much as the fault of our politicians. We should tolerate, even celebrate, any politicians who test their ideas robustly enough to prove that some of them don't work. But, of course, we do not.

*Donald Green, Professor of Political Science at Yale, tells me that one question in the social sciences has been thoroughly tested with field experiments: how to get out the vote. So politicians can use rigorous evaluation methods when it suits them.

It's a sad truth that one of the most successful pilot schemes of recent years was implemented not by politicians but by a celebrity chef and a television crew. Jamie Oliver, chirpy Essex boy turned darling of the British middle class, created a national phenomenon in 2005 when he tried to persuade schools to serve healthier meals. Almost accidentally, he created a reasonable approximation of a controlled experiment. He convinced schools in the London borough of Greenwich to change their menus, and then mobilised resources, provided equipment and trained dinner ladies. Other London boroughs with similar demographics received none of these advantages. Indeed, because the resulting television programme wasn't broadcast until after the project was well under way, they probably knew little about it.

Two economists, Michele Belot and Jonathan James, picked up the data generated by the cheeky chef's campaign and analysed it, discovering that if primary-school kids eat less fat, sugar and salt, and more fruit and vegetables, they are ill less often and do somewhat better at English and science. These conclusions would be more robust if the trial had been rigorously controlled, but until Jamie Oliver came along, none of the country's politicians had shown much interest in the experiment. Tony Blair, then British Prime Minister, fell over himself to endorse the campaign. He had been in power for eight years at the time.

If formal experiments hold few joys for traditional leaders, informal feedback will often fail to reach them, too. Few advisers face Peter Palchinsky's fate, but even so his compulsion to blurt out the truth is rare. There is a limit to how much honest feedback most leaders really want to hear; and because we know this, most of us sugar-coat our opinions whenever we speak to a powerful person. In a deep hierarchy, that process is repeated many times, until the truth is utterly concealed inside a thick layer of sweet-talk. There is some evidence that the more ambitious a person is, the more he will choose to be a yes-man – and with good reason, because yes-men tend to be rewarded.

Even when leaders and managers genuinely want honest feedback, they may not receive it. At every stage in a plan, junior managers or petty bureaucrats must tell their superiors what resources they need and what they propose to do with them. There are a number of plausible lies they might choose to tell, including over-promising in the hope of winning influence as go-getters, or stressing the impossibility of the task and the vast resources needed to deliver success, in the hope of providing a pleasant surprise. Actually telling the unvarnished truth is unlikely to be the best strategy in a bureaucratic hierarchy. Even if someone does tell the truth, how is the senior decision-maker supposed to distinguish the honest opinion of a Peter Palchinsky from some cynical protestation calculated to win a budget increase?

Traditional organisations are badly equipped to benefit from a decentralised process of trial and error. Static, solved problems are ideal for such organisations; as are tasks where generalised expertise counts for much more than local knowledge. But such 'Coca-Cola problems' are increasingly rare in a rapidly changing world, which is why – as we shall see – many businesses are beginning to decentralise and strip authority away from managers. In the next chapter, we'll see how adaptive organisations need to decentralise and become comfortable with the chaos of different local approaches and the awkwardness of dissent from junior staff. We'll also see the heroic effort required to force a traditional hierarchy to change its mind.

But there is a more fundamental problem here than the right way to design an organisation, because it isn't just organisations that struggle to acknowledge and adapt to their mistakes. Most individuals suffer from the same problem. Accepting trial and error means accepting error. It means taking problems in our stride when a decision doesn't work out, whether through luck or misjudgement. And that is not something human brains seem to be able to do without a struggle.

9 Why learning from mistakes is hard

I spent the summer of 2005 studying poker. I interviewed some of the best players in the world, attended the World Series of Poker in Las Vegas, analysed 'pokerbots' – poker-playing computers – and chronicled the efforts of highly rational players, such as Chris 'Jesus' Ferguson, a game theorist with a PhD who is a world champion and a formidable one-on-one player.

While poker can be analysed rationally, with big egos and big money at stake it can also be a very emotional game. Poker players explained to me that there's a particular moment at which players are extremely vulnerable to an emotional surge. It's not when they've won a huge pot or when they've drawn a fantastic hand. It's when they've just lost a lot of money through bad luck (a 'bad beat') or bad strategy. The loss can nudge a player into going 'on tilt' – making overly aggressive bets in an effort to win back what he wrongly feels is still his money. The brain refuses to register that the money has gone. Acknowledging the loss and recalculating one's strategy would be the right thing to do, but that is too painful. Instead, the player makes crazy bets to rectify what he unconsciously believes is a temporary situation. It isn't the initial loss that does for him, but the stupid plays he makes in an effort to deny that the loss has happened. The great economic psychologists Daniel Kahneman and Amos Tversky summarised the behaviour in their classic analysis of the psychology of risk: 'a person who has not made peace with his losses is likely to accept gambles that would be unacceptable to him otherwise'.

Even those of us who aren't professional poker players know how it feels to chase a loss. A few years ago, my wife and I had booked a romantic weekend in Paris. But she was pregnant, and a couple of hours before we were due to catch the train she began feeling sick. She was throwing up into a plastic bag in the taxi on the way to the station. But when I met up with her, she was determined to go to Paris because our tickets weren't refundable. She didn't want to accept the loss and was about to compound it.

Being an economist is rarely an advantage in a romantic situation, but this was perhaps an exception. I tried to convince my wife to forget about the tickets. Imagine that the money we had spent on them had been lost for ever, I told her, but also imagine that we stood on the steps of Waterloo station with no plans for the weekend, when somebody came up to us and offered us free tickets to Paris. That was the correct way to think about the situation: the money was gone; and the question was whether we wanted to travel to Paris for no further cost. I asked my wife whether she would accept such an offer. Of course not. She was feeling far too sick to go to Paris. She forced a faint smile as she realised what I was telling her, and we went home. (As if to confirm that we had made the right decision, the nice people at Eurostar refunded our tickets anyway. And a few months later, my wife somewhat more pregnant, we got to Paris in the end.)

The behavioural economist Richard Thaler, with a team of co-authors, has found the perfect setting to analyse the way we respond to losses. He studied the TV game show *Deal or No Deal*, which is a great source of data because the basic game is repeated incessantly, with similar rules, for high stakes, in over fifty countries. *Deal or No Deal* offers contestants a choice of between twenty and twenty-six numbered boxes, each containing some prize money, ranging from pennies to hundreds of thousands of dollars, pounds or euros. (The original Dutch version has a jackpot of five million euros.) The player holds one box, not knowing how much money is inside. Her task is to choose the other boxes in any order she likes. These are then opened and discarded. Every time she opens a box containing a token amount, she celebrates, because that means her own mystery box doesn't contain that low prize. Every time she opens a box with a large prize, she winces, because that reduces the odds that her own box will be lucrative.

All of this is pure chance. The interesting decision is the one that gives the game show its title. From time to time, the 'Banker', a mysterious and anonymous figure, calls the studio to offer the contestant cash in exchange for the unknown sum inside her box. Will it be a deal, or no deal?

The psychology of the game is revealing. Let's take a look at Frank, a contestant in the Dutch version of *Deal or No Deal*. After a few rounds, the expected value of his box – that is, the average of all the remaining amounts – was just over €100,000. The Banker offered him €75,000 – serious money, but less than 75 per cent of his box's expected value. He turned it down. Then he received a nasty shock. Frank opened a box containing €500,000, the last big prize remaining. His expected winnings plunged to just €2,508. The Banker's offer plunged, too – from €75,000 to €2,400. Relative to Frank's likely winnings, this was a more generous offer than the previous one – 96 per cent of the expected value of playing on – but Frank rejected it. The next round, Frank spurned a Banker's offer that was actually greater than the average value of the remaining boxes. And in the final round, Frank's two remaining possibilities were €10 or €10,000. The Banker offered him a more-than-generous €6,000. Frank turned it down. He left the studio with €10. After being stunned by the loss of a guaranteed €75,000 and a decent chance of a €500,000 prize, Frank started taking crazy gambles. Frank had gone on tilt.

Frank's behaviour is typical. Thaler and his colleagues looked at how people responded to the Banker's offers immediately after making an unlucky choice, a lucky choice, or a choice that was broadly neutral. They found that the neutral choosers tended to be quite keen to accept the Banker's deal. Lucky choosers were cocky: they were more likely to turn down the Banker and keep going. But it was unlucky choosers who stood out. They were extremely unlikely to accept an offer from the Banker.* Why? Because if they did, it would lock in their 'mistake'. If they kept playing, there was a chance of some sort of redemption. The pattern was all the more striking because the Banker tended to make more generous offers to losers – lower in absolute terms, of course, but closer to the average of the remaining boxes. Objectively, players who had just made an unlucky choice should have been more willing to deal than anyone, because they were receiving more attractive odds from the Banker.

Perhaps this is a phenomenon restricted to game shows and the poker tables of the Rio in Las Vegas? No such luck. The economist Terrance Odean has found that we tend to hang on grimly, and wrongly, to shares that have plunged in the hope that things will turn around. We are far happier to sell shares that have been doing well. Unfortunately, selling winners and holding on to losers has in retrospect been poor investment strategy.

All four examples – poker, Paris, *Deal or No Deal* and share portfolios – show a dogged determination to avoid crystallising a loss or drawing a line under a decision we regret. That dogged determination might occasionally be helpful, but it is counterproductive in all these cases and in many others. Faced with a

---

*Typical contestants accepted the Banker's offer 31 per cent of the time. 'Winners' accepted the offer 25 per cent of the time. 'Losers' accepted only 14 per cent of the time, despite receiving objectively more generous offers.

mistake or a loss, the right response is to acknowledge the setback and change direction. Yet our instinctive reaction is denial. That is why 'learn from your mistakes' is wise advice that is painfully hard to take.

10 A recipe for adapting

We face a difficult challenge: the more complex and elusive our problems are, the more effective trial and error becomes, relative to the alternatives. Yet it is an approach that runs counter to our instincts, and to the way in which traditional organisations work. The aim of this book is to provide an answer to that challenge.

The adaptive, experimental approach can work almost anywhere, so we'll look at a huge range of problems. We'll meet the rebellious colonels who risked their careers – and their lives – to change the shape of the war in Iraq; and the doctor whose desperate gamble in a wartime prison camp should serve as an example to the staff of the World Bank today. We'll discover what the disasters at Three Mile Island and Deepwater Horizon have to tell us about preventing another Lehman Brothers disaster. We'll learn from a watchmaker, a street urchin, a Wall Street rebel, two aircraft designers and a failing choreographer. We'll study the corporate strategies of companies from Google to a simple high-street cobbler. We'll search for solutions to problems from the banking crisis to climate change.

Along the way, we'll also be learning about the recipe for successfully adapting. The three essential steps are: to try new things, in the expectation that some will fail; to make failure survivable, because it will be common; and to make sure that you know when you've failed. Palchinsky would have recognised these steps, but they involve formidable obstacles. To produce new ideas we must overcome our tendency to fall in step with those around us, and overcome those with a vested interest in the status quo. Making failure survivable sometimes means taking small steps, but not always: many innovations emerge from highly speculative leaps, and surviving such leaps is not easy. Nor is it easy to survive a failure in the financial system. And distinguishing success from failure, oddly, can be the hardest task of all: arrogant leaders can ignore the distinction; our own denial can blur it; and the sheer complexity of the world can make the distinction hard to draw even for the most objective judge.

Along the way, I hope that we'll learn something about how to adapt and experiment in business and in our own lives. Faced with the costs and risks of trial and error, should you and I try to experiment and adapt more than we do? What price would we pay in our quest to succeed?

Notes to Chapter 1

323 Von Hayek quote: Friedrich von Hayek, *The Fatal Conceit* (Chicago: University of Chicago Press, 1991).

323 The electric toaster seems a humble thing: http://www.toaster.org/1900.php.

325 'It warms bread when I plug it into a battery': telephone interview with Thomas Thwaites, 30 June 2009.

325 The range of products: Eric Beinhocker, *The Origin of Wealth* (London: Random House, 2007), p. 9.

327 We're proud of the change we've brought: Barack Obama, 'Speech at the White House Correspondents' Dinner, 2009'. Available at: http://politicalhumor.about.com/od/barackobama/a/obama-white-house-correspondents-transcript_2.htm.

328 Perhaps we have this instinct: Beinhocker, *The Origin of Wealth*, p. 9.

329 Perhaps the best illustration of this: Philip E. Tetlock, *Expert Political Judgement* (New York: Princeton University Press, 2005).

330 'The best lesson of Tetlock's book': Louis Menand, 'Everybody's an Expert', *New Yorker*, 5 December 2005.

331 Just two years later, *Business Week*: 'Oops! Who's Excellent Now?', *Business Week*, 5 November 1984; Christopher Lorenz, '"Excellence" Takes a Knock', *Financial Times*, 1 November 1984.

331 The 'who's excellent now?' experience is reinforced: Leslie Hannah, 'Marshall's "Trees" and the Global "Forest": Were "Giant Redwoods" Different?', in N. Lamoreaux, D. Raff and P. Temin (eds), *Learning by Doing in Markets, Firms and Countries* (London: University of Chicago Press, 1999).

332 At the time of writing, it was not even in the top five hundred: FT Global 500, 2008. Available at: http://media.ft.com/cms/8aa8acb8-4142-11dd-9661-0000779fd2ac.pdf.

332 Ten of Hannah's top hundred: Paul Ormerod, *Why Most Things Fail* (London: Faber and Faber, 2005), p. 12.

332 Consider the early printing industry: Ormerod, *Why Most Things Fail*, p. 15.

333 It eventually found one: Tom Scocca, 'The First Printed Books Came with a Question: What Do You Do with These Things?', *Boston Globe*, 29 August 2010. Available at: http://www.boston.com/bostonglobe/ideas/articles/2010/08/29/cover_story/?page=full.

333 At the dawn of the automobile industry: Ormerod, *Why Most Things Fail*, p. ix.

334 The modern computer industry is a striking example: Beinhocker, *The Origin of Wealth*, p. 333.

334 Meanwhile, Xerox, struggling to survive: John Kay, *The Truth about Markets* (London: Penguin Allen Lane, 2003), pp. 101–103.

335 It took several decades: http://www.toaster.org/museum.html.

335 Biologists have a word for the way: there is no shortage of popular accounts of evolution. I have relied here on Eric Beinhocker's excellent summary in *The Origin of Wealth*.

337 Yet the blind evolutionary process produced: see Karl Sims, 'Evolving Virtual Creatures' Computer Graphics', *Siggraph '94 Proceedings*, July 1994, pp. 15–22. Available at: http://www.karlsims.com/papers/siggraph94.pdf. Videos available at: http://www.karlsims.com/evolved-virtual-creatures.html.

339 Given the likely shape: Beinhocker, *The Origin of Wealth*, ch. 9.

342 He discovered the same thing: Ormerod, *Why Most Things Fail*, chs. 9 and 10.

343 If companies really could plan successfully: Ormerod, *Why Most Things Fail*, ch. 11; and Paul Ormerod and Bridget Rosewell, 'How Much Can Firms Know?', Working Paper, February 2004. Available at: http://www.paulormerod.com/pdf/intent6mar03.pdf.

344 A railroad foreman named Phineas Gage: Malcolm McMillan of Deakin University maintains a treasure trove of information about Gage. Available at: http://www.deakin.edu.au/hmnbs/psychology/gagcpage/.

345 When Palchinsky sent back his findings: Loren Graham, *The Ghost of the Executed Engineer: Technology and the Fall of the Soviet Union* (Cambridge, MA: Harvard University Press, 1993), pp. 51–5.

349 'For a day and a half': quoted in Graham, *The Ghost of the Executed Engineer*, p. 69.

349 When the US historian Stephen Kotkin: Stephen Kotkin, *Steeltown USSR* (Berkeley: University of California Press, 1991), p. 254.

350 In Magnitogorsk, there were two types: Graham, *The Ghost of the Executed Engineer*, p. 75.

350 There had been no trial: Graham, *The Ghost of the Executed Engineer*, p. 46.

352 'You can be watching TV: Andy Warhol, *The Philosophy of Andy Warhol* (New York: Harcourt, 1975), p. 100.

354 He had been in power for eight years at the time: Tim Harford, 'How a Celebrity Chef Turned into a Social Scientist', *Financial Times*, 7 November 2009. Available at: http://timharford.com/2009/11/how-a-celebrity-chef-turned-into-a-social-scientist/;   and Michele Belot and Jonathan James, 'Healthy School Meals and Educational Achievements', Nuffield College Working Paper. Available at: http://cess-wb.nuff.ox.ac.uk/downloads/schoolmeals.pdf.

354 There is some evidence that the more ambitious: see James Surowiecki, *The Wisdom of Crowds* (London: Abacus, 2005), pp. 253–4. Surowiecki refers to two studies that reach this common-sense conclusion, but I have not been able to discover a precise citation.

355 Even when leaders and managers: Mancur Olson, *Power and Prosperity* (New York: Basic Books, 2000), pp. 138–9.

356 I spent the summer of 2005 studying poker: Tim Harford, 'The Poker Machine', *Financial Times*, 6 May 2006. Available at: http://timharford.com/2006/05/the-poker-machine/; and Tim Harford, *The Logic of Life* (New York: Random House, 2008).

356 The brain refuses to register: Gary Smith, Michael Levere and Robert Kurtzman, 'Poker Player Behavior after Big Wins and Big Losses', *Management Science*, Vol. 55, No. 9 (September 2009), pp. 1547–55.

356 The great economic psychologists Daniel Kahneman and Amos Tversky: Daniel Kahneman and Amos Tversky, 'Prospect Theory: An Analysis of Decision under Risk', *Econometrica*, Vol. 47, No. 2 (1979), p. 287.

357 Found the perfect setting to analyse the way we respond to losses: Thierry Post, Martin J. Van den Assem, Guido Baltussen and Richard H. Thaler, 'Deal or No Deal? Decision Making under Risk in a Large-Payoff Game Show', *American Economic Review*, Vol. 98, No. 1 (March 2008). Available at: http://ssrn.com/abstract=636508. Having written about Thaler's research before, and even presented a radio documentary on the show, I am indebted to Jonah Lehrer and his book *How We Decide* (Boston, MA: Houghton Mifflin Harcourt, 2009) for emphasising how striking this result really is.

359 Unfortunately, selling winners and holding on to losers: Terrance Odean, 'Are Investors Reluctant to Realize Their Losses?', *Journal of Finance*, Vol. 53, No. 5 (October 1998), pp. 1775–98. Available at: http://faculty.haas.berkeley.edu/odean/Papers%20current%20versions/AreInvestorsReluctant.pdf.